NUMBERS 116 & 117

Yale French Studies

Turns to the Right?

Yale French Studies

Michael A. Johnson and Lawrence R. Schehr, *Special editors for this issue*

Alyson Waters, *Managing editor*

Editorial board: Thomas Kavanagh (Chair), R. Howard Bloch, Edwin Duval, Tara Golba, Christopher L. Miller, Jean-Jacques Poucel, Julia Prest, Maurice Samuels, Yue Zhuo

Assistant editor: T. Chapman Wing

Editorial office: 82-90 Wall Street, Room 308

Mailing address: P.O. Box 208251, New Haven, Connecticut 06520-8251

Sales and subscription office:

Yale University Press, P.O. Box 209040

New Haven, Connecticut 06520-9040

Published twice annually by Yale University Press

Designed by James J. Johnson and set in Trump Medieval Roman by The Composing Room of Michigan, Inc. Printed in the United States of America by the Vail-Ballou Press, Binghamton, N.Y.

ISSN 044-0078

ISBN for this issue 978-0-300-11823-0

**MICHAEL A. JOHNSON AND
LAWRENCE R. SCHEHR**

Editors' Preface: Turns to the Right?

The four decades since the "events" of May '68 have seen some seismic shifts in history, politics, the arts, and dynamics of interpersonal relations. If the events of that spring and summer ultimately did not pan out in a rosy revolution, as some had thought it might, many things have changed, from the fall of communism, to the formation of a Europe far greater than the Common Market, to shifting dynamics between East and West. In France, in particular, we have noticed an increasing phenomenon over the past decade or so that seems to be symptomatic of a malaise in some quarters, one that relates, perhaps, to a perceived loss of French identity and the possible loss of the French exception. Such a sense of national loss has led, in many cases, to what appears initially to be an ideological shift to the Right. This apparent shift plays out in the arts, especially in literature, both high and low, in philosophy, in various arguments for and against progressive mores in twenty-first century France, and even in some cases, returns toward a more "normalizing" version of psychoanalysis. In a France that is more and more integrated into a more general European model, there has been, in a number of quarters, a dialectical turn of the screw that has produced fascinating aesthetic and philosophical projects.

Thus we have seen writers like Richard Millet, Michel Houellebecq, Maurice Dantec, and Marc-Édouard Nabe come to the fore, each of whom espouses a position of return that, while not necessarily exactly the position of the Front National, certainly seems to put in question universal republican values for all. Similarly, the work of Pascal Bruckner and André Glucksmann represents a return to a philosophy that sheds not only its post-68 overtones (Jacques Derrida, Gilles Deleuze, and especially Michel Foucault) but also what was inherited

YFS 116/117, *Turns to the Right?* ed. Johnson and Schehr, © 2009 by Yale University.

from Sartre and the Existentialists. And even the gradual—or even precipitous—shifts of Philippe Sollers, Julia Kristeva, and Elisabeth Badinter, as well as certain critiques recently offered of postcolonial discourses, fit this revisionist model.

Arguably, even the work of "bad girl" writers like Christine Angot and Virginie Despentes might be symptomatic of a return to "me" and away from "us," as would the work of the author Renaud Camus and the graphic novelist Fabrice Neaud, both of whom refuse notions of gay solidarity associated with post-68 movements, while relying on surprisingly genealogical notions of identity: for Neaud, the robust figure of the genealogical tree, and for Camus, the purity of the French language. And if we have evoked Le Pen in a mention of the Front National, if we might evoke José Bové as well, we are quick to add that this movement is not so much a reactionary move but a new set of ideological discourses that is, in its own way, an illustration of reformulated subjectification in the postmodern era.

For these reasons, the essays in this volume do not simply diagnose a general *droitisation* of the French cultural landscape, as though one could find a stable vantage point from which to make such a diagnosis. Rather, they indicate a sense of disorientation, or perhaps, of *reorientation*, in regards to the traditional Left-Right distribution of political sensibilities inherited from the Enlightenment. The danger of grouping such diverse thinkers and writers as Alain Finkielkraut, Luc Ferry, Maurice Dantec, Marcel Gauchet, and Alain Badiou, under the banner of "new reactionaries" as Daniel Lindenberg does in his highly criticized pamphlet, *Le rappel à l'ordre: enquête sur les nouveaux réactionnaires*, is that we reduce complex arguments, whose "spirit" may be either progressive or conservative, reactionary or revolutionary, (and based on what may be ancillary, non-essential, aspects of their arguments) to a single "tendency."[1]

Indeed, as Bruno Chaouat and François Noudelmann both remark in their contributions to this volume, it is no easy task to distinguish between the yearning of conservative or reactionary discourses and the melancholic opposition to the "neoliberal, capitalistic status quo" professed by the new Left. Both positions hark back to tradition and to some version of Frenchness, genealogical or otherwise. However, it must be said, although these two positions may appear the same, and

---

1. Daniel Lindenberg, *Le rappel à l'ordre: enquête sur les nouveaux réactionnaires* (Paris: Seuil, 2002).

perhaps even respond to the same socio-political phenomena, they are not the same.

Along these lines, the apparent rhetorical similarity between "conservative" and "revolutionary" critiques of the *esprit de mai* demands particularly attentive reading in order to parse out differences where they matter. As Kristin Ross argues, critics of the "68 spirit" such as Ferry and Renaut, and in a more refined manner, Lipovetsky, misconstrue the event, missing what was in fact profoundly new and productive about that historical moment (namely the unprecedented, although transitory, *rapprochement* of students and workers).[2] And while Badiou's diagnosis of ageless narcissistic individualism and of privatized existences in post-68 culture may resemble Lipovetsky's on many accounts, he is nonetheless faithful to an entirely different 1968 than the popularized mass media version put forward by both the *nouveaux philosophes* and Sarkozy, as Adrian Johnston's essay in this volume argues.

If debates surrounding the legacy and collective memory of May '68 are now taking dramatically new forms, we might also say that the general value of collective memory and the prioritization of certain "sites of memory" has shifted in some way as well. Bruckner's critique, as Richard J. Golsan describes it in his essay, pits memory against history, arguing that the "duty to memory" has enabled some insidious rewritings of history, distorting the past in the name of the political and ideological purposes of the present. At stake here, in the reconfiguration of collective memory and the scrambling of sites of memory, is the present as a site of possibility, a present for which Verena Conley's essay compellingly argues.

Also central to a number of these essays are questions of political affect and sensibility. It is a matter of political sensibility, for example, that we associate moral critique with right-wing thought. This is why Jean-Claude Michéa's work—fueled by a strong moral critique—has attracted so much positive attention from French right-wing thinkers, even as he claims to write in the service of an original socialism, according to Bénédicte Coste. We might say the same about Bruckner, Dantec, Millet, and Neaud and many of the writers discussed in this volume whose moral critiques place them under suspicion in the eyes of a Left shaped as much by an affective *habitus* as it is by the intellectual. Lindenberg's pamphlet is a case in point here.

2. Kristin Ross, *May '68 and its Afterlives* (Chicago: University of Chicago Press, 2004).

The essays in this volume, while certainly neither exhaustive nor encyclopedic, engage a variety of phenomena, all of which relate to this multiple turn in heretofore unforeseen directions. Together these essays represent a call for responsible reading of these new formulations, even those that challenge ingrained political sensibilities.

Our heartfelt thanks for their contributions to this volume go to the translators Andrew Pigott and Michael Gott.

I. *States of Affairs*

FRANÇOIS NOUDELMANN

A Turn to the Right: "Genealogy" in France since the 1980s

The fortieth anniversary of May '68 had the equivocal flavor common to all such commemorations, as it resuscitated the past only to bury it ever more deeply. With the passing of yet another decade, we recall an era during which political and social emancipation seemed a feasible and legitimate goal; but after all the festivities, we feel that we will never see its like again; and we resign ourselves to thinking that the next decade's anniversary, in 2018, will be all the more commemorative, and for that, all the sadder. The fortieth anniversary nonetheless sparked unforeseen levels of interest: with his virulent denunciations of the forgotten event, France's then president-elect, Nicolas Sarkozy, paradoxically made it relevant again.

In blaming May '68 for all the woes of contemporary society, Sarkozy rekindled the debate over the legacy of those moments. Sectarianism, unbridled capitalism, the school crisis, the breakdown of authority, and the deterioration of morals all bear the mark of this nihilistic period. Such an ideological fairy tale would have appeared for exactly what it was—namely, a mediocre bit of electioneering—had a cadre of former May '68ers not already endorsed it, most notably among them, that emblem and rallying-figure of right-wing French politics, André Glucksmann. Glucksmann's change of heart incited many like-minded progressives to desert the cause as well, as they fled a defeated Left and accepted the political favors of the party now in power. Referring to this catharsis of social democracy, the philosopher Alain Badiou could thus dub Sarkozy a "Rat Man."[1]

The defeat of leftist theory and leftist politics was certainly a moment of truth. A number of intellectuals and elected officials had long

1. Alain Badiou, *De quoi Sarkozy est-il le nom?* (Paris: Lignes, 2007).

YFS 116/117, *Turns to the Right?* ed. Johnson and Schehr, © 2009 by Yale University.

since swapped their progressive ideals for other objectives, such as defending the homeland or protecting the secularist, republican culture of France's public schools. This oft-observed ideological rupture, along with the spectacle of a Right pronouncing itself disabused and complex-free, is symptomatic of a deep-seated cultural mutation that was twenty-five years in the making. Politics is only a part of this mutation and, in fact, a paradigm shift has occurred. The history of ideas has used the prefix "post-" to describe every cultural trend since postmodernism; indeed, today one encounters as many "post-'s" as one did "-isms" among the avant-gardes. Yet the figure of the "post," this "coming after," seems to be the verbal symptom of a deeper difference relative to time. This is why the "rightward turn" entails not only the aforementioned ideological reorientation, but also an acute tension at the heart of French society between a conservative penchant for continuity and a new mode of becoming that threatens to disrupt national identities.

A FRENCH RESTORATION

Conservative restoration can certainly be seen in France today, and it is at work in all fields of knowledge, politics, and culture; it operates according to an alliance among trends that are often contradictory. The 2008 issue of *La revue internationale des livres et des idées* bore the ironic title: "Should we scrap deconstruction, literary studies, poststructuralism, the '68 mindset, postcolonial studies, and other sectarian and relativist afflictions?"[2] The tone is there; it is the moment for a massacre: the moment when modernist idols can be vilified without guilt. This modernity, which is fragile precisely because of its break with tradition and the spirit of entrenchment, has not ensured its legacy as such. Certainly, it helped transform many facets of society—families, lifestyles, the school system—; but it could not reclaim these changes as its own handiwork. As Serge Audier demonstrates in his excellent study, *La pensée anti-68*, it always managed to rouse the ire of the Left and the Right in equal measure.[3] Both right-wing nationalism and left-wing statism have consistently denigrated the cultural and political production of the leftist student revolts of the 60s.

---

2. Anon., "Faut-il flinguer la déconstruction, les études littéraires, le post-structuralisme, la pensée 68, les études postcoloniales et autres plaies communautaristes et relativistes?" *La revue internationale des livres et des idées* 5, May–June 2008.

3. Serge Audier, *La pensée anti-68* (Paris: La découverte, 2008).

Detractors of the movement condemn its intellectual influence, even if the scope of that influence remains unclear. A book as simplistic as Alain Renaut and Luc Ferry's *La pensée 68* (1985), gathering various authors under the umbrella of "anti-humanist" writers, joins media ideologues in bemoaning the decline of Western civilization and pinning the blame squarely on May '68—resembling, in this, those members of the wealthy classes who blamed all economic crises on the *Front populaire* of 1936.[4] In that vein, Alain Finkielkraut, France's version of Allan Bloom, became famous for his attack on Claude Lévi-Strauss's supposed "relativism" (*La défaite de la pensée*, 1987).[5] Indeed, this apocalyptic tone has seduced a number of philosophers, who nowadays prefer the complacency of preaching to the disquiet of philosophical inquiry. Régis Debray diagnoses a glitch in the transmission of cultural meaning;[6] Marcel Gauchet notes a generational crisis, and so on;[7] intellectuals strive to outdo one another with their laments—over the break-down of authority, over the blurring of sexual distinctions, over the deterioration of language, and over the general lack of respect for ancestors or national sovereignty.

The extent of this ideological reversal comes to light when we consider the example of Jean-Paul Sartre, the most famous intellectual of all: a critical conscience that remains steady in the face of universal contradictions. Sartre condemned his inner "intellectual," defining himself as "a man made of other men, worth them all and worthier than none."[8] He fled institutional centers of power and influence, and recognized no other legitimacy than that of the streets. His death in 1980 is emblematic of France's rightward turn. From then on, intellectuals could reclaim the role of doomsday prophet; in other words, they could peer around the corners of time and foresee an ever-encroaching societal decay. The historical recurrence of such a figure, once embodied in Spengler's *Decline of the West*,[9] should not obscure what has been at stake these past two decades: the alarmist discourse levels a critique at democracy itself, that is to say, at that political freedom giving anyone a right to power. In *La haine de la démocratie* (2005), Jacques Rancière flawlessly analyzes the disdain that these new

---

4. Luc Ferry and Alain Renaut, *La pensée 68* (Paris: Gallimard, 1985).
5. Alain Finkielkraut, *La défaite de la pensée* (Paris: Gallimard, 1987).
6. Régis Debray, *Les cahiers de médiologie* 11, (Paris: Gallimard, 2001).
7. Marcel Gauchet, *Le débat* 132, (Paris: Gallimard, 2004).
8. Jean-Paul Sartre, *Plaidoyer pour les intellectuels* (Paris: Gallimard, 1972).
9. Oswald Spengler, *The Decline of the West* (New York: Knopf, 1926).

"intellectuals" harbor toward consumer society and its popular culture, which, they claim, has perverted the great ideals of democracy.[10] The position of this contemporary Platonistic philosopher, which purports to uphold some higher imperative—reason, moral law, the sovereign good—made its entrance just as the intellectual fell lower in the hierarchy of power: supplanted by political science "experts," such intellectuals seek to legitimize their now precarious station as prince's counselors by re-branding themselves as defenders of universal values.

The conservative restoration logically implies a politics of knowledge, insofar as it dissociates fields and perspectives that the democratic insurrection, acting without institutional consent, had tended to intertwine. Those who sully May '68 seek thereby to reaffirm the sovereignty that is disciplinary as much as it is national. In the sixties, collaboration between philosophy and the social sciences, as well as the theoretical ambition of literary studies, had fostered exchanges among various fields of knowledge, and valorized "margins," "boundaries," and the "outside." Today, the disciplines have rediscovered their own territory. Under the rubric of philosophical or literary history, strict disciplinary temporalities have reasserted themselves, framed by state structures (the *agrégation* exam, the National Council of Universities) that ensure that each department will teach a homogeneous curriculum.

This public framing of knowledge participates in a general affirmation of national identity, at times touted as "the French exception," whose representatives it carefully selects. One might have expected that the international success enjoyed by many a sixties-era French philosopher would have been money in the bank for quite a while, but their eviction from the French university system and long exodus to the United States made them suspect. The very fact that Deleuze, Foucault, Derrida, Cixous, Lyotard, Lacan, and Kristeva fall within the purview of "French Theory" marks their extraneousness. The French intelligentsia's aversion to all things American leads to haughty dismissals of cultural studies, gender studies, and minority studies. Such antipathies, moreover, stoke French Republicanism. Dubbing himself a "national republican," Régis Debray embodies this collusion of multiple nationalisms—be they of academic, cultural, or political valence.

By denouncing "French Theory," French institutions have ironi-

---

10. Jacques Rancière, *La haine de la démocratie* (Paris: La Fabrique, 2005).

cally aligned themselves with the enemies of "continental" thought: proponents of analytical philosophy, those who denounce post-structuralism and deconstruction as "literary philosophies" devoid of scientific rigor, have gained recognition in the academy. Jacques Bouveresse's polemic against Derrida, which runs from *Prodiges et vertiges de l'analogie* (1999) to his latest study, *La connaissance de l'écrivain* (2008), is an obvious example.[11] The trend, moreover, has spread beyond the confines of strict philosophical debate. Martha Nussbaum's work—nowadays widely disseminated in France—has extended the scope of the analytical tradition to a domain where heretofore it did not venture, as she reestablished contact between philosophy and literature. In fact, under the tutelage of literary theorists and postmodern thinkers, the joint ventures of literature and philosophy reached their apogee. Caught up in the theoretical exuberance of the sixties and seventies, intellectuals mixed psychoanalysis, sociology, and linguistics; they opened dialogues among proponents of existentialism, structuralism, Marxism, and diverse hermeneutic strategies; they even took part in creative projects, such as the New Novel or the New Theater. But learned neophytes explain how, at best, those philosophies and those literatures were comprised of little more than smoke and mirrors, and how, at their worst, they imprisoned the human spirit within lifeless textualism. To such aberrations, they oppose the traditional categories: narration, character, humanist representation, and moral exemplarity.

In this way, the restoration has orchestrated contradictory attacks by French Kantian humanists and analytical philosophers. Not all of its purveyors, however, strike a bellicose note. Sometimes, former practitioners of "French Theory" affect a contrite aggiornamento, casting their youthful excess in an unfavorable light. Tzvetan Todorov, who introduced the methods of formal analysis into literary studies, recently expressed his regrets in *La littérature en péril* (2007), where he condemns the transgressions of textualism.[12] Similarly, the legacy of Roland Barthes—an emblem of textual criticism if ever there were one—has been the subject of numerous revisionist debates. Antoine Compagnon, once a member of Barthes's inner circle, had already sought to establish a healthy balance between readerly "good sense"

11. Jacques Bouveresse, *La connaissance de l'écrivain* (Paris: Agone, 2008) and *Prodiges et vertiges de l'analogie* (Paris: Raison d'agir, 1999).

12. Tzvetan Todorov, *La littérature en péril* (Paris: Flammarion, 2006).

and the pretensions of theory. In *Le démon de la théorie* (1988), Compagnon showcased his expertise as he usefully contextualized the theoretical moment within the history of scholarship.[13] Even so, under the aegis of a wise neutrality, it strongly intimates that our recess hour has ended. The careful parsing of Barthes's legacy appears all the more clear when critics begin to dissociate Barthes the modernist—a great fan of the avant-gardes—from Barthes the traditionalist—a reader and admirer of Chateaubriand. The figureheads of modernity, Compagnon explains, have often assumed their status with grave reservation; for they have always essentially been conservative in their outlook.[14] Whether vengeful or reasonable in character, the restoration has succeeded, and is now part of our intellectual history.

THE "PATRIMOINE" AND ITS GLORY DAYS

Cultural shifts and revisions of the past are part of history. The rightward turn of the 1980s, however, did not limit itself to a mere reconfiguration of the past; it altered the very meaning of the word. In effect, it has produced excesses inversely proportional to those of the early Modernists and transformed time into an Absolute unencumbered by continuity. Modernists of the late nineteenth and early twentieth centuries had gone so far as to abolish the past: no longer did it suffice to oppose one's elders; one had to disavow any and all forms of heritage, without exception. Radical proponents of a new *tabula rasa* thus advocated the destruction of libraries and museums in favor of the new. Today, the dichotomy between the old and new guards has collapsed, thereby inverting the arrow of time: for there is no need to uphold the superiority of a tradition to which our present already belongs. The future also has succumbed, becoming little more than a backward march, a future anterior that offers no novelty that is not instantly reabsorbed into the past.

The 1980s ushered in a cult of what has been passed down culturally from generation to generation: *patrimoine*, the French concept of cultural heritage. Since then, rites of commemoration have covered the widest array of historical events, and have engendered countless archives. Historian François Hartog has demonstrated how altered social practices and new institutions have enshrined this cultural mu-

13. Antoine Compagnon, *Le démon de la théorie* (Paris: Seuil 1998).

14. Compagnon, *Les antimodernes: de Joseph de Maistre à Roland Barthes* (Paris: Gallimard, 2005).

tation.[15] Patrimonial schools, patrimonial politics, and patrimonial holidays have become the basic components of French national culture. The phenomenon is certainly not peculiar to France. It would seem, in fact, that the notion of *patrimoine* has everywhere grown in scope and significance. Indeed, UNESCO now defines the cultural heritage as a "natural" entity (on a par with a country's geographical layout, for example). And any contemporary production can feasibly be preserved in the national archives. In this way, the present is lived in as a stock of the past for the future.

The cult of cultural heritage casts a touristy pall over French cultural products, which it destines inexorably for the museum. Even as France puts its most famous architects proudly on display, it bans them from its cityscape. The grand projects born of Mitterrand's ambition have quickly reverted to a cautious urbanism exemplified by today's Paris. Compared to Barcelona or London, France's capital is becoming a vast museum, as rapidly and as thoroughly as Rome. In fact, Paris's failed candidature for the 2012 Olympic Games relied on a film by Luc Besson that presented a postcard image of France and its old cultural icons; whereas London emphasized its cultural and ethnic diversity.

The *Amélie* syndrome has given a dominant nostalgic tone to French cinema. It comes as no surprise that the most popular films are those that applaud traditional identities; accordingly, *Bienvenue chez les Ch'tis* (2008), a film bursting with local color, recently broke all previous records at the box office. Certainly, the cultural products of every nation tend to do the same; in France, however, nostalgia for the past weighs as heavily on (so-called) "artistic" cinema as on its popular counterpart. Again, the past in question is not the past per se, but a new manner of apprehending time as an object of commemoration. And so it is that recent films by Arnaud Desplechin (*Un conte de Noël* [2008]) and Olivier Assayas (*L'heure d'été* [2008]) primarily deal with problems of family and heritage, and thus differentiate themselves from New Wave cinema, which tended rather to parody and subvert those themes.

Before, individuals *had* a past; now they *are* their past. That temporal shift inflects France's genealogical turn more sharply even than its rightward turn, though both are traceable to the 1980s. With its propensity for reversing political affiliations, the intellectual contro-

15. François Hartog, *Régimes d'historicité* (Paris: Seuil, 2004).

versy surrounding the Jewish question has in this regard proven most revelatory. Sartre's former secretary, Benny Levy, symbolizes this in a spectacular fashion as he went from a revolutionary militantism motivated by universal principles to a return to his cultural identity and a rediscovery of the faith of his forefathers.[16] Often presented as a conversion from Mao to Moses, this charismatic intellectual's about-face converged with other such reversals, relatively common to members of his generation. Disillusioned by the militant universalism he once professed, one that could not rid the world, or even itself, of anti-Semitism, he abandoned the philosophy of Sartre for that of Levinas, and finally, for Judaism. Benny Levy's case, of course, differs from the singular brand of French nostalgia discussed above, in that he would eventually make *aliyah*, and leave France for Israel. It nonetheless conforms to the general principle that, somewhere along the line, genealogies have become the sources of present identity.

The debate rages on today, stoked (for instance) by Jean-Claude Milner's book, *Les penchants criminels de l'Europe démocratique* (2003),[17] which pits the Jewish tradition, with its emphasis on study and the intergenerational transmission of knowledge, against a murderous and ever-forgetful modernity. In its exalted form, this debate posits an extensive, Pauline universalism—one "neither Jewish nor Greek" and espoused by the likes of Alain Badiou[18] and Michel Deguy[19]—against the *intensive* universalism practiced by the people of the Book. In its debased form, the debate has seen those of the former camp, who refuse to sever the Jewish tradition from universal history, denounced for their anti-Semitism. It has also rallied a number of intellectuals hostile to what they call "progressive Islam." In this vein, the genealogical turn has spawned competing strains of cultural memory. Regions, religions, and ethnicities are the new constituents of identity, irrevocably linked to familial traditions.

Faced with the proliferation of mutually antagonistic genealogies, it behooves us to peer beyond what, on their surface, those genealogies express. With this conflict, in fact, a truth doggedly repressed by the French Republic has resurfaced, a truth that has been set by a government ministry supposed to define it. No less than the cultural plural-

16. Benny Levy, *Être juif* (Lagrasse: Verdier, 2003).
17. Jean-Claude Milner, *Les penchants criminels de l'Europe démocratique* (Lagrasse: Verdier, 2003).
18. Badiou, *Saint Paul, la fondation de l'universalisme* (Paris: PUF, 1998).
19. Michel Deguy, *Un homme de peu de foi* (Paris: Bayard, 2002).

ism of our moment, France's return to cultural roots—in other words, its self-imposed confinement to the patrimonial museum—bespeaks a troubled and hemorrhaging present, one divided between multiple histories that no longer fit in the Republican mold. The genealogical turn merely projects a nostalgic desire for wholeness, contested by France's actual heterogeneity. It is most likely not even a "turn," but rather a crossroads, a traffic jam, or a re-drawn map of national identities.

FRANCE AT HOME AND ABROAD

My portrayal of a France obsessed by its homegrown genealogies might surprise those who, on the contrary, lament the passing of its historical sense; many, in fact, complain that French tradition has deteriorated, that their children no longer even know the *Marseillaise,* that its language, culture, and politics have been standardized, even Americanized. Both trends, however, attest to the same phenomenon. Even alarmist discourses concede that France, long held to be a singular and exemplary nation, has begun to evolve away from its standard Republican myths. That evolution, moreover, is not imposed by supranational politics; rather, it originates from within French society itself. Only the most nationalist of politicians oppose federation with the rest of Europe. However, internal crises linked to immigration have tarnished those founding principles, *"Liberté, Egalité, Fraternité."*

The riots of 2005, otherwise known as "the suburban revolt," belied Republican ideals by demonstrating that the legal equality conferred by citizenship might not protect citizens against racial and social discrimination, for those who revolted were indeed French citizens: "children of the Republic," as then President Chirac dubbed them. The Republican insistence on common origins (resulting in the prohibition of ethnic statistics) fell into a trap of its own creation when confronted with the realities it had repressed. Some intellectuals condemned what they saw as an ethnic and religious uprising; but France was caught off-guard by groups with no stated political objectives, who, in their violence, expressed a desire not only to obtain commodities, but also simply to destroy them. The specter of multi-ethnic society had crossed the English Channel, and France, finally, could no longer ignore it.

For ten years or so now, the Republican ideal of integration has fallen increasingly out of favor. Veils worn at school, strife between communities, and a growing tide of anti-Semitism have eroded the confidence once placed in secular and egalitarian models of governance. The patrimonial and memorial thrust that ought to have reunified French national history and placed it again on one continuous timeline has paradoxically sparked dissension among competing genealogies. With its belated recognition that the French government did collaborate in the deportation of Jews, France opened its historical floodgates: these days, other repressed histories are clamoring for acknowledgment. Thanks to the influence of civil society lobbying groups, the likes of which, until recently, did not even exist in France, France's colonial past and its role in the slave trade are finding their way into the history textbooks. Similar developments include the founding of an independent *Conseil représentatif des associations noires* ("Representative Council of Black Associations"). The new *Conseil* has not yet had any discernable impact on the political scene, since no politician of African descent has won a seat at the National Assembly; though it perhaps benefits from an Obama-like effect: eighty percent of the French electorate declared themselves ready to vote for the African-American candidate if given the chance.

These "other" Frances are seeking more and more to render their experience in art. Some directors, eschewing the intimist psychology common to most French cinema, have taken on this socially volatile material. Abdellatif Kechiche's *L'esquive* (2004), for instance, takes place in a housing project, where a class of adolescents recites a play. The bodies, expressions, and accents of these children of immigrants flesh out the roles of Marivaux's *Le jeu de l'amour et du hasard.* Avoiding facile representations of delinquency, Kechiche causes the voice of the minority to erupt from within the most refined sentences ever penned in French. Laurent Cantet's *Entre les murs,* winner of the 2008 *Palme d'or* at the Cannes Film Festival, also takes place in a poor and troubled school, and thus shows faces typically unseen, as it lends expression to voices typically unheard. Free of any impulse to sanctify or canonize their subjects, these films open up the *banlieue* and bring the social periphery to our center of attention.

In its diversity of expressions, the genealogical turn thus uncovers multiple historical identities; that diversity, moreover, refuses to fit within the tidy confines of the Hexagon. In spring 2007, a manifesto titled "Pour une littérature-monde" ("For a World-Literature") appeared, one that championed the decline of French parochialism, and the corresponding advent of a new cultural worldliness.[20] Though it certainly attacked the psychological navel-gazing currently in vogue among the French literati, the real target of "Pour une littérature-monde" was the notion of *francophonie.* Its signatories argue that *la francophonie,* created to safeguard the French language against outside influences, reproduces the old colonial distinction between writers based in the Hexagon and all their "Francophone" counterparts abroad, who just happen (as if coincidentally) to write in French. Thus a *French* literature independent of territorial boundaries would regroup those writers who find a common source of angst and inspiration in the transformations of today's world: Tahar Ben Jelloun (Morocco), Maryse Condé (Guadeloupe), Ananda Devi (Mauritius), Nancy Houston (Canada), Dany Laferrière (Haiti), Jean-Marie-Gustave Le Clézio (France), Amin Maalouf (Lebanon), Alain Mabanckou (the Congo), Anna Moï (Vietnam), Nimrod (Tchad), Boualem Sansal (Algeria), Abdourahman Waberi (Djibouti), to name a few. Their texts are not reduced to the nationality of the authors, and they modulate identity within the flux, exile, chaos, and unpredictable encounters that comprise global history. Such texts would overwhelm, shatter, indeed *archipelagize* metropolitan France.

The inspiration for this world-literature, Edouard Glissant, embodies the synthesis of the universal and the particular. His philosophy and poetics of his *Tout-Monde* ("All-World") forges an identity as it redistributes the relations between the global and local.[21] Combating introverted and incestuous genealogies, he attunes continental thought to its inner archipelagoes and liberates difference from the monotony of the same. Most probably, Glissant's own Martiniquan heritage has informed his project: situated in and out of France, he heralds an irreversible creolization that no genealogical turn could ever deflect or resist.

Try as it may, the conservative restoration that began in the 1980s cannot encase the present within some patrimonial reification; nor will it stifle those cacophonous voices that today hail difference and becoming. Neither modern nor anti-modern, these voices refurbish the legacy of the sixties, even as they repudiate its utopian excesses. The be-all-and-end-all of politics, structural absolutism, and theoretical supremacy no longer hover on their horizon; yet they embrace a

---

20. Collective, *Pour une littérature-monde* (Paris: Gallimard, 2007).
21. Edouard Glissant, *Poétique de la relation* (Paris: Gallimard, 2005).

concept of time that remains open to the possibility of newness. Certain scholars, for instance, continue to deconstruct old humanist precepts without unleashing the dreaded scourge of anti-humanism: witness recent work in anthropology, for instance: Françoise Héritier on gender[22] or Philippe Descola[23] on the overlap of species. Indeed, the conservative restoration has failed even to gain a decisive political victory; for not all veterans of the student revolts of the sixties have taken the rightward turn, or found religion, or undertaken the defense of imperiled traditions.

Indeed, some notable thinkers have held steady to the course of liberty, autonomy, and emancipation. Though having garnered little media attention before his recent suicide, André Gorz nonetheless wrote decisively on the history of capitalism, as he reflected on its evolution and proposed alternatives to the paradigm of full-time employment. From his early comradeship with Sartre, to his later work on political ecology, Gorz tweaked and renewed revolutionary thought. Today, more and more political activists are turning to his treatises, *Adieux au prolétariat* (1980) and *Les métamorphoses du travail* (1988), for inspiration.[24] Gorz also dialogued with a philosopher whose personal history remains deeply intertwined with the revolutionary sixties: Antonio Negri, who converted the fictions of a radiant and univocal future for all into a program whereby the world's multitudes might take an active role in matters relating to globalization.[25] These philosophers based in France kept loyal to the spirit of the sixties, even as, in many ways, they outgrew it. Allied with thinkers from diverse backgrounds, not all of whom share their revolutionary heritage, they accept *and* criticize the world to come, and they listen all the while to the crossing of identities and the appearance of new subjectivities.

The true stuff of thought is revealed by its tone. If today's genealogists prophesy apocalypse, those who embrace becoming make manifest their joy: a sign of those healthier passions that Spinoza opposed to sadness. The ideological mutation of the 1980s is a symptom, not a return to some national essence. French identity is reconfiguring

<hr>

22. Françoise Héritier, *Masculin-Féminin* (Paris: Odile Jacob, 2008. 2 vols).

23. Philippe Descola, *Par-delà nature et culture* (Paris: Gallimard, 2005).

24. André Gorz, *Adieux aux prolétariat* (Paris: Seuil, 1980) and *Les métamorphoses du travail* (Paris: Galilée, 1988).

25. Antonio Negri, *Goodbye Mr. Socialism*, trans. Paola Bertilotti (Paris: Seuil, 2007) and *Du retour* (Paris: Calmann-Levy, 2002).

itself, as it has always done. It will never be the property of any government agency, the state, or a museum. Its culture, heritage, and future can thrive in France, outside of France, and even without France. Though in exile in the United States, did Thomas Mann not proclaim that, in times of purifying genealogy, "German culture is where I am"?

—Translated by Andrew Pigott

VERENA ANDERMATT CONLEY

"Soigne Ta Droite"

After World War II, Francophiles in the United States associated France with a strong leftist culture whose labors culminated in the events of May 1968. A dramatic change of climate has since ensued. The "Winter Years" that swept over the country in the 1970s have given way to a more confused political and cultural status quo where lines distinguishing the Left from the Right are not easily drawn. Attempts at reviving militantism, from Sartrean existentialism or Fanonian-style postcolonialism, to the poetic revolutions of the 1960s, have proven difficult in a country under the sway of consumer economics and globalization that produced a new crop of thinkers and writers, from Luc Ferry and Alain Renaut to Michel Houellebecq, Maurice Dantec, and others who are most openly critical of their elders' militantism.

In this essay, I propose to revisit French culture of the past three decades to argue that the 1960s were not really a triumph of the Left but a sign of its demise: a consumer culture—of which the names cited above are a product—truly displaced the communism and existentialism that had defined the postwar years. It also undermined the revolutionary ideals of the 1960s. If words can be borrowed from Jacques Rancière, consumerism redistributed French society. In such a climate, what has become of leftism? Or, to put it another way, what is the relation between this new shift to the Right with consumerism and what remains of the Left? Are the terms coined during the French Revolution in fact still applicable?

After World War II and the demise of the Vichy regime associated with members of the bourgeoisie, there was a resurgence of a strong leftist culture grouped around the two poles of existentialism and Marxism. Jean-Paul Sartre's attacks on the Right associated with

YFS 116/117, *Turns to the Right?* ed. Johnson and Schehr, © 2009 by Yale University.

Nazism were coupled with his attempts to influence the course of French history through literature, as he made clear in *Qu'est-ce que la littérature?* (1947). In addition to his many direct involvements in social and political matters of the day, Sartre intervened through his writings, from *Henri Martin* (1953), a polemical book in which he came to the defense of a communist sailor wrongly accused by conservative officers of treason because he distributed anti-colonial tracts in Vietnam, to a strident denunciation of colonialism in his preface to Frantz Fanon's *Les damnés de la terre* (1961) and other works. A few years later, in his autobiographical essay, *Les mots* (1964), Sartre ruefully confessed that for a long time, he had taken his pen for a sword. Existentialism both worked with, but also rivaled and fought against, Marxism in its Stalinist form advocated by the French Communist Party in the shadow of the Russian dictator. Following the Liberation, the "heroism" the Russian people had displayed in the harsh winter of 1942–43 during the battle of Stalingrad that marked a turning point in the war, appealed to the French intelligentsia. The memory of this heroism faded and rumors of torture in the socialist paradise reached French soil. Nonetheless, during the postwar years, many intellectuals such as Louis Aragon and his Russian-born wife, Elsa Triolet, as well as other former surrealists, among others Paul Eluard, were avid supporters of the Communist Party. Subordinating their country to Russia and international communism, they participated in huge peace protests in this increasingly rigid Cold War period where lines were clearly drawn. They staunchly defended Russia as the bearer of peace against the United States, seen as the aggressor.

Many of these intellectuals and writers rallied around the influential weekly newspaper, *Les lettres françaises,* founded during the Occupation by Jacques Decour, a communist intellectual executed by the Nazis, and Jean Paulhan; later, Aragon took the paper under his wing. The paper had enormous currency in the postwar years because of its mythic origin. With the progressive discovery of the abuses by Stalin, many contributors left the weekly. After revelations of torture following the dictator's death in 1953, Aragon somewhat belatedly tried to reorient the paper's increasingly embarrassing position, a move that led to a split with the Communist Party. It is against this double political *engagement* by existentialists and Marxists with their highly politicized, thematic literature and, at least on the side of the communists, a blind allegiance to the Party that in the 1960s in the midst of decolonization and destalinization, another Marxism saw the light of day under a double influence of philosophy and psychoanalysis that led to experimental writing. Making fun of the ideals of their elders, from Jean-Paul Sartre and his existential humanism to the communists with, in retrospect, their untenable discourse as evidenced in *Les lettres françaises,* a group of young intellectuals introduced notions of difference, desire, and language. Critics and writers associated with the review *Tel Quel,* including Philippe Sollers, Julia Kristeva, and even Jacques Derrida, rejected the full historical subject as well as an unqualified obedience to a political party.

The linguistic and writerly turn of the 1960s under the influence of Claude Lévi-Strauss, Martin Heidegger, and a rereading of Freud, resulted in a new textual "leftism" whose proponents vowed to avoid the mistakes of their predecessors. Their critical and writerly practices undermined dialectical reasoning and any resolution of opposites. The subject, they claimed, was divided or deferred. They replaced *la politique,* the politics of politicians, with *le politique,* a political element of, and in, the text. Their focus on language led them to problematized relations to the referent. In the words of the late Félix Guattari, one had to avoid a reductionist militantism to become "analytically militant" by continually adjusting what he called "processes of subjectivation" and theorizing in an evolving historical and political situation.

Experimental writing as an invention of new processes of life was seen as an act of resistance in itself, beyond the meanings of words. To create, as Gilles Deleuze put it, is to resist. Art invents life. Hélène Cixous made herself a strong advocate of writing in an essay entitled, "*Sorties*" (1975; "*Forays,*" 1986). In spite of her exuberant tone, in an exchange with Catherine Clément at the end of their co-authored book entitled *La jeune née* (1975), Cixous was pessimistic. A few years after the events of May 1968 that were seen by some as the apogee of this new textual leftism with its poetic revolution, she declared that she feared for the future of writing in a world of marketing and intensified capitalism that signaled a turn to the right:

> Right now, I am pessimistic. There is, in a very generalized manner, a loss of voice in the world of writing, of literature, of creation. It is symptomatic and it will have effects; it isn't by chance that reading is on the retreat in almost all countries of the West. So that means that all the governments united, whether Right or reformist, are saying: "You, if you still have eyes, shut them, and intellectuals of all countries, your mouths, and don't start making analyses, and besides, it

isn't worth the trouble." One sees the development of an international intrigue that is leading toward capitalist imbecilization in its most inhuman, most automatic, most formidable form. The selling out of all the countries, their handing themselves over the way France has done with the Unites States, is also done on condition of a silent complicity.[1]

The future showed her to be prescient. The waning of communism coincided with the arrival in France of consumerism and a global capitalism that simultaneously marked the end of social experimentation. The latter was replaced by the programming of desire away from its socio-existential and psychoanalytical inflections to one based on marketing and profit. French bourgeois society was less liberated from symbolic networks and social hierarchies than transformed by others based on flexible capital and often quantifiable success. As Paul Virilio repeatedly remarked, the old bourgeois society that was the target of existentialism, communism, *and* of textual Marxism, is replaced by a new pyramid, based as much upon the *speed* of accumulation as on accumulation itself. This new pyramid put in place after the 1970s is composed of politicians, the military, CEOs, and media people, including media intellectuals and artists. It is comprised of those at the top who have the power of decision and those at the bottom who are compelled to consume. Yet by the end of the twentieth century, more and more people, from workers to recent immigrants, live outside of this pyramid altogether. With the progressive reordering of French, as well as European and world culture, celebrity is a measure of success. The militant intellectual gives way to the media intellectual and the star. Ideas cannot be thought outside of money. Crucial to the intellectual star are photo-ops and lucrative sales of books inside and outside of the Hexagon.

This turn to the Right that occurred just at the time when leftism seemed to have won its battles after May 1968, was based on global capitalism that progressively transformed earlier bourgeois subjects regulated by a century-old symbolic order into market-driven citizens. Over the last few decades of the twentieth century, because of economic redistribution, this global capitalism with its money flows became increasingly accompanied by population flows that, in France, translated into waves of immigrants, often from the country's former

---

1. Hélène Cixous and Catherine Clément, *The Newly Born Woman*, trans. Betsy Wing (Minneapolis: University of Minnesota Press, 1986), 160.

colonies, but also from other places in Asia and from the former USSR. These new arrivals, compelled to move for economic reasons, wound up in the infamous *banlieues* at the very moment that many unskilled jobs in France were eliminated or outsourced due to globalization. The presence of these immigrants prompted strong resistance among certain parts of the French population that became obsessed with everything "national" at the same time that the concept of the nation-state was undergoing dramatic changes. With globalization, the state is more and more at the mercy of transnational companies; as a result, its citizens' rights are being threatened. The reaction of the "average Frenchman" to this reconfiguration of France, with its economic and social dilemmas, produced yet another turn to the Right, in addition to the one induced by a consumer economy itself.

Much has been written about this second turn to the Right, often associated with a proper name, Jean-Marie Le Pen, that resulted in new forms of racism and economic exclusion. In the pages that follow, I propose to focus on the first turn when a new form of global capitalism did away with the social experimentation hailed by existentialists, communists, and *soixante-huitards* alike. This turn also put an end to artistic experimentation in the form of "writing." A new capitalism that took over the world in the 1970s and 1980s with the Reagan Revolution (1981–89) culminated in the fall of the Berlin Wall in 1989 that marked—however temporarily—the triumph of economic liberalism and undid the basis for the very distinctions between Left and Right.

With help of the media, advertising, technology, and the concept of *speed*, Virilio, but even more so, Jean Baudrillard, describe this state of things as a "certain tendency" of the world, an orientation or direction against which there is no recourse. Unlike poststructuralism associated with philosophical and psychoanalytical texts that argue for openings and becomings in a dynamic system of differences, postmodernism, a term popularized by Baudrillard, refers to a historical period that terminates the heroic age of modernism of which Sartre and French communism were the last avatars. It also replaces the turbulent revolutions of the sixties. Postmodernism ushers in a kind of political lassitude, even a residual melancholia. In a world of input and output, humans cannot but note the futility of all political endeavor. With this postmodern condition, when, as Baudrillard writes in 1977, everything works according to structural laws of value, space for political intervention has been eradicated.[2] To undo the unified historical subject of existentialism and Marxism, poststructuralism had set out to complicate the referent (or ordinary human being) that it saw as the powerful product of a bourgeois strategy. With postmodernism however, the territory itself is said to have disappeared and the map is all that remains.[3] Even art, which since the French Revolution had been the site of resistance and change, was co-opted by money. Paintings, Jean-François Lyotard wrote in 1985 in the catalog to an exhibit at Beaubourg, entitled, *Les immatériaux* (1985), are equated with a check. The subversive function of art as an invention of life (a function that had been assigned to the artist in France since the nineteenth century) has been abandoned or, at least, weakened.

In a world under the sway of the media and based on interchangeable regimes of signs, human relations are also said to deteriorate. Symbolic orders and kinship structures that regulated French society for centuries are on the wane. This in itself does not have to be negative. In the 1960s, feminists and other special interest groups fought hard to abolish many of these structures decried for being patriarchal and for subjugating and imprisoning women. However, their replacement by other structures derived from marketing was increasingly deplored by women and men alike. In this new society, the more traditionally marked places are replaced by what the anthropologist Marc Augé has called "non-places [*non-lieux*]," such as airports, trains, supermarkets, and other zones of transit.[4] In postmodern societies, identities formed in symbolic networks are replaced by others that are based, like apartment buildings in Paris, on access codes. Solitary and narcissistic individuals controlled by marketing replace those that moved in a more organic fabric of traditional society. For Augé, this does not constitute the end of society but signals its transformations. What previously made sense has lost its meaning. Contemporary society is confronted with an overabundance of events and a proliferation of spaces and novel forms of identities and relations. It will, Augé

2. Jean Baudrillard, *Simulations*, trans. Paul Foss, Paul Patton, and Philip Beitchman (New York: Semiotext(e), 1983).

3. By means of the allegory of the territory and the map in the tale, "On Rigor in Science," by the Argentine writer Jorge Luis Borges, in *Dreamtigers*, trans. Mildred Boyer and Harold Morland (Austin: Texas University Press 1990), Baudrillard shows how only the map subsists and the territory is lost.

4. Marc Augé, *Non-Places*, trans. John Howe (New York: Verso, 1995).

argues, make sense again in a new space/time, but no structure has yet been put in place.

So far, I have drawn the trajectory of this argument through contrastive readings of Sartre, *Les lettres françaises*, but also of Gilles Deleuze and Félix Guattari, Hélène Cixous, Jean Baudrillard, Jean-François Lyotard, and Marc Augé, in order to set the stage for the recent turn to the Right in France. I can now look at two of the new thinkers and writers who embody this turn: Luc Ferry and Michel Houellebecq. They both came of age in a market economy and write from its condition. Though they do not entirely approve of it, they are most critical of their predecessors and of what they dismiss as the latter's ill-conceived militantism. I shall conclude by seeing how the generation of May 1968 fares in today's political and cultural climate and whether some earlier forms of resistance to capital can be updated and used to create less a turn to the Left than simply a new turn.

Luc Ferry is the prototype of the new intellectual who has both enabled and espoused this French "turn to the Right" through his writings and his actions. His categorical and ongoing dismissal of what he calls "the anti-humanism of *la pensée 68*" culminated in a book with the same title, co-authored with Alain Renaut and published in French in 1985.[5] The two philosophers invoke Sartre to argue for a return to the "individual" (who would have remained unaffected by consumerism), "values" (the slogans of the conservative wing of the American Republican party resound between the inverted commas), and a secular "humanism" (rife with the glory of truth, dignity, and essence) that differential thinking had long before called into question. They contrast the individual with the subject and not, as the post-68 thinkers did, with the citizen. Ferry wants to revive the individual by way of an existential humanism that had come under attack in the sixties in order to close the "revolutionary" parentheses of that era, which had carried a critique of the fulsome individual, the French state, consumerism, and colonialism. Throughout his work, Ferry argues strongly for a return to *virtue* and *values*. Against the revolutionaries of 1968, especially Deleuze and Guattari, whom he links with Nietzsche, Heidegger, and a certain Nazism, Ferry argues for a non-metaphysical, non-tyrannical humanism, derived from Kant—rather than from Descartes

5. Luc Ferry and Alain Renaut, *French Philosophy of the Sixties: An Essay in Anti-humanism*, trans. Mary H. S. Cottan (Amherst: University of Massachusetts Press, 1990).

—and from Sartre. This new humanism privileges freedom, ethics, and liberal democracy. In *The New Ecological Order*, Ferry accuses his elders of siding with communism and, especially, with Nazi fascism.[6] The fascist ties of revolutionary ecology in 1968 thinkers are developed at length by way of an attack on deep ecology and on American eco-feminists. Ferry argues instead for a "soft" ecology that would tax cars for emission of carbon dioxide and prevent industries from dumping too much toxic waste in conspicuous places. He is adamant about replacing revolutionary ideals with democratic reforms from within. Ferry speaks from the vantage point of his Parisian debates. Never addressed is what happens in places that do not have Western-style democratic practices. Dismissing postmodernism equated with "posthumanism," Ferry also denounces a return to a pre-modern vision of the world. Writing indirectly against Bruno Latour, he adopts a slogan to announce that "we are still modern" (xix). He never questions his use of "modernism" or of the universal "we." He debunks at length "non-sensical" thinkers such as Michel Serres and his idea of a "natural contract."[7] In a sentence he might well wish he had not written, he announces that "It is strange to see that ideas of environment and ecological protection always stem from the West and not from developing countries" (xxv). It is in conversation with a scientist, Jean-Didier Vincent, in their co-authored book with the lofty title *Qu'est-ce que l'homme* (2000; What is Man) —and heaven forbid, not the "human being" that would, at least, include *la femme*—that Ferry addresses preemptively a vague charge of "philosophism."[8]

Reduction of a world replete with its messy complications to easy binary oppositions lends to his writings a strong didactic and pedagogical value. The universal concepts that make up his rhetoric appear to predispose him to a public career in politics and education. In 1982, he joined the Saint-Simon Foundation, a French think tank created by the historian François Furet. The club, founded in 1981 after the election of François Mitterrand and dissolved in 1999, was meant to bring together the university, businesses, and public administration to foster "democracy" and economic liberalism in order to combat to-

---

6. Ferry, *The New Ecological Order*, trans. Carol Volk (Chicago: Chicago University Press, 1995).

7. See Michel Serres, *The Natural Contract*, trans. Elizabeth McArthur and William Paulson (Ann Arbor: University of Michigan Press, 1995).

8. Ferry and Jean-Didier Vincent, *Qu'est-ce que l'homme* (Paris: Odile Jacob, 2000).

talitarianisms. It was to join people with money to those who, for lack of liquidity, had "ideas." It is this very combination in which money tends to select the proper "ideas" that accelerates an inevitable turn to the Right even within France's Left and questions the accepted distinctions between the two.

In one of his more recent books, *Qu'est-ce qu'une vie réussie?*, published in 2002 by Grasset just as he was about to become minister of education, Ferry inquires about the meaning of life in an age of consumerism, media, and technology.[9] The meaning of life has not disappeared, though the question has to be rephrased. Ferry insists on salvaging humanist values that for him, in spite of Baudrillard's claim to the contrary, still have currency. Careful to distance himself from the contemporary slogan that pushes humans toward the categories of wealth, success, and prestige, he shows that one can harmonize life's forces in such a way as to realize one's creative abilities and to derive from them a sense of satisfaction. The unspoken term of his argument is that the self-creativity of the individual is valid only for those who have at least the means to accede to such a possibility. Failing to enter into a discussion about how most humans do not have such a privileged option, Ferry speaks for those who already have the means. He comes to the defense of humanist values and the good life at a time when most humans live in anomie or, in the words of Virilio, in a world, most of which has become an insalubrious *banlieue.*

The book is a critique of the Nietzschean turn in French thought. Less dismissive than he was in earlier books, Ferry now recognizes both some of Nietzsche's contributions and, closer in time, those of Deleuze; yet he continues to insist on the new humanistic values that he finds in Greek philosophy. Ferry makes a case for a turn to philosophy instead of religion in an age of unbridled consumerism. Appealing to values of "self-discipline" and "mastery," to manly virtues and values, Ferry encourages his readers to acquire "a certain serenity" and accede to grace. Ferry writes: "This whole book has attempted to offer the reader the possibility of appropriating the great responses to the question of the good life [*vie réussie*] presenting those responses as singularities so as to enable the reader to make personal choices in an enlightened fashion" (283). He adds:

---

9. Ferry, *What Is the Good Life?*, trans. Lydia G. Cochrane (Chicago: University of Chicago Press, 2005).

If we must discover the human world, enrich our experience, broaden our views—thus constantly encounter a diversity of cultures and beings —it is because we possess (unlike the oyster) the curious faculty of detachment from the particularities of origin. It is a talent that, in spite of the anxiety it arouses, keeps encouraging us to perfect ourselves, to enrich our lives—and to travel, to borrow Naipaul's image—rather than to remain clinging to the rock [like the oyster] we grew up on. (284)

This beautiful and harmonious view of *la vie réussie* is carried over into the domain of art:

It is because they are "singular" authors or composers, in this narrowly defined sense (that is, rooted in their culture of origin and their epoch, yet destined to speak to all men of all times by virtue of the universality of their message) that we still read Plato or Homer, Molière or Shakespeare, and still listen to the works of Bach or Rameau. The same is true of all great works and all great monuments. One can be French and Roman Catholic and still be profoundly moved by the temple of Angkor Wat, the great mosque of Kairouan, a book by Gabriel Garcia Marquez, or a fine example of Chinese calligraphy. (282)

Ferry's notion of a universal culture of the kind that is usually displayed on coffee tables or presented on PBS, has a very strong Western focus and, in spite of fleeting allusions to Naipaul and the Khmer temples or an "example" (but nothing more than the sample) of Chinese calligraphy, refuses diversity that would present other universalities at the heart of Western universalism. Ferry claims that living in the instant, in a state of grace, is a mark of a successful life. To illustrate his argument, he chooses to end his book by quoting stanzas 5 and 6 from a poem by Victor Hugo, "Booz endormi" ("Boaz asleep"), from *La légende des siècles (1859)*. The passage he quotes deals with the superiority of Boaz as an old man over young men. Sublime and with glowing eyes, he attracts women more than his younger counterparts:

Women looked at Boaz more than all the young men.
For the young man is handsome, but the old is sublime.
. . . . .
And though you see a fire in the eyes of young men,
In the eyes of an old man you can see a glow.[10]

10. Ferry, *What is the Good Life,* 287. Victor Hugo, quoted in English translation from "Boaz Asleep," in *Selected Poetry in French and English,* trans. and introd. Steven Mond (New York: Routledge, 2002).

To illustrate his point, Ferry turns to a mythical and biblical patriarch. He quotes Hugo's poem in such a way as to excise Ruth, the strong woman character introduced by the poet.

Ferry writes from the top of the new social pyramid diagrammed by Virilio. He inserts himself even more acutely at the top of the new social structure when he is named to the distinguished post of French Minister of Education for the conservative government of Jacques Chirac and his Prime Minister, Jean-Pierre Raffarin, from 2002–2004. Ferry specifically defended French humanist and republican laws on secularity and conspicuous religious symbols in schools. While in office, he showed how the good life and humanistic values are in harmony by adopting a much criticized, rather lavish lifestyle. At the same time, he tried to rein in the French teachers' union by accusing the left wing brought in by the 1968 cultural revolution of undermining the proper role of schools. The schools, he was quoted as saying, should not be assuring the personal fulfillment of individual children but the handing down of a body of knowledge and culture.[11] Ferry's liberal self-fashioning is based on authoritarian values, a combination already analyzed by Virilio and Baudrillard, who show how such conservatism is often invoked to smooth over economic liberalism. With the reshuffling of the Raffarin cabinet following the elections of 2004 that signaled a seeming turn to the Left, Ferry, as a most controversial minister, had to resign.

How to live, think, and write in an era of unbridled materialism is also a question raised by the writer Michel Houellebecq, who does not enter into Ferry's rarefied spheres. He sees the world of consumerism and rejects the revolutionary ideals of the 1960s associated with previous forms of militantism that he ascribes indiscriminately to postwar communism and May 1968.[12] Houellebecq situates his novels squarely in the context of economic liberalism. His decadent protagonists move in postmodern landscapes, from Spain's Costa Dorada (Gold Coast) to the beaches of Thailand. The background is that of tourist hotels and bars, the very non-places described by Augé. Houellebecq's novel, *Platform*, becomes a critique of market culture, with its emphasis on careerism and money.[13] For the protagonist,

11. Hugh Schofield, "France's Teachers Go on Strike Again," BBC News, May 6, 2003 (http:news.bbc.co.uk/2/hi/europe/3002079.stm).

12. Maurice Dantec also criticizes militantism though he searches for new literary forms that would go with a technological society resisted by a conservative French nation in *Périphérique* (Paris: Flammarion, 2003), 103–122.

13. Michel Houellebecq, *Platform*, trans. Frank Wynn (New York: Alfred Knopf, 2003).

named Michel, like the author, the world resembles one giant non-place:

> After the check-in formalities, I wandered around the shopping arcade. Even though the departures hall was completely roofed over, the shops were built in the form of huts, with the teak uprights and roofs thatched with palm leaves. The choice of products ranged from international standards (scarves by Hermès, perfumes by Yves Saint-Laurent, bags by Vuitton) to local products (shells, ornaments, Thai silk ties); every item had a barcode. All in all, airport shops still form part of the national culture; but a part that is safe, attenuated, and wholly adapted to global consumption. For the traveler at the end of his journey, it is a halfway house (*espace intermédiaire*), less interesting and less frightening than the rest of the country. I had an inkling that, more and more, the whole world would come to resemble an airport. (93–94)

Houellebecq shows no concern for the social, economic, or ecological nightmares created by the development of these places. He decries the militantism of the sixties that wanted to change the evolution of the world, but also the careerism of economic liberalism. A modern day "stranger," he wants to live happily in the world through sex.

In *Platform*, published in France in 2001, Houellebecq's protagonist also asks, in his fashion: what is the good life (*une vie réussie*)? Rejecting the solution provided by culture or by economic liberalism, he opts for happiness through sex, even if it is linked to sex-tourism. Not by chance, Michel works for the French Ministry of Culture. While on a tour in Thailand where he has many sexual encounters, he meets a woman, Valerie, with whom, after his return to Paris, he has a satisfying sexual relationship that brings them mutual happiness. Michel derides career-driven protagonists like Valerie before her conversion to sex, and especially her co-worker Jean-Yves, who thinks only of "having a good career [réussir une carrière]" (316). Jean-Yves makes plenty of money but is estranged from his wife, has no sex, and is profoundly unhappy. Michel tries to analyze Jean-Yves's motivation. With razor-sharp insights that here and there punctuate the novel's unstoppable sex scenes, the narrator concludes that Jean-Yves is motivated by a desire to construct something: "All in all, it was a respectable motive, not unlike the one that explains the very advance of human civilization. The social reward bestowed on him was a large salary; under other regimes it might have taken the form of an aristocratic title" (219).

In the novel that is a thinly disguised platform for his own ideas (lubricated with a little sex), Houellebecq presents his criticism of market economy as well as of politics in general in dialogical form. When the protagonist's lover, Valerie, tells him that the battle she is waging will be the last, he has wit enough to accede to irony: "It reminded me of history books in which politicians declared that this would be the 'war to end all wars,' the sort that was supposed to lead to a definitive peace" (202). He reminds her that it was she who told him that "capitalism by its very nature is a permanent state of war, a constant struggle that can never end" (202). Valerie agrees, but adds: "But it's not always the same people doing the fighting" (202).

These moments of critical acuity alternate with long passages of description of the postmodern world replete with non-places, marketing, and sex tourism. Deriding Kant's idea of a common will, Houellebecq writes in favor of a soft *consensus.* His protagonist is proud of not voting, and considers elections as excellent television shows (235). Moreover, he declares his dislike of militants who wanted to make society evolve in a given direction, and does not like their way of interesting themselves in general causes. "What did I, for my part, have to reproach the West for? Not much—but I wasn't especially attached to it (and I was finding it more and more difficult to understand how one could feel attached to an idea, a country, anything, in fact, other than an individual" (236). Michel dislikes the West because it is expensive and cold, and prostitution is bad. It is hard to smoke in public places and impossible to buy drugs; people work too much; there is too much noise and public safety is poorly implemented. He considers society to be a natural environment in which the idea of solidarity is never entertained. Perhaps, he concludes, society cannot survive with individuals like himself. But, at the same time, he can survive with a woman whom he would like to make happy. Though also critical of the 1960s, especially of revolutionary idealism and militantism, the narrator does not feel like tearing himself away from nature. He is more like the oyster Ferry criticizes for not wanting to leave its rock.

At the end of the book, Houellebecq's cynicism prevails. At this very moment of happiness, in a beautiful setting on the seashore in Thailand, the protagonist looks in the direction of Valerie, the woman with whom he wants to share (sexual) happiness, and a sudden terrorist attack kills her along with many other tourists. Appealing to a cliché, Houellebecq brings love and death together. The narrator returns briefly to Paris but eventually decides to go back to Thailand. He philosophizes on the individual and the world: "It is possible to live in the world without understanding it; all you need is to be able to get food, caresses, and love" (257). And he concludes:

> To the end, I will remain a child of Europe, of worry and of shame. I have no message of hope to deliver. For the West, I do not feel hatred. At most I feel a great contempt. I know only that every single one of us reeks of selfishness, masochism, and death. We have created a system in which it has simply become impossible to live, and what's more, we continue to export it. (258)

He uncovers the double standard of those who want to moralize actions such as the organization of sex tourism in Thailand. After the terrorist attack, the French press is indignant about the tour operators who—like Jean-Yves—facilitate the sex trade. Houellebecq accuses journalists and politicians, from Françoise Giroud to Lionel Jospin, of condemning the sex trade out of self-interest, for they suddenly appeal to morality in a capitalist society that has no values outside of money (348–49). Michel keeps his distance from the world and its dubious values, and can now accept death.

Writing for Houellebecq is less an artistic experiment than an activity turned toward media success, sensationalism, and money. In *Platform*, in a society governed by liberal economic competition, sexual relations become competitive as well. Houellebecq openly praises sex and the extension of sex tourism into poor and developing countries. The treatment of such rightist themes earned him a solid though controversial reputation and a court case. Can we compare this reputation to those of Baudelaire and Flaubert, accused of outrage to public morality? Both the poet and the writer are on today's list of classics of French literature. While Baudelaire and Flaubert revealed the bigotry of the moral system of bourgeois society and experimented with writing, Houellebecq exposes without judgment the crude predatory behavior that hides under the cloak of liberalism in journalistic prose. Hailed by some as the greatest writer today and denounced by others as depraved, Houellebecq clearly replaces the sense of community at the heart of Marxism and socialism with a core of raw competition.

What, in such a conservative climate, we can now ask, happens to the artists and theorists of the 1960s when they are confronted by market culture? To begin, we can look at a film by Jean-Luc Godard from which I borrowed the title for this essay, *Soigne ta droite* (*Keep Your

Right Up [1987]), a phrase that carries echoes of a boxing match as a metaphor for the violence and competition in today's society under the spell of economic liberalism. Godard, as most of his biographers and filmographers would have it, made his "great, heroic films," from *Breathless* and *Two or Three Things I Know About Her* to *Weekend* or *La Chinoise*, in the 1960s. They attack the social, political, and economic systems of France, Europe, and the world by way of filmic experimentations, that is, with the complication between sound and image, as well as by employing Brechtian processes that disrupt the narrative and introduce a distance between film and viewer in order to dismantle representation in the service of the reigning bourgeoisie. *Soigne ta droite* makes fun of a market economy that perverts humans and kills art. To foster its effects, the film features many of Godard's earlier props, from cars to electronic equipment and videos in scenes reminiscent of the antics of Jerry Lewis. It also contains literary allusions so numerous as to give the viewer the impression that the film-maker has withdrawn into his own world of poetry. The film follows the protagonist, "The Idiot"—with echoes of Dostoyevsky—(also called, "The Prince," a filmmaker played by Godard himself) who has to deliver his film by the end of the day. It stages all the characters of the new social pyramid that, subtended by greed, along with economic and demographic pressures, produces a double turn to the Right. When the sense of community at the basis of social experimentation and Marxism is replaced by competition, all values are turned upside down.

One scene will illustrate this point.[14] A protagonist earlier referred to as "L'individu," played by the late Jacques Villeret, is gathering wood and pruning shrubs in the country when a couple drives up in a red Mercedes convertible. The woman (Jane Birkin) asks for directions to Paris. She recognizes the Individual whom she greets as *La fourmi.* He, in turn, addresses her as *La cigale.* The Ant and the Cicada refer to the well-known fable by Jean de La Fontaine—one of Ferry's favorite authors—whose moral lessons every child schooled in France had to memorize. Its seemingly timeless message is that the hard-working Ant will have something to eat during the barren days of winter, whereas the prodigal Cicada, who wasted all summer singing, will go hungry. In *Keep Your Right Up*, the moral is reversed. The Cicada engages the Individual in conversation. Unlike the hard-working Ant, she owes her wealth and success to her connections. The Cicada in-

---

14. Jean-Luc Godard, *Soigne ta droite* (*Keep your right up*, 1987), scene 8, "Woods."

troduces her companion as the son of TWA and Hennessy Cognac before launching into a vapid narrative about all the places she has to visit and the people she will meet who will be useful to her. Godard sharply criticizes the new elite composed indiscriminately of business people, politicians, media people, and even nobility. The Cicada tells the Ant that they live in the Visconti mansion, that she has to visit Dior to buy some dresses, and that she will go to the opera with the ambassador from Brazil who will introduce her to Francis Ford Coppola. They will get seats to the finals of Wimbledon, if they have time, because her fiancé's uncle is connected with the Queen of England. Albeit indirectly, Godard scathingly criticizes a society dominated by money and social networking. It is the Ant, the hard working Individual, who will go hungry. When the Cicada asks if he needs anything from Paris as she and her lover roar off in their Mercedes, the Ant shouts after them: "Phone Mr. La Fontaine for me and tell him he is an asshole." Here, the moral of the story is reversed. It is the hardworking individual, outside the new social pyramid, who will go hungry. The worker, who had been the hope of postwar intellectuals, is doomed. The good life is on the side of wealth and networking.

Soigne ta droite seems to imply that nothing is possible in the violent 1980s outside of an ironic presentation of the new situation of greed, injustice, and the workers' demise. The artist-filmmaker seeks solace in shots of nature. Burlesque scenes showing the greed and sex of a materialistic society are intertwined with some hauntingly beautiful images of a recurring seascape, often seen through slightly open French doors behind which, at times, a young girl is seen looking in. Godard does not go beyond denouncing the new media society in which no resistance is possible. Or is it? The film ends with the assertion that the light will stab the night in the back. A sunrise—or a dawn—announces the possibility of a renewal with a whisper from which new voices will rise. Godard quotes a recurring line from Lautréamont's *Chants de Maldoror*, "I salute you, ancient ocean." In a long tribute to the ocean, the poet, in voluntary exile, finally announces that he is about to return to human society with all its brutal aspects. Praising the greatness of the ocean that he contrasts with the weakness and conceit of humans, the poet will make "a great effort, and accomplish dutifully [his] destiny on this earth."[15]

15. Isidore Ducasse, Comte de Lautréamont, *Les chants de Maldoror.* Chant 1, 9., trans. Guy Wernham, 1943, 12–26.

In a society under the sign of money and profit, artists can do nothing but withdraw. As Godard playing himself in *Prénom Carmen* (1983; *First Name: Carmen.*) states with a heavy Swiss accent: "Les temps sont durs pour des œufs comme nous" (Times are tough for blockheads like us). Life is difficult for inventive artists and thinkers in a postmodern era with its emphasis on money and profit. The whisper will resume in the future. In the present, melancholia is the only posture possible.

Or is it? We can, to conclude, turn briefly to some writers and critics who are survivors of the 1960s and who, though they agree that there is no organized resistance to global economic liberalism, are not content with lofty pedagogy, sheer cynicism, or melancholia. These include Gilles Deleuze and Félix Guattari decried by Ferry, as well as Hélène Cixous, Etienne Balibar, and Jacques Rancière, who have attempted to go beyond a broadly conceived militantism of soft or dubious ethical claim. Resistance is not possible from the outside (through protest and demonstrations), but more from the inside (through tactical operations). At stake for them is the opening of small spaces from which to think otherwise and to influence the construction of subjectivities and new alliances. Deleuze argued for the opening of *vacuoles* in the micropolitics of the everyday; Guattari, for deviating by creating new sensibilities and forms of intelligence on the part of artists and critics who are engaged in the production of subjectivities; Cixous—rephrasing Beckett—, for writing as something small but precious; Balibar, for rephrasing burning questions; and Rancière, for reconfiguring through art what is thinkable at a given moment.

The late Michel de Certeau used to say that one should never take people for idiots ("Il ne faut jamais prendre les gens pour des imbéciles"). Though people are consumers or even live in anomie, they create their own openings and invent life. They rephrase, reconfigure, and introduce fissures in dominant discourse. Current liberal democracy is one in which an elite and a world government of wealth govern in the name of the people. What passes for democracy is often forced consensus. When faced with this tendency, some artists and critics espouse a turn to the Right while some of their elders seek refuge in melancholia. In both cases, the present as a site of the possible is eschewed. Of importance, still others assert, is not to flex one's muscles or *soigner sa droite,* to put one's right up, but to deviate gently, with civility, by means of something small but precious, so as to accede to a good life by making the present into a site of possibility.

MICHEL GUELDRY

The Americanization of France

A writer thinking about the concept of "Americanization" must immediately ask several methodological questions, for this subject, which seems at first glance to be "obvious," is in fact often poorly conceptualized and deliberately manipulated. This initial methodological clarification concerns Americanization in general, but given the limits of this article, I shall focus on describing the Americanization of the French economy and French culture, which this phenomenon has affected with particular force.

METHODOLOGICAL QUESTIONS

The first question involves the *definition* of Americanization, which is inseparable from the *process* of the spread of American goods and culture: what is exported and imported, and why? Indeed, the "how" and the "why" of Americanization emerge from the difference between what America exports and what local players assimilate. Does the United States disseminate practices and values that are beneficial to all, or practices and values that may be good or bad but that are, above all, dominant? If capitalism and pluralist democracy, the founding American principles of the American experience, mean the end of History—according to Francis Fukuyama—then Americanization would be synonymous with the "natural" imposition of the correct direction of History (*sens de l'Histoire*). And if Western ideology (rationalism, individualism, and so forth) has to replace distinct local particularities, then the United States would be blazing a trail for all of humanity rather than being the source of the Great Secret. Therefore, through its "universal" practices and ecumenical values, the spread of Americanization would be a ruse by History used to put an

YFS 116/117, *Turns to the Right?* ed. Johnson and Schehr, © 2009 by Yale University.

end to History itself (*le bon sens de l'Histoire*). Such an interpretation of Americanization might better serve U.S. nationalism than the truth, however. Conversely, to interpret Americanization as a deadly coca-colonization or a soft brand of fascism would also be a caricature of the situation; hence there is a pressing need to define what exactly the process of Americanization involves. For example, France has imported Coca-Cola and hip hop but not baseball, which is all the rage in a Communist country like Cuba and a non-Western country like Japan, while China has imported capitalism but not democracy. The United States, therefore, exports certain economic practices to which one must adapt in order to survive, but also other values and practices that may be ignored or bypassed. No one is forced to eat at McDonald's, watch *Desperate Housewives*, or play with Barbie. Thus there is selectivity and a capacity for choice in the reception of Americanization, which reveals itself as a heterogeneous and multileveled phenomenon—from Americanization of the core of a country's culture and practices to various forms of assimilation/adaptation to outright rejection. So how do we distinguish forced Americanization from the voluntary variety, the natural evolution, pre-emption, hijacking, and quasi-imitation undertaken in order to remain true to oneself? Are there forms of Americanization and/or resistance unique to France? These questions call for the identification of diverse forms of Americanization and local strategies of reception, resistance, and appropriation of America *extra muros*.

This leads to a second question, which is one of cause and effect. When globalization emanates from Japan or India, is this a form of Americanization that has ricocheted or is it a phenomenon of a different nature? Whatever the answer, this question applies to the United States as well: Rome is no longer in Rome, as du Bellay would have it, and in many ways American culture is no longer made only "in the USA." American values, practices, and products are recycled and marketed *ad infinitum*, to the point of being unrecognizable and then reintroduced to the United States. An Americanoid vulgate circulates, aping, deforming, and amplifying the American original. Not long ago, for example, France was reading Inspector Maigret, while today it produces Americanized detective series, complete with guns and pyrotechnics, and *Loft Story* or *L'île de la tentation* imitate the worst of American television. Americanization therefore emerges as a vital but not singular component of a world culture, of a mercantile cosmopolitanism, of a hodge-podge of cultures, which is overdetermined but not totally controlled by America. While Americanization may be the principal engine of this phenomenon, it is also relayed by numerous local engines with the capacity to act locally and rather independently.

Is this partial modification of French culture by American culture —an acculturation—accompanied by a degradation of the host culture —a dis-culturation? And how does one situate attendant forms of transculturation, the process whereby a community borrows forms, values, or materials from a dominant culture? And how then do we understand Franco-American hybrids? For example, in May 2008, the singer Sébastien Tellier, who speaks English quite badly, was chosen to represent France in the Eurovision Song Contest with a song called *Divine,* sung in English. Thus French popular music, sung in English, benefits from official subsidies and support. According to *Le monde,* at the July 2008 FrancoFolies festival in La Rochelle, which has been the bastion of Francophone song for more than twenty years, unknown young artists performed free concerts near the old port, on a stage sponsored by MySpace. The bill featured only French groups, a fact that was not immediately evident from the groups' names: The Dodoz from Toulouse, Shaolin Temple Defender from Bordeaux, The Sugar Plum Fairy Project from Tours, and Guadaloupean singer Tom Franger, who sang in Creole-inflected English, not to mention Uncle Ben, Uncle Slam, Little, and Pony Pony Run Run.[1]

NEOLIBERAL CAPITALISM, A SELF-CERTAIN AND DOMINANT SYSTEM

In order to understand the profound penetration of the American economic model in the Hexagon, let us recall the recent past. From 1945 until the early 1980s, France was marked by "social Colbertism." While the French general economic framework was capitalist, the market, private enterprise, competition, class tensions, and individual risk and initiative, were limited and counterbalanced by the economic intervention of the State (Colbertism), a complex welfare state and a specific "third way" that was neither Soviet communism nor U.S. capitalism. Colbertism was visible in nationalization programs,

---

1. Yves Eudes and Odile de Plas, "La chanson française *in english*," *Le monde* (September 3, 2008). Out of 25 participants in the festival, 13 performed in English, while two mixed their native language with English, and the Russian, Dima Bilan, won the festival prize with his English song, *Believe.*

government-controlled monopolies such as the SNCF, central planning, large public projects (the Concorde, etc.), the defense of *champions nationaux* [big national "favorite" industries], public controls and subsidies, defense of the domestic market against outside competition, the orientation of Europe toward French interests, monetary manipulation, a Left-Right consensus for state intervention, and the domination of government ministries and public enterprises by the Republican elite with a strong state-centered culture.

This social Colbertism inspired economic politics, which had, as its social complement, the collective protection of the welfare state. In order to counter the harmful influence of the Communist Party, to integrate the proletariat and working classes into the Republic, and to legitimize the capitalist system in a populace scarred by class struggle and civil strife, the Republic needed to be social, according to article 2 of the Constitution of 1958. Social Colbertism was therefore the national formula for modernization, reconciling the French state-based economic tradition that had preceded capitalism by 150 years, with free-market economics. The State derived its legitimacy from three complementary sources: political (rule of law, democratic pluralism, and freedom of expression), economic (neo-Colbertism), and social (the welfare state). This synthesis was the French version of European social democracy. Yet starting in the 1980s it would be undermined by the convergence of five factors.

First among these factors were the oil crises of 1973 and 1979. France was able to forestall the consequences of these crises for several years but the foundations of its former prosperity were crumbling.

The second factor was competition from Japan. Starting in 1981–82, the massive importation of quartz watches, cameras, video cameras, and automobiles spread economic anxiety among French politicians, business leaders, and workers. This shifting of the balance of power sparked what was called the "battle of Poitiers." In this city, where Charles Martel defeated the Saracens in 732, a small customs office was entrusted with the formidable task of inspecting thousands of Japanese videocassette recorders. The importations were impeded by an act of administrative subterfuge, as the overworked office let the machines out in piecemeal fashion onto a French market that was, in fact, quite receptive. Yet this feeble defense could not contain the tidal wave provoked by the strength of the Japanese economy.

The third element was the failure of the "break with capitalism" in François Mitterrand's socialist economic politics from May 1981 to

March 1983. For almost two years, the socialist state recruited incessantly, increased salaries and social services, and reduced the length of the workweek, and, in so doing, sparked a flight of capital and a severe degradation of public finances. In March 1983, with nowhere to turn, Mitterrand adopted a policy of economic austerity, indexed the franc to the deutschmark with newfound budgetary discipline, halted state generosity, and celebrated entrepreneurship. The Socialists reconciled with business—and with reality, as their opponents snickered—at the very moment when the economic crisis, unemployment, Europe, and globalization were all settling in for the long haul. Thus social Colbertism began a long and painful unraveling.

The era of national largesse also drew to a close because of the imposition of a competitive capitalist model, which came from the United States and the United Kingdom to challenge the rest of the world. Margaret Thatcher and Ronald Reagan intended to destroy social democracy, diminish the role of the state, and revitalize the market through privatization, deregulation, and fiscal policy favorable to business and the upper classes. This neo-liberal capitalist model grew stronger in the 1990s with the help of the pro-market legislation of the Single European Act of 1986 and a forced march toward a single currency that started in 1992. In order to satisfy the five "convergence criteria" of the Maastricht Treaty, a prerequisite for adopting the single currency, France adopted an orthodox monetary policy, tightened public and social spending, and disengaged from numerous public enterprises and social programs. According to critics, as it embraced this tough monetarist discipline, France sacrificed the real economy—the production of goods, services, and jobs—to the defense of the franc against international markets, the speculative financial economy, and the casino capitalism of the 1980s and 1990s. A number of new expressions came into use, describing the rising social crisis, nationalist-populist protests and identity malaise: *les déçus du socialisme* (socialism's disillusioned believers), *l'austerité* (austerity), *les nouveaux pauvres* (the new poor), *les exclus* (the excluded), the RMIistes (recipients of welfare allocations known as *revenu minimum d'insertion*), *restos du cœur* (soup kitchens founded by the comedian Coluche), the generalized consensus of *la pensée unique,* the proposed alternative economy of *l'autre politique, les souverainistes*, Neo-Jacobins, *l'euroscepticisme, la fracture sociale,* and so forth. Coluche, Abbé Pierre, José Bové, and Olivier Besancenot became the spokespersons and rescuers of a civil society that had been abandoned, while, in some lofty hideaway, the French elite, often under criminal investigation for corruption and venality, partied and praised privatization, competition, globalization, and the Maastricht treaty.

The fatal blow to social Colbertism would be globalization, symbolized by China's admission to the World Trade Organization in 2001, the increased competition from the BRICKS (Brazil, Russia, India, China, Korea and South Africa) economies, and the rising price of raw materials, energy (the third oil crisis), and food in the first decade of the twenty-first century. From that point on, the relatively continuous economic growth and social enrichment of the years known as the "*Trente glorieuses*" (1945–1973) were shown to have been a short-lived socio-economic oasis in the economic history of France and Europe.

In his 2007 book, *Ensemble,* Nicolas Sarkozy writes, "the crisis of the Republic is inseparable from the calling into question of progress. During the *Trente glorieuses,* sons saw in their fathers' eyes the promise of a better future. Today what they see in their fathers' expressions is dread of exclusion or fear of losing their social position."[2] Thus Sarkozy proposes a revitalized and reformed capitalism, holding that the two are compatible: "I believe in competition. . . . I believe in the market economy, where the customer is king" (65–66). Meanwhile he admits the destructive character of 1990s monetarism (114–15), the over-evaluation of the euro (130–131), and laissez-faire policy (144–45). His opponents, however, denounce him as the culmination of thirty years of French-style economic neo-liberalism, the return of a carnivorous Right that has learned the American model only too well. Hence the numerous nicknames denouncing what opponents consider his materialist vulgarity: *Sarko l'Américain; Starkozy;* President *fric, frac, frime;* Carla Bruni-Sarkozy, his wife, is part of the champagne Left (*bobo*), Sarko is bling-bling. One finds neologisms and Anglicisms such as *Sarkollywood; Sarkonomics; le président too much; le président Top Gun; le président people,* and the use of English in these critical expressions is quite significant.

A 2008 special issue of the *Canard enchaîné* devoted to "Président Fric-Frime" carried the subtitle "Sarko and money. It's for real"—a reminder of an outburst by the President over his relationship with Carla Bruni. A caricature shows "le petit Nicolas," with his arms wide open, flashing a greedy smile while exclaiming, "Work more and you'll become rich . . . and then you can become my friends!" Pierre Musso,

---

2. Nicolas Sarkozy, *Ensemble* (Paris: XO Editions, 2007).

less politically engaged than this satirical weekly, raises numerous parallels between *Sarkozysme* and *Berlusconisme,* notably their managerial approach to politics. "Sarkoberlusconisme" corresponds to the "five key themes for business," including "strategic planning" and "reengineering." They share a "management dogma" going "well beyond the sphere of business" and seeing itself as "a new rationality developed in the West and laying claim to universality." Through these two members of the same posse, "business culture has left the 'micro' sphere of business and become simply a culture or even a Western religion with a global scope." At the heart of management is the "culture of daring, of challenge" and the "entrepreneurial dynamic" of "competition," the "self-made man" and the triumph of "business imagination in the hollowed political domain."[3]

Reaganomics claimed to liberate the economy from limits and laws judged artificial or imposed by public policy and to shrink back the political sphere to its "natural" regalian functions (defense, security, etc.). Nowadays, this neo-liberal business ideology inspires, drives, or directly absorbs a significant portion of the political domain. Election campaigning has turned into political marketing, management and implementation of policy are being privatized or catching up with entrepreneurial practices, and the materialistic trivialities of capitalism conspire to demobilize the citizenry. This consumerist pseudo-apoliticism is illustrated in an ironic quatrain featured on the web site of Strip-Tease, a variety show seen on France 3, a French TV channel: "Si la part de la politique/Dans Strip-Tease est si famélique/C'est que ce monde est allergique/A ce qui n'est pas dithyrambique [If the role of politics/In Strip-Tease is so anorexic/It's because the world is allergic/To that which is not dithyrambic]."[4] However one interprets Sarkozy, it is undeniable that in France, as elsewhere, the impact of American neo-liberalism has been such that the language and the values of private business have triumphed in a mood of increased economic competition and social malaise.

CULTURE: INDIVIDUALISM OF THE MASSES

Some observers argue that the only culture common to all of Europe today is the American commercial-media culture. Its *lingua franca*

---

3. Pierre Musso, *Le Sarkoberlusconisme* (Paris: Editions de l'Aube, 2008). "Challenge" and "self-made man" are in English in the original.

4. http://strip-tease.france3.fr/, accessed June 6, 2008.

would be "Globish," a global English that is a repertoire of several hundred words shared by a large number of Europeans (and by the world), allowing one to travel, conduct business, and communicate across cultures. This means forgetting the common—Celtic, Germanic, Latin, Slavic—foundation of Europe, Greco-Roman antiquity, Judeo-Christianity, the Renaissance, the Reformation, the Enlightenment, the Arts, the shared adversity of Fascism and Communism, and so forth.

As a matter of fact, a triple temporal and cultural gap continued to exist until about the middle of the 1960s. The first gap was between the core of the global system (the United States) and its periphery, the rest of the planet. The products, ideas, values, practices, and fashions of the United States took years to cross the Atlantic and to fully penetrate Europe, and took even longer to reach outer peripheries (countries) even further removed, while the peoples frozen by communism were excluded altogether. Decades later, diffusion from the United States (or elsewhere) has become much faster, as the latest movie, computer game, or hit single can go viral and be launched simultaneously across the globe. The second gap was the one separating Paris from the provinces. In the capital, life was about innovation and importation, while in the provinces it was about the soft light of sleepy afternoons. In *Le cheval d'orgueil*, Pierre-Jakez Hélias (1914–1995) describes his Breton childhood in which his Brittany of the 1920s very much evokes the Brittany of Paul Gauguin (1848–1903), who lived there from 1886 to 1891. Since then, development, improvements in the infrastructure, and the standardization of communications and culture have significantly closed the gap between the provinces and Paris. The third gap is a longstanding generational one. In the United States, France, and elsewhere the baby boomers were "the children of Marx and of Coca-Cola" (Godard), while their parents and grandparents had been (de)formed by World War I, the Great Depression, and World War II. This "greatest generation" was ill-equipped to understand the generation born into post-WWII prosperity. The parents and grandparents faced William II, the Czar Nicholas II, the Bolshevik revolution, Mussolini, Hitler, Stalin, and Tojo. They went scared and hungry for years, married at twenty, and often became parents nine months later. Their children came of age in a time of free sex thanks to the pill, did drugs, listened to rock-n-roll, practiced yoga, spoke English, and questioned the illusions of progress. In other words, they seemed to live on another planet. Yet these baby boomers grew up and settled down. These hippies-turned-yuppies, who have become parents in turn, have more in common with their children than with their own parents: peace, economic plenty, consumer-leisure society, market superficiality, moral relativism. The cultural consequences of advanced capitalism—fashion, music, drugs, shallowness, narcissistic rebellion, and adventure, coupled with contemporary (pop) psychology—prolong, exploit, and accentuate the great upheaval of the 1960s and the post WWII economic boom, they do not depart from them. Intergenerational relations have changed since relationships between the norm and alternative, dissident, or marginal expressions have shifted. Cuisine fusion, Zumba fitness, sudoku, ikebana, and other "exotic" imports and hybrids today have less capacity to surprise than the Beatles did in 1963. Meanwhile, minority sexualities have been (relatively) mainstreamed, and "rebellious" music makes money for the matrix.

The cultural Americanization of France has therefore developed within the context of these three factors: 1) The narrowing of the gap between the United States and the rest of the world, achieved with the emergence of a decentralized system of production of Americanized goods and services and the development of properly French capacities of filtration, "hybridization," and production; 2) the growing technological integration, cultural sophistication, and social transformation of France; 3) the standardization of generational values and practices, whereby the once-clear gap between parents and children was blurred by the rise in the level of general culture and by the balkanization of cultural norms.

"IMBÉCÉLÉBRITÉ": FIFTEEN MINUTES OF HEXAGONAL FAME

For a long time, France has established high culture from Paris—the urbane culture of the dominant and cultivated classes—as the official culture. Meanwhile popular, regional, and rural cultures were relegated to the margins or to a status of folkloric curiosity. This "classical" culture was intensely logocentric, rooted in the written word, verbal analysis and prowess, and canonic texts. Today popular culture, decentralized and commercialized, is taking its revenge. This culture is mediatized and iconocentric, based on the image and on what in French is known as *le look*. In the United States, television has become a member of the family, an authority figure, and a role model for behavior and consumption. Structured discourse has made way for confessional feeling, television therapy, strangeness, and dysfunction all shamelessly flaunted in a murky postmodern stew that is narcissistic, ludic, consumerist, and anomic.

Over the past fifteen to twenty years, French television has come to display the very same characteristics, summed up by the neologism "imbécélébrité." Combining "imbécilité" with "célébrité," the term designates those who will go to any length to achieve their "fifteen minutes of fame" (Warhol) on television. The first notable program of this sort was *Loft Story* (2001–02 on M6), followed by *Nice People* (2004, on TF1 and imitating the film *L'auberge espagnole*), *Les colocataires* (2004 on M6), *Secret Story* (starting in June 2007 on M6), *L'île de la tentation* (TF1), *Koh-Lanta* (TF1), and the like. Since 2005, M6 has been airing *L'amour est dans le pré*, a show featuring women and farmers setting up house in the country. The producers strive to create incompatible couples for shock effect and to boost ratings. This program was adapted from *Farmer Wants a Wife*, created in the United Kingdom in 2001 before spreading to numerous European countries and the United States. Between 2001 and 2007, TF1 broadcast *Le maillon faible*, a copy of the British program, *The Weakest Link*, on which participants are humiliated by a cruel host before being eliminated by fellow contestants' schemes. The globalization of these themes and programs is clear, and their bad taste is without limits.[5] Trash-TV is the most recent avatar of mediocrity in the media, as well as proof that commercial television is driven by the logic of competitive capitalism.

WHAT IS READ, WHAT IS SAID

Two contemporary novelists, Christian Authier (1969–) and Fréderic Beigbeder (1965–) offer opposed yet complementary perspectives on France's unique and selective process of Americanization. The first writer, introverted, anxious, critical, and nostalgic, spews the absurdities of our age. The second is a mischievous and merrymaking dandy who revels in a postmodernity that is insolent, narcissistic, and sensual. This contrast recalls an adage by eighteenth-century French moralist Vauvenargues (1715–47), for whom the world is a comedy for the *homme d'esprit* and a tragedy for the *homme de cœur*.

Authier bemoans the corruption of feelings by technology: "As the advertising slogan goes, 'Love is as easy as a phone call.' The cell

5. In Greece, for example, Annita Pania (1970–) is one of the queens of trash-tv, and her first book is entitled *The Revenge of Toilet Paper*.

phone brought about urgency, impatience, tension and non-stop acceleration."[6] He continues: "For years, editorials and very serious commentaries from philosophers and sociologists have gone on about new behaviors linked to the Internet, and especially, to cell phones. . . . Under the pretext of bringing us closer and keeping us in permanent contact, these technologies have separated and spread us thin" (106). In another novel, he laments the replacement of speech with "commercialized gibbering, an incessant soundtrack of supermarkets, ring tones, and mood music,"[7] and he expresses stupefaction at the zombies with "earpieces screwed to their cell phones" (151–52). This novel's anti-hero, Christophe, swamped with work (49, 59–60) and harried by "slick-talking, narcissistic ham actors spouting banalities" slides into "nausea" (145) and isolates himself in his unrest (67, 79) before it all ends badly for him. His tragic destiny symbolizes the failures of our time, threatened by "grafting of goods and commerce" (15), vulgar materialism, and "hatred of life" (58). Confronted with this state of affairs, the author retreats into recrimination and nostalgia. Beigbeder, on the contrary, successfully straddles the worlds of television, marketing, literature, and corporate promotion. He is chronicler of the literary and the urbane, organizer of Parisian soirées at a place called Caca's Club (!), host of *Hypershow*, a quirky prime-time talk show on Canal+, and his official web site is whimsically known as SNOB (site non officiel (de) Beigbeder). His writing sketches a generation obsessed with money and image, one that scoffs at everything and casts a sarcastic, cynical, and sensual eye on the quirks of contemporary French life. Beigbeder's book *99 francs* is actually autobiographical fiction. It was released in 2000, but in subsequent editions, the book cover is mockingly edited to show 14.99€ marked down twice to the discounted price of 6€.[8] This grinningly ferocious critique of the world of publicity flays the whole of modern commercial culture: "Everything is temporary and everything is for sale. Man is a product like any other, with a sell-by date" (16). The protagonist Octave mockingly proclaims,

> I'm an adman; and yes, I pollute the universe. I'm the guy who sells you crap. Who makes you dream of things you'll never have. The skies are always blue, the chicks are never ugly. It's perfect happiness,

6. Christian Authier, *Une si douce fureur* (Paris: Stock, 2006), 103.

7. Authier, *Les liens défaits* (Paris: Stock, 2006).

8. Frédéric Beigbeder, *99 francs* (Paris: Grasset, 2000). See also *Mémoires d'un jeune homme dérangé* (Paris: La Table Ronde, 2003).

> touched up in PhotoShop. Polished images, music in the air. . . . I'm
> three trends ahead of you, and I always manage to keep you frustrated.
> Glamor is a country where one never arrives. . . . Making you drool is
> my religion. Nobody in my profession wants you to be happy, because
> happy people don't consume. Your suffering boosts business. Hedo-
> nism isn't humanism, it's about cash flow. (17)

This likeable golden boy, a product of the Reagan money culture, enjoys spitting in the faces of others:

> I spend my life lying to you and I'm well compensated for it. I earn
> 13,000 euros a month (not to mention my expense account, company
> car, the stock options and the golden parachute). The euro was in-
> vented to make the salaries of the rich six times less indecent. . . . I
> forbid you to be bored. I block you from thinking. The terrorism of
> trends helps me sell emptiness. (18–19)

Thirty years ago, we already found evidence of this dismal reputation of the marketing and advertising industry in the title of publicist
Jacques Séguéla's 1979 book: *Don't Tell My Mother That I'm in Advertising . . . She Thinks I Play the Piano in a Brothel.* Tellingly, Séguéla served as director of communications for Mitterrand's 1981 presidential campaign.

The Americanization of French sensibility has also manifested itself in "chick lit," which has been quite successful in France. With
Gossip Girl, It Girl (Cecily von Ziegesar), *Garces Academy* and *La
liste VIP* (Zoey Dean), *California Girls* (Hailey Abbott), *Les menteuses*
(Sara Shepard) and *Les petites diablesses* (Nancy Holder), the *Girl
Attitude* collection aims to be "Cosmo[politan] for everybody." The
collection promises paradise, which means "gossip, sex, youth, love,
guys, girls, and VIPs."[9] These are just a few examples of this Americanization by which French bookstores now offer books inspired in
large part by themes and categories from the United States.[10]

René Étiemble, who in 1963 denounced the scourge of *franglais*,
would never have imagined the extent of its spread. Take for example
the 2008 catalog of back-to-school products of the Toulouse Virgin
Megastore. To study Molière or Corneille, students have a choice be-

9. See www.girlattitude.com
10. Here, for example, is a short list of new themes and books one may find in the
average FNAC: les Cultural studies, la face cachée de Google (collectif Ippolot @
Manuels Payot), la condition noire en France, les *animatueurs* de télévision, le *story-
telling,* la *Petite anthologie du flingage sur Facebook* (Pierre de Taillal aux éditions
Bourin), la révolution wikipedia.

tween (English-named) brands such as *Esprit Street Wear, Branché Girly,* and *Bad Girl & Fantasy.* The latter offers a range of school notebooks such as *Ruby Gloom, Bad Alice, Kamafun,* and *Miss Tic* as well as *Gothic Flames* pens and a *Propyspirit* pencil cases to stow in the *Ruby Glow* backpack. Younger children have their own *Hello Kitty* line of school supplies to help them read Babar. The *Poodle* backpack comes with a *prix small* of 39.99€. And the days of Bic pens are over. Children can choose from a line of pens with brand names such *Easy Clic, S'moove Easy, V Pen,* or *Magic +,* also for a *prix small.* And the list goes on: the so-called *presse people* category includes periodicals such as *France Dimanche, Voici, Closer, Ici Paris, Public, Gala, Point de Vue,* and *Bon Week* (which is considered a *féminin-people*). *Paris-Match* also belongs in part on the list, for its contribution to the *pipolisation* of customs and discourse. Mediatization, star-and image-making, and gossip, all *à l'américaine,* along with the erosion of private life and the confusion of genres, voyeurism, sexual obsession, politics as circus, and emotional manipulation over substance all fall under this umbrella. Examples abound, including the mystery of François Mitterrand's hidden daughter, the Sarkozy family saga, and Rachida Dati's pregnancy (along with the rumor that former Spanish Prime minister José Maria Aznar is the father). Proper language is degraded by youth- and English-inflected media neologisms: "la presse trash"; a "bimbo" is "trash" and is the opposite of the "it-girl"; something difficult or unpleasant is "gore"; busy professionals are "booké" or "hyperbooké"; songs are "mixé," and so forth. One either has "le look" or must be "relooké." One also finds routine references to "serial killer," "profilers," "thriller," and "snipers." Phrases like "c'est pas top" (or even "tip top"), "c'est hard," "c'est cool" abound, and there is even mention of a "talk show" on "prime time." In short, portions of French culture have become remakes of American culture in a widespread detour toward *le faux cool.* As Belinda Cannone put it, "La bêtise s'améliore" ("Stupidity is getting better").[11]

INTELLIGENT AMERICANIZATION

Fortunately, this nihilist-comsumerist reverse utopia has not absorbed everything. One can certainly point to countless examples of good, positive Americanization in the Hexagon, but I shall make mention of only a few of these. First of all, liberal democracy and defense of under-

11. Belinda Cannone, *La bêtise s'améliore* (Paris: Stock, 2008).

represented groups' rights have made progress. Notable examples include the notion of *parité* (whereby political parties are supposed to present an equal number of male and female candidates for elections) and progress in the realm of rights for sexual minorities. For instance, one witnesses the permanence of the issue of gay rights by comparing two landmark movies, Edouard Molinaro's 1978 film, *La cage aux folles*, where homosexuality and homophobia were the stuff of comedy, but presented in a positive light, and Francis Veber's 2000 film, *Le placard*, where affirmative action for gays in the workforce and anti-gay violence are considered as well. Another area is parental rights for same-sex couples: Vincent Garenq's 2008 film, *Comme les autres*, shows how much this cause, while still not yet supported by a majority of the population, has advanced in French society. Some minorities have affirmed their cultures and demanded their place in the sun.

Secondly, since the Jazz Age of the 1920s, France has continued to admire, import, and emulate excellent American music and dance forms. This includes more than just the big international U.S. stars, but also uniquely American genres. After all, the first French record label devoted to gospel music is called *We have a dream*, while 2008 marked the sixth year for the *"Nuit du Gospel"* (*www.lanuitdu gospel.com*), a tour of American gospel artists. Another example is the major *Festival de country music*, featuring stars from American television (including John Schneider of *The Dukes of Hazzard*, known in French as *Shérif, fais-moi peur*), and held in the village of Mirande in July 2008, in the heart of the agricultural department of Gers, land of traditional gastronomy and architecture and home of the singer Francis Cabrel. The festival's web page advertises (in Franglish) thirty hot-air balloons, truck, car, and bike "shows," as well as "western dance" activities, including line dancing and a "Saloon" called "le country club." Additionally, a great number of dance studios in France offer *le rock acrobatique, le lindy hop*, and *le west coast swing*, while international line-dancing championships are held in the Paris suburb of Levallois-Perret. Finally, in the realm of literature, translations allow the French access to classics such as Faulkner and Fitzgerald, as well as to today's fiction writers, along with works on feminism, psychology, couples, relationships, gender studies, personal development, New Yorker cartoons, and guides to the Internet. And the publisher *First* has popularized an array of topics via their *Pour les nuls* (. . . *for Dummies*) collection (*www.efirst.com*).

For four centuries, between the Age of Exploration and the beginning of the twentieth century, Europe shamelessly colonized the world and imposed its religions, customs, and languages everywhere it could. Among its former colonies, the United States has been the most successful, and American dynamism has in turn affected Europe. If the United States is the heir to and the extension of Europe (after the continent started two suicidal world wars), it is understandable that Europe, in turn, could be Americanized by its brilliant offshoot. And this is all the more true given the heterogeneous, plural, and contradictory qualities of postmodern identity. One can be Peruvian, yet of Japanese origin; one can be Israeli and Palestinian Muslim, Palestinian and Christian, Mexican and American, African and white, or German and Kurd. French citizens must therefore recognize the inherent complexity of France's identity and think more complexly about elusive categories such as interior, exterior, orthodoxy, canon, high and low cultures, and, by extension, even Americanization. Difficult as they may be to define, French identity and Americanization remain distinct categories, and in numerous domains, the little Gallic village is still holding out against the latest incarnation of the Roman invader.

—Translated by Michael Gott

II. French Intellectuals

ADRIAN JOHNSTON

The Right Left: Alain Badiou and the Disruption of Political Identities

NEITHER HIPPY NOR SQUARE— CULTIVATING NEW POLITICAL TASTES

Alain Badiou, like the Socrates of his dear Plato,[1] is masterful at being a gadfly. An active Maoist militant in the France of May '68 and its protracted 1970s aftermath, Badiou no longer is an uncompromising adherent of Maoism or traditional Marxism-Leninism. Nonetheless, he persists unfashionably preaching, and practicing, the virtues of communism *qua* radically egalitarian forms of politics.[2] Unlike the *nouveaux philosophes* he despises as Thermidorean betrayers of what really happened during May '68, he is unrepentant about his Maoism, unwilling entirely to disavow a stance associated with the horrifically failed Cultural Revolution; and, he controversially refuses to apologize for his previous support of Cambodia's Khmer Rouge. Badiou continues to be scathingly critical of any kind of centrism making its peace with the pairing of free markets and representative democracy, a combination he calls "capitalist-parliamentarianism,"[3] launching salvo after salvo of blistering attacks upon the values and beliefs underpinning multi-culturalist humanism, with its historicist relativism, widely embraced by the not-so-radical Left of the recent past and present.[4]

Among his many contributions to conversations concerning a

1. Alain Badiou, "Plato, Our Dear Plato!" trans. Alberto Toscano, *Angelaki: Journal of the Theoretical Humanities* 11/3 (2006): 39–41.

2. Badiou, *De quoi Sarkozy est-il le nom?* (Paris: Nouvelles Éditions Lignes, 2007), 130–133, 150–151, 154–155. Hereafter referred to as *Sarkozy* in the text.

3. Badiou, *Metapolitics,* trans. Jason Barker (London: Verso, 2005), 17; Badiou, "Of an Obscure Disaster: On the End of the Truth of the State" trans. Barbara P. Fulks, *Lacanian Ink* 22 (2003): 75–76.

4. I would like to thank Kathryn Wichelns for her attentive, patient help with editing and revising this piece.

YFS 116/117, *Turns to the Right?* ed. Johnson and Schehr, © 2009 by Yale University.

range of topics, Badiou's incisive polemical interventions bearing upon politics disturb assumed senses of the lines of demarcation distinguishing Left from Right. If readers of Badiou experience difficulties when trying to situate him in relation to familiar political categories, this is likely a symptom of how his "metapolitical"[5] reflections constitute, in part, a sustained critique of the established frameworks of categories for conceiving of political differences in the liberal-democratic societies of late capitalism. Taken together, a number of recent responses to Badiou testify to his having managed to unsettle standard distinctions between the Left and the Right by defying unproblematic classification according to these distinctions. Interestingly, there is a remarkable convergence of concerns *vis-à-vis* Badiou. Those responding from both sides of the Left-Right divide focus on the same set of terms and themes in Badiou's writings.[6] Whenever a consensus unexpectedly congeals between normally opposed political orientations, one should pay careful attention to what is at issue.

On the (center-) Left hand, authors such as Simon Critchley,[7] Peter Dews,[8] Éric Marty,[9] and Yannis Stavrakakis[10] all voice worries about the uncompromising militancy of Badiouian political pronouncements. Such commentators fear that the notions of courage, discipline, fidelity, sameness, and universality Badiou weaves together, notions central to Badiou's overarching philosophical system as well as to his (meta)politics, are inherently rightist. Even a critical reader as sympathetic to Badiou's philosophy and distinctive brand of leftism as Bruno Bosteels observes that aspects of how Badiou articulates his theory of the event strongly resemble features of rightist "ultraradicalism."[11] For the collective political imagination of post-1960s America in particular (but

5. Badiou, *Metapolitics*, xxxix, 10–11, 23, 55, 61–62.

6. Badiou, *"L'intellectuel de gauche va disparaître, tant mieux,"* *Le monde*, July 7, 2007 (http://www.lemonde.fr/societe/article/2007/07/14/l-intellectuel-de-gauche-va-disparaitre-tant-mieux_935544_3224.html).

7. Simon Critchley, "Demanding Approval: On the Ethics of Alain Badiou," *Radical Philosophy* 100 (2000): 27; Critchley, "A Heroism of the Decision, a Politics of the Event," *London Review of Books* 29/18 (2007): 33–34.

8. Peter Dews, "Uncategorical Imperatives: Adorno, Badiou, and the Ethical Turn," *Radical Philosophy* 111 (2002): 36–37.

9. Éric Marty, *Une querelle avec Alain Badiou, philosophe* (Paris: Gallimard, 2007), 19–20, 22–23.

10. Yannis Stavrakakis, *The Lacanian Left: Psychoanalysis, Theory, Politics* (Albany: State University of New York Press, 2007), 154–55.

11. Bruno Bosteels, "Radical Antiphilosophy," *Filozofski Vestnik: Radical Philosophy*, ed. Peter Klepec, 2008.

also, to varying extents, of the countries of Western Europe, too), being a good leftist is associated with, among other things, presumably healthy aversions to hierarchical organizations and to the wielding of violent, ruthless means against adversaries. From this sort of perspective, order and force tend to be considered fascist and/or totalitarian. Arguably, the segment of the left side of today's political spectrum, ranging from mainstream American Democratic voters to academic proponents of post-Marxist theories of "radical democracy," has inherited proto-conceptual aesthetic and affective inclinations—one could loosely describe these as "political tastes"—stemming from a characterization and self-conception of the Left dating back to the Vietnam era. To risk relying on a somewhat reductive phrasing, leftist unease with Badiou's militant rhetoric usually arises from those portions of the Left that still conceive of themselves within the constricting parameters of the old "hippies versus squares" cultural lifestyle stand-off (a deadlock enshrined in American politics with Richard Nixon's launching of the "culture wars" through his invocation of the "silent majority").

On the Right hand, Philippe Raynaud, to take one example, agrees with Badiou's center-Left critics that his is a philosophy valorizing a heroism that doesn't seem compatible with properly leftist sentiments. In the course of addressing Badiou's "metapolitics of revolution," Raynaud suggests that "the opposition between heroism and the search for well-being or the denunciation of bourgeois life as animal life are not especially related to the Left's critique of modern society and instead evoke the incandescent forms of conservative thought."[12] In a similar vein, it might be appropriate to mention at this point that one of Badiou's favorite cinematic genres is the classical Western, with its glorification of bravery set in the wild wilderness of untamed, lawless lands. Moreover, the ethics entwined with his politics has as its fundamental commandment the bare injunction to "Continue!"—or, to borrow a phrase from American political sloganeering, to "Stay the course!" That is to say, the sole categorical imperative Badiou puts forward is one demanding that actors persevere in conserving and drawing out the consequences of previous, come-and-gone events.[13] He even insists on the existence of eternal trans-

<hr>

12. Philippe Raynaud, *L'extrême gauche plurielle: Entre démocratie radicale et révolution* (Paris: Éditions Autrement, 2006), 166.

13. Badiou, *Ethics: An Essay on the Understanding of Evil*, trans. Peter Hallward (London: Verso, 2001), 44, 47, 50, 90–91; Alain Badiou, *Circonstances, 1: Kosovo, 11 septembre, Chirac/Le Pen* (Paris: Éditions Léo Scheer, 2003), 11.

historical political values, upholding allegedly stable "communist in-variants"[14] and embellishing his fiery treatises with language taken straight from Platonism and Christianity. Nowadays, living in the aftermath of a Christian, play-cowboy President who incarnates the most conservative, backward-looking tendencies within the Republican Party of the United States, how can one not suspect that Badiou, regardless of what he thinks of himself, has more in common with the Right than with the Left? In response to this question, it is tempting to pose another question: What, if anything, ought contemporary leftists to learn from the political practices of right-wing agents and organizations?

Particularly within the context of first-world academia, Badiou's appeals to willful, heroic decisions and commitments—"The Decider" might again come to mind—as necessary for any genuinely emancipatory politics are in danger of sounding out-of-date, if not reckless. For theorists steeped in philosophies wary of purportedly *passé* notions such as free will and eternal idea(l)s, a body of theory openly acknowledging its indebtedness to Plato, Descartes, Hegel, and Sartre, among others, seems anachronistic at best. Furthermore, these types of scholars sometimes protest that no precise philosophical principles guarantee in advance an assured, *a priori* difference between the brave resolution to recognize select happenings as events and subject oneself to them, as spoken of by Badiou, and such catastrophic historical-political disasters as Nazism and Stalinism (the latter two being lumped together, in a gesture of equivocation that is not in the least bit innocent, under the heading of "Totalitarianism"). Badiouian-style politics seems to be read by these protesting theorists as an instance of, to resort to the pejorative Habermasian label, "left-wing fascism" (a recently published review essay in *The New Republic* accusing Slavoj Žižek of being, among other things, a fascist—Badiou too is mentioned in this essay—epitomizes precisely this sort of center-left reaction against the varieties of radical leftist politics endorsed by Badiou and Žižek).[15] What prevents Badiou's doctrine of eventual subjectification from becoming a hymn inspiring excesses of brutal, dehumanizing terror?

14. Badiou and François Balmès, *De l'idéologie* (Paris: François Maspero, 1976), 66–67, 69–70; Badiou, "Of an Obscure Disaster," 62.

15. Adam Kirsch, "The Deadly Jester: The Most Despicable Philosopher in the West," *The New Republic*, December 3, 2008 (http://www.tnr.com/story_print.html?id=097a31f3-c440-4b10-8894-14197d7a6eef).

The above issues will be dealt with herein via a combined dual focus on Badiou's relatively early Maoist writings and his 2007 booklet *De quoi Sarkozy est-il le nom?*, written in response to Nicolas Sarkozy's successful run for the French presidency. Throughout his electoral campaign to replace Jacques Chirac, Sarkozy repeatedly called for a break with the lasting legacy of May '68. Indeed, the master signifier of Sarkozy's campaign was *"rupture."* The candidate promised to combat the purportedly hedonist ideology of the May '68 radicals, with its ostensible moral-relativist celebration of self-indulgent wallowing in an orgy of unproductive pleasures. Sarkozy's May '68 is also that of the well-paid, repentant ex-Maoists anointed by the French mass media as the recognized representatives of that singular time and place in the living historical memory of France. Despite his virulent hatred of both Sarkozy and the New Philosophers, Badiou agrees with them on at least one point: There is something to be broken with here. However, Badiou proposes a "rupture" specifically with the popularized, falsified rendition of May '68 (the one misrecognized by Sarkozy as the actual, factual version) that lowers it to the status of an adolescent sex-drugs-and-rock-and-roll youth rebellion, the French/European equivalent of an American anti-war movement insidiously overshadowed and obfuscated by Woodstock, Timothy Leary, and *Easy Rider.* For Badiou and certain others, including Jacques Rancière (with Badiou, another former student of Louis Althusser), there is a different May '68: a month in which students and workers together organized a massive, coordinated refusal to occupy their assigned positions in the capitalist socioeconomic division of labor[16] (along these lines, *De quoi Sarkozy est-il le nom?* contains the assertion that May '68 was "one of the last real manifestations of the specter of communism" [49–50]). Badiou further proposes a break with the underlying consensus binding together the Right, as represented by Sarkozy, and the center-Left, as represented by many *nouveaux philosophes* and their ilk (including Sarkozy's foreign minister, the nominally socialist Bernard Kouchner, himself a former student radical). The result of Badiou's twofold rupture is a vision of a truly leftist politics in which the radical Left becomes increasingly better able to mount effective challenges to the hegemonies of liberal-democratic late-capitalism the more it gets over its immobilizing hippy hangover. In short, it is the post-1960s blurred vision of the Left that

16. Kristin Ross, *May '68 and its Afterlives* (Chicago: University of Chicago Press, 2002), 2–3, 10–12, 73–74.

renders models of centralized organization and incitations to painful sacrifice all somehow "fascistic."

"IT JUST FEELS WRONG"—
WORKING-THROUGH LEFTIST INHIBITIONS

Badiou himself is at least as unsettled by the topic of affect as those readers who feel ill at ease with his invocations of certain emotions and sentiments relative to politics. A profound ambivalence in connection with affective phenomena betrays itself in Badiou's *œuvre* through a series of inconsistent oscillations and shifts at the level of his conceptualizations of affects.[17] Whether and how a consistent Badiouian theory of (political) affects can and should be forged out of this tangled knot of conflicting statements by Badiou bearing on affective phenomena is one of the guiding preoccupations of what follows.

What, precisely, makes leftists sympathetic to liberal democracy and secular humanism uncomfortable with Badiou, apart from his obvious scorn for these two ethico-political formations? One of the main sources of this discomfort is a set of associated, interlinked concepts, motifs, and terms in Badiou's philosophy. To start with, Badiou consistently has refused to shy away from endorsing, sometimes even enthusiastically, the use of violence. In his early Maoist writings, the aggressive negativity of fissuring destruction is hailed as the driving motor of the dialectics of history; the partisan truths of the communist tradition, in their actualized efficacy, are portrayed as unavoidably violent and dictatorial.[18] His more recent political statements plead for an emancipatory leftist re-appropriation of the popularly maligned signifier-notion "Terror"[19] (although, *contra* the Maoism of his philosophical and political youth, he has since de-emphasized the primacy

17. I deal extensively with a lot of what is involved here in my book *Badiou, Žižek, and Political Transformations: The Cadence of Change* (Evanston: Northwestern University Press, 2009).

18. On the necessary violence of communism, see the following : Alain Badiou, "Projet d'intervention d'Alain Badiou au 6e Congrès du P.S.U.," *Contribution au problème de la construction d'un parti marxiste-léniniste de type nouveau* (Paris: François Maspero, 1970), 46; Badiou, *Théorie de la contradiction* (Paris: François Maspero, 1975), 17, 26, 86–87; Badiou, Joël Bellassen, and Louis Mossot, *Le noyau rationnel de la dialectique hégélienne* (Paris: François Maspero, 1978), 46–47; Badiou, *Théorie du sujet* (Paris: Éditions du Seuil, 1982), 149, 308, 345; Colin Wright, "Resurrection and Reaction in Alain Badiou: Towards an Evental Historiography," *Culture, Theory & Critique* 49/1 (2008): 76.

19. Badiou, *Metapolitics*, 138. See also, Badiou, "Philosophy and the 'war against terrorism,'" *Infinite Thought: Truth and the Return of Philosophy*, ed. and trans. Oliver

of destruction, nowadays denying that it is the principle animating force of historical temporalities[20]). Badiou goes so far as to characterize terror—the ambiguity of this word, which can designate either an experiential state of feeling or a practical way of doing, perturbs the very core of his account(s) of affects—as an integral aspect of every post-eventual truth-process pursued by a militantly faithful subject-of-an-event.[21] When it comes to the emancipatory aspirations of any genuinely egalitarian political project, he warns that, "you cannot expect politics to be soft-hearted, progressive, and peaceful if it aims at the radical subversion of the eternal order that submits society to the domination of wealth and the rich, of power and the powerful, of science and the scientists, of capital and its servants."[22] Of course, his idea here is that a reflexive pacifism dictated by the automatic acceptance of the centrist moral axiom that violence is "never the answer" and unemployable for any decent leftist with a good conscience amounts, in the end, to conceding the terrain of the present to those willing to employ violence, however overtly or covertly, for their own gain. An inflexibly principled refusal to fight cedes the *status quo* to those whose pursuits of their interests are not constrained by such principles.

Not only does Badiou shamelessly appeal to a violent destructiveness unrestrained by a quasi-theological ethics of alterity that emphasizes humility in the face of the differences of others (*Ethics*, 25–28), but he also insists on the indispensability of discipline for effective political *praxis*—an insistence that likely does not go down well with those audiences for whom this word conjures up images of goose-stepping soldiers in anonymous columns, mechanically embodying the state's power to kill its dehumanized enemies. It is these imagistic associations that prompt hasty recourse to the overused epithet "fascist." Badiou's recurrent emphasis on the political-practical importance of discipline, a note present in his earlier writings as well as

---

Feltham and Justin Clemens (London: Continuum, 2003), 144–145; Badiou, *Logiques des mondes: L'être et l'événement, 2* (Paris: Éditions du Seuil, 2006), 34.

20. Badiou, *Being and Event*, trans. Oliver Feltham, (London: Continuum, 2005), 407–408; Badiou, *The Century*, trans. Alberto Toscano (Cambridge: Polity Press, 2007), 54–55, 64–65; Badiou, "Destruction, Negation, Subtraction," lecture, European Graduate School, 2007 (http://www. youtube.com/watch?v=zefBDXmoQaE).

21. See Badiou, *Théorie du sujet*, 309–310; Badiou, *Logiques des mondes*, 96–99; Oliver Feltham, *Alain Badiou* (London: Continuum, 2008), 78.

22. Badiou, "One Divides Itself into Two," in *Lenin Reloaded: Toward a Politics of Truth*, ed. Sebastian Budgen, Stathis Kouvelakis, and Slavoj Žižek (Durham: Duke University Press, 2007), 13.

in his current interventions, implicitly demands the refusal of being inhibited and paralyzed by these associations.

In the 1970s, Badiou savagely attacks the then-ascendant anti-Oedipal duo of Gilles Deleuze and Félix Guattari for their promotion of a theoretical apparatus he deems to be laden with disastrous political consequences, particularly in the context of a France in which the enthusiasms unleashed by May '68 evaporated into a stifling atmosphere colored by pessimistic disavowal and cynical reaction. The 1975 booklet *Théorie de la contradiction* condemns this duo, with their poststructuralist libidinal anarchism according to which all unifying disciplinary powers are to be condemned with equal vehemence in the name of fragmentary, chaotic multitudes (i.e., the "molecular," "rhizomatic," etc.), as being just as theoretically and politically conservative as the classical structuralist doctrines with which they supposedly break. For Badiou, structuralism is conservative insofar as its ahistorical formalism effectively denies the possibility of radical systemic changes undetermined by pre-existent synchronic scaffoldings; for it, there are only continuous "permutations" internal to structure and nothing more (*Théorie de la contradiction*, 71). From Badiou's vantage-point, the Deleuzo-Guattarian alternative merely puts forward yet another invariant structural configuration, a timeless form in which the two non-dialecticized sides of the One and the Many stay put in their assigned places.[23] Unlike dialectical materialism correctly conceived as the crucial theoretical basis of an actually effective Left (*Théorie de la contradiction*, 77–82), Deleuze and Guattari moralistically reject *prima facie* every manner of disciplined organization (*Théorie de la contradiction*, 74–76) (Bosteels, with respect to Badiou's writings from this period,[24] and Peter Hallward, with respect to Deleuze's philosophy,[25] both insightfully and persuasively develop these aspects of the Badiouian critique of Deleuzian thought).

23. Badiou, "The Flux and the Party: In the Margins of *Anti-Oedipus*," trans. Laura Balladur and Simon Krysl, *Polygraph: An International Journal of Culture and Politics* 15/16 (2004): 78; Badiou, "Le fascisme de la pomme de terre," *La situation actuelle sur le front philosophique*, ed. Groupe Yenan-Philosophie (Paris: François Maspero, 1977), 44–46.

24. Bruno Bosteels, "Logics of Antagonisms: In the Margins of Alain Badiou's 'The Flux and the Party,'" *Polygraph: An International Journal of Culture and Politics* 15/16 (2004): 96, 102; Bosteels, "Post-Maoism: Badiou and Politics," *Positions: East Asia Cultures Critique* 13/3 (2005): 603.

25. Peter Hallward, *Out of This World: Deleuze and the Philosophy of Creation* (London: Verso, 2006), 162–63.

Two years later, in a collection published by François Maspero entitled *La situation actuelle sur le front philosophique*, Badiou presents two back-to-back essays in which he ferociously denounces anti-Oedipalism as a leftist deviation compatible and complicit with capitalism. "The Flux and the Party: In the Margins of *Anti-Oedipus*" viciously mocks the radical pretensions of Deleuze and Guattari's intoxicated odes to lawless energetic fluxes and flows. He writes, "Unforeseeable, desiring, irrational: follow your drift [*dérive*], my son, and you will make the Revolution" ("The Flux and the Party," 76). It gets much harsher. Opposing "Marxism-Leninism," with its "idea of the class party," to "the anti-dialectical moralism of the theoreticians of desire" (a "Moralism, yes, and of the dullest kind" [78]), Badiou says of seemingly transgressive libidinal anarchism:

> All this cultural racket, all this subversive arm-pumping, only to slip us, at the end, that Freedom is Good and Necessity Evil?
>
> Freedom, and by the way, what Freedom? "Subject-group," Freedom as Subject. Deleuze and Guattari don't hide this much: return to Kant, here's what they came up with to exorcise the Hegelian ghost.
>
> For quite a while, I wondered what was this "desire" of theirs, stuck as I was between the sexual connotations and all the machinic, industrial brass they covered it up for that materialist feel. Well, it's the Freedom of Kantian critique, no more, no less. It's the unconditional: a subjective impulse that invisibly escapes the whole sensible order of ends, the whole rational fabric of causes. It's pure, unbound, generic energy as such. That which is law unto itself, or absence of law. The old freedom of autonomy, hastily repainted in the colors of what the youth in revolt legitimately demands: some spit on the bourgeois family. (79)

He subsequently reiterates his criticism according to which Deleuzo-Guattarian post-structuralism is far from being a genuine, resistant alternative to structuralism. Rather, theirs is "the moralism of desire, a structuralism full of shame" (80). As such, Deleuze and Guattari should be treated as "hateful adversaries of all organized revolutionary politics" (84).

The title of the next essay, "Le fascisme de la pomme de terre," suggests that the rhizomatic politics of libidinal anarchism is tantamount to making way for the triumph of the most aggressive elements of the Right (potatoes are a variety of rhizome, hence the title). Penned under the pseudonym "Georges Peyrol," the essay opens with assertions to the effect that pitting the Many against the One, a variant of which would be the favoring of undisciplined fragmentation over disciplined group order, is, in reality, the expression of a petty-bourgeois mentality and class position (42–43). In Badiou's eyes, the political tastes of this theoretical aesthetic barely conceal attitudes that only those who feel no pressing need for a coherent, forceful, and targeted confrontation with the order of things can afford—"Behind the hatred of militancy the hatred of class struggle badly hides itself" (43). By dissolving the antagonistic conflicts and splits between classes as socio-economic factions within the murky, formless masses of multiplicities (46–52), Deleuze and Guattari, with their hippy-esque aversion to directed organizational hierarchies impatiently dismissed as nothing more than expressions of the desires of authoritarian personalities for Nazi-like law and order, concede in advance the domains of public life to those others willing to seize it for themselves. Hence, however subjectively radical the denouncers of the family and everything that goes with it experience themselves as being, they are, objectively speaking, complicit in sustaining the control of those they superficially oppose —or, more accurately, those they refuse effectively to oppose. For Badiou, real opposition requires something along the lines of a unified militant collectivity or organization. This leads him to maintain that, "It's logical: you cannot think and exalt the pure multiple (the Rhizome) without casting yourself down into the flattest conservatism, the most entirely sure of all that is" (47).

Despite the numerous changes major and minor in Badiou's thinking after his Maoist phase of the 1970s—various commentators have already thoroughly catalogued these shifts—the notion of discipline remains an explicit constant resurfacing in some of his most up-to-date reflections. In a 2007 interview, Badiou states, "I think that creative politics, the politics that changes the world, will not be at all the politics of spontaneity or of enthusiasm. In the end, it is a question of a politics of discipline."[26] In the aftermath of his early labors, Badiou has taken quite a stretch of distance from orthodox Marxism-Leninism as well as the Maoism of his past. Nevertheless, both here (in 2007) and in the 1970s, his defense of the political indispensability of practical discipline audibly echoes Leninist and Maoist warnings against spontaneist anarchism, with its poisonous mixture of idealist(ic) utopianism, bourgeois

26. Badiou, "*The Concept of Model*, Forty Years Later: An Interview with Alain Badiou (with Tzuchien Tho)," in *The Concept of Model: An Introduction to the Materialist Epistemology of Mathematics*, ed. and trans. Zachary Luke Fraser and Tzuchien Tho (Melbourne: Re.press, 2007), 104.

individualism, and lack of discipline, as a detrimental leftist deviancy veering off the proper path toward communism.[27] Other contemporaneous statements by Badiou hint at an additional reason for tethering radical militant leftism to discipline, apart from the fact that an undisciplined politics is unable and/or unwilling to fight back against fierce rightist reactionaries. As he articulates it in another recent interview, "People who have nothing—no power, no money, no media—have only their discipline as a possibility of strength."[28] When referring to the *sans papiers* in the context of an analysis of the ongoing drama of the global financial crisis, he likewise appeals to "the new discipline of those who have nothing."[29] Communism is nothing if not the politics of those "who have nothing"—or, as the famous lyrics of the Internationale have it, those who are nothing from the perspectives of reigning situations: "We are nothing, let us be everything."

In his first systematic philosophical work, 1982's *Théorie du sujet*, Badiou elaborates at length a politically-motivated account of a "Promethean ethics" of courage (*à la* a defiance of whatever "gods" are the powers-that-be) [336–37; 344]). This ethics is bound up with a set of connected concepts: in particular, courage and "confidence" (*confiance*). Badiou defines confidence as a "pre-political disposition" (338), a state or position inclining in the direction of possible political projects (this definition can be read as hinting at affective conditions preparing pre-eventual persons to be ready, willing, and able to respond to events as subjects).[30] This disposition, arguably affective, underpins the entirety of Badiouian practical philosophy (i.e., his interrelated ethics and politics, which he would resist presenting as a monolithic "practical philosophy" per se), not only as articulated in 1982—in

27. V.I. Lenin, *The State and Revolution: The Marxist Theory of the State and the Tasks of the Proletariat in the Revolution*, *Lenin: Selected Works* (New York: International Publishers, 1971), 298, 306, 345; Lenin, "'Left-Wing' Communism—An Infantile Disorder," *Lenin: Selected Works*, 524–525; Mao Tse-Tung, *Quotations from Chairman Mao Tse-Tung*, ed. Stuart R. Schram (New York: Bantam Books, 1967), 144; Mao Tse-Tung, "Rectify the Party's Style of Work," *Selected Readings from the Works of Mao Tsetung* (Peking: Foreign Languages Press, 1971), 220; Mao Tse-Tung, "On the People's Democratic Dictatorship: In Commemoration of the Twenty-eighth Anniversary of the Communist Party of China," in *Selected Readings from the Works of Mao Tsetung*, 379–80.

28. Badiou, "Interview with Alain Badiou (with Diana George and Nic Veroli)," *Carceraglio*, October 16, 2006 (http://scentedgardensfortheblind.blogspot.com/).

29. Badiou, "*De quel réel cette crise est-elle le spectacle?*," *Le monde*, October 18, 2008 (http://www.entretemps.asso.fr/Badiou/Crise.htm).

30. Johnston, *Badiou, Žižek, and Political Transformations*.

Théorie du sujet, he declares that, "Confidence organizes the entirety of the ethical field" (345)—but in its current version(s) as well.

In the wake of 1988's *Being and Event*, and most notably in his concise book on *Ethics*, Badiou identifies "fidelity" (*qua* persistent perseverance along the post-eventual paths paved by subjective struggles on behalf of specific amorous, artistic, political, and scientific truths) as the sole thing categorically commanded by any and every ethic of an event-disclosed truth and its ensuing processes. Hence, as far as he is concerned, fidelity is constitutive of ethics *tout court*.[31] Later, in 2006's *Logiques des mondes*, Badiou sings the praises of heroism, encouraging people to become "anonymous heroes" (445), brave champions of causes greater than themselves who put aside the limited interests of their egotistical individuality (including desires for fame, glory, splendor, and martyrdom) in favor of something immanently transcending the banal, brute life of Darwinian flesh. In the conclusion to this substantial sequel to *Being and Event*, Badiou evinces his awareness of many leftists' reservations regarding his apparently old-fashioned preaching of the virtues of heroism when he remarks, "It is sometimes said to me that I see in philosophy only a means of reestablishing, against the contemporary apology for the ordinary and the futile, the rights of heroism. Why not?" In the immediately subsequent paragraph, the penultimate one of the conclusion, he adds:

> In effect, I place heroism on the side of discipline, the sole weapon of Truth and of peoples, against power and wealth, against insignificance and mental dissipation. It is again necessary to invent this discipline . . . this discipline no longer distinguishes itself from our desire to live. (*Logiques des monde*, 536–37)

The conclusion itself is entitled "What Is It to Live?." Badiou's answer to this question is that only living life under the guidance of an "Idea" as an ideal of infinitely more worth than life itself counts as truly living (*Logiques des monde*, 529–30; 532–33)—by contrast with merely being biologically alive in a state of comfort and safety as the sole sense of living valued under the authority of what Badiou, in the preface to *Logiques des mondes*, baptizes "democratic materialism," the dominant ideology of capitalist biopolitics.[32] Already in *Théorie du*

---

31. Badiou, *Being and Event*, 232–39; Badiou, *Ethics*, 41–42, 44–48, 52, 78–79, 90–91.

32. Badiou, *Logiques des mondes*, 9–10, 12–13, 15, 16–17, 593; See Adrian Johnston, "The Weakness of Nature: Hegel, Freud, Lacan, and Negativity Materialized," in

sujet, as well as in *Logiques des mondes*, confidence, the confidence to continue later spoken of by Badiou in terms of fidelity and heroism, is grounded in discipline (*Théorie du sujet*, 346). But, what grounds faithful discipline? This query requires an examination of Badiou's portrait of courage, insofar as adhering to disciplinary strictures arguably does not occur in the total and complete absence of sufficient affective fortitude and sheer strength of will.[33]

THE COURAGE FOR COURAGE—AFFECTS, VIRTUES, AND POLITICS

I have treated Badiou's conceptions of affects in general and of courage in particular at length elsewhere.[34] In the present context, attention will be paid to his use of the term "virtue," a term that features prominently in the portrayal of courage contained in 2007's *De quoi Sarkozy est-il le nom?*. When referring to courage alongside "anxiety," the "super-ego," and "justice" as the four "categories of the subject-effect" in *Théorie du sujet* (307)—these four categories reappear in slightly modified terminological guises in *Logiques des mondes* as "affects" that "signal the incorporation of a human animal into the subjective process of a truth" (96–97)—Badiou denies such phenomena the status of being "virtues," "capacities," "experiences," or "states of consciousness/conscience" (*Théorie du sujet*, 307). Rather, in Badiou's philosophical lexicon, these are names for processes as ways of doing instead of fashions of feeling (the subsequent 2006 labeling of these four categories as affects perhaps marks a shift, however subtle, as regards this topic). *Théorie du sujet* goes on to say three more things related to the delineation of courage, things pertaining to the related concept-term "confidence" (*confiance*): First, "In the matter of Marxist politics and the class subject, the one manner of giving up is to lose confidence" (338); Second, "confidence concentrates itself in fidelity to courage" (339); Third, "The essence of confidence is having confidence in confidence" (341). In addition to the first claim's insistence on the indispensability of *confiance* for committed leftist political

---

Hegel and the Infinite: Into the Twenty-First Century, ed. Clayton Crockett, Creston Davis, and Slavoj Žižek (New York: Columbia University Press, 2009 [forthcoming]).

33. Johnston, *Badiou, Žižek, and Political Transformations*; Peter Hallward, "What's the Point?: First Notes Towards a Philosophy of Determination," in *Material Worlds: Proceedings of the Conference Held at Glasgow University, 2005*, ed. Rachel Moffat and Eugene de Klerk (Newcastle: Cambridge Scholars Publishing, 2007), 153–58.

34. Johnston, *Badiou, Žižek, and Political Transformations*.

praxis temporally elongated so as to be effective, the second two claims, taken together, signal that confidence and courage involve reflexive dynamics in which feelings and doings enter into dialectical, co-determining relations with each other (and this in spite of Badiou's basic, enduring disregard for affects).[35]

During a discussion of *Théorie du sujet,* Alberto Toscano addresses the Badiouian characterizations of anxiety, courage, the super-ego, and justice. He underscores what could be described as Badiou's de-affected conception of affect:

> [L]ike his theory of the subject, Badiou's theory of affect is also post-Cartesian, which is to say that it treats the subject as a formalization and an aleatory trajectory, meaning that "affect" does not refer to an experience, a capacity, a spiritual or mental disposition.[36]

Toscano's representation of Badiou's position here is entirely accurate. However, is this affect-less theory of affect internally consistent and defensible? In addition to Mehdi Belhaj Kacem's reworkings of the Badiouian philosophical framework carried out in connection with an alternate psychoanalytic depiction of affective and libidinal life[37]— this sort of re-working is called for by Oliver Feltham[38]—Sam Gillespie's posthumously published book *The Mathematics of Novelty* contains some very insightful remarks regarding this issue. Gillespie observes that, "when Badiou speaks of something that happens, his terms reveal an uncharacteristic display of sentiment,"[39] especially when the philosopher speaks of his personal experience of the event of May '68:

> Badiou seems to be appealing to categories of affect that presuppose a subject of experience who is gripped or seized by something incalculable, who becomes a catalyst for all possible action. What seems to be potentially overlooked, then, within the overall sterile, formal frame-

35. Johnston, *Badiou, Žižek, and Political Transformations.*

36. Alberto Toscano, "The Bourgeois and the Islamist, or, The Other Subjects of Politics," in *The Praxis of Alain Badiou,* ed. Paul Ashton, A.J. Bartlett, and Justin Clemens (Melbourne: Re.press, 2006), 344.

37. Mehdi Belhaj Kacem, *L'affect* (Paris: Éditions Tristram, 2004), 16, 92–93, 163–64, 169, 172–73, 178, 182; Kacem, *Événement et répétition* (Paris: Éditions Tristram, 2004), 153, 171, 198–99, 242.

38. Oliver Feltham, "Enjoy Your Stay: Structural Change in *Seminar XVII,*" in *Jacques Lacan and the Other Side of Psychoanalysis: Reflections on Seminar XVII,* ed. Justin Clemens and Russell Grigg (Durham: Duke University Press, 2006), 192.

39. Sam Gillespie, *The Mathematics of Novelty: Badiou's Minimalist Metaphysics* (Melbourne: Re.press, 2008), 103.

work of the ontology of *Being and Event* is any possible theory of affect that could account for that very act of gripping the subject. This absence is telling when it comes to addressing the manner in which subjects are gripped by events. (Gillespie, 103)

What holds above for *Being and Event* does as well for *Théorie du sujet*, in addition to the majority of Badiou's writings since the 1980s. For a number of reasons that become more apparent in his contemporary rendition of courage as a virtue rather than an affect, Badiou understandably does not want to reduce politically efficacious instances of courage to brave feelings and fear-resistant emotional states alone. And yet, Kacem, Feltham, and Gillespie, among others,[40] justifiably indicate that the dynamics of eventual subjectification cannot credibly be divorced in their entirety from affective undercurrents helping to enable and then serving to buttress the faithful endeavors of subjects-of-events. A compromise between Badiou and his more sympathetic critics is possible: a variant of virtue ethics (in some ways, a precise inversion of classical Aristotelian virtue ethics) in which, for example, courage-as-feeling and courage-as-doing are bound together in a mutually-reinforcing, as it were, virtuous circle.

In more recent reflections on the affective and the political, reflections in which the topic of courage is a central matter of concern, Badiou once again expresses his wariness of emotions, particularly when they have to do with ethics and politics. In *De quoi Sarkozy est-il le nom?*, he refers to the "without-principle of affect" (12–13), proceeding to herald "an orientation of thought and existence able to affirm itself beyond affects" (20). Similarly, in the preface to 2008's *Petit panthéon portatif*, Badiou voices a pronounced lack of trust in "passions."[41] The text on Sarkozy is especially interesting as regards the Badiouian engagement with affect. Whereas *Théorie du sujet* lumps the concept-term "virtue" together with other words referring to emotional experiences and phenomena, Badiou has come to utilize "virtue" to designate something separate and distinct from the affective. Early on in his 2007 musings on the French election, he declares that, "Courage is without doubt the principle virtue today" (*Sarkozy*, 20). He later avows his intention to "conserve its status as a virtue" (*Sarkozy*, 96). But, who or what in the past is thereby being conserved? Surprisingly, the answer

---

40. I undertake an immanent critique of the Badiouian handling of affects in *Badiou, Žižek, and Political Transformations*.

41. Alain Badiou, *Petit panthéon portatif* (Paris: La fabrique éditions, 2008), 7–8.

might very well be "Aristotle" (Feltham indeed is justified in comparing certain aspects of Badiouian philosophy to Aristotelian virtue ethics[42])—and this despite both Badiou's prevailing preference for a Plato-Descartes-Hegel axis over an Aristotle-Kant one, as well as the absence of Aristotle's name in the context of these statements about courage. Perhaps this hypothesized link is yet another factor responsible for progressive academic leftist discomfort with Badiou: What could be more conservative than an apparently aristocratic value-system extolling the aesthetically appealing excellences of a contemplative existence and elaborated by an ancient Greek male with the luxury of leisure-time for such pursuits?

Prior to turning briefly to Aristotle's *Nicomachean Ethics* in light of the practical sides of Badiou's philosophy, a condensed explication of the latter's sketch of courage as a virtue is warranted. In *Logiques des mondes* and elsewhere, Badiou pleads for a contemporary reinvention of heroism.[43] However, in *De quoi Sarkozy est-il le nom?*, he explicitly contrasts courage and heroism[44]: The former is a virtue as a sustained position or stance maintained by a persisting and persistent post-eventual subject ("endurance in the impossible"), while the latter is a fleeting pose or momentary posture inspired in a passing flash (*Sarkozy*, 96–97). However, Badiou subsequently concedes that an initial dose of heroism is required to catalyze one's "conversion" to a virtuously courageous subjective mode of proceeding (*Sarkozy*, 98–99). Herein, the characterization of heroism arguably betrays a quiet reliance on a presumption that a minimal degree of bravery already is possessed, prior to eventual interpellation, by those who, on the basis of this affective condition, are able to allow themselves to be shattered by and taken up into an event and its ensuing practical consequences.[45] In this same text, Badiou nonetheless denies that courage, as a virtue in his sense, is a disposition already possessed to greater or lesser extents by individual human animals as pre-eventual not-yet-subjects (*Sarkozy*, 95–97).

As Bosteels notes in connection with this 2007 tract by Badiou, "Ultimately . . . the difference between heroism and courage is a mat-

42. Feltham, *Alain Badiou*, 77.

43. Badiou, *Logiques des mondes*, 445, 536–37; Badiou, "The Contemporary Figure of the Soldier in Politics and Poetry," lecture, University of California at Los Angeles, January 2007 (http://www.lacan.com/badsold.htm).

44. Bosteels, "Force of Nonlaw: Alain Badiou's Theory of Justice," *Cardozo Law Review* 29/5 (2008): 1915–916.

45. Johnston, *Badiou, Žižek, and Political Transformations.*

ter of time" ("Force of Nonlaw," 1916). Along these lines, Badiou even asserts that, "The primary material of courage is time" (*Sarkozy*, 97). Therefore, courage is something other than the physiological and psychological substances usually associated with ideas of affects. Being courageous means not being quickly discouraged in too short a time in the face of the obstacles, resistances, and failures inevitably to be met with on the hard road of an event-inspired trajectory subtracted from the prevailing temporalities of the default rhythms of life according to socio-historical business-as-usual. Badiouian courage is a matter of *praxis*, of temporally extended and elaborated practices stubbornly pursued by subjects. As a "true virtue," it is a verb, not a noun: a practical way of proceeding (*Sarkozy*, 97–98). More specifically, courage is not a "state" as an emotional experience or affective condition attached to individual bodies and consciousnesses (although, as alleged in the paragraph above, Badiou seems clandestinely to smuggle back in courage-as-feeling [i.e., an affect], as distinct from courage-as-doing [i.e., a virtue], when speaking of how a jolt of heroism is requisite for jarring one into virtuously emboldened modes of thinking and acting). Additionally, brave activities, as those manifest deeds of which courage as a virtue consists, create a "new time"[46] (i.e., a post-evental temporality immeasurable according to the temporal-historical standards of established situations/worlds).[47] However, this subject-supported newness is reliant upon a certain oldness, namely, the faithful preservation-through-practice of appeared-and-disappeared past events. For Badiou, creation requires conservation. In a piece for an issue of *Les temps modernes* devoted to the memory of Jean-Paul Sartre, one of his acknowledged "masters,"[48] Badiou remarks, "that which is the most horrible in the world of Capital, which is our world, is its perpetual and monotonous artificial youth. Every radical politics will restore, in the infinite measure of the generic, the time of aging necessary to truths" ("Saisissement," 19).

46. Badiou, *De quoi Sarkozy est-il le nom?*, 46, 97, 99; Alain Badiou, "New Horizons in Mathematics as a Philosophical Condition: An Interview with Alain Badiou (with Tzuchien Tho)," *Parrhesia* 3 (2007): 8.

47. Johnston, *Badiou, Žižek, and Political Transformations*.

48. Badiou, "Saisissement, dessaisie, fidélité," *Les temps modernes* 46/531–533 (1990): 15, 18, 20–21; Alain Badiou, *Beckett: L'increvable désir* (Paris: Hachette, 1995), 7; Alain Badiou, "Can Change be Thought?: A Dialogue with Alain Badiou (with Bruno Bosteels)," in *Alain Badiou: Philosophy and Its Conditions*, ed. Gabriel Riera (Albany: State University of New York Press, 2005), 242; Badiou, *Logiques des mondes*, 426, 580.

With all of this in mind—Badiou himself ties together these various propositions regarding courage in a short summary of his own (*Sarkozy*, 100)—a rapid and simplifying glance at Aristotle is in order. The first two chapters of the second of the ten books composing the *Nicomachean Ethics*, the founding document of traditional virtue ethics, concisely articulate the notion of virtue in manners useful for working through some of the difficulties in Badiou's tangled knotting-together of conceptions of affect, virtue, and ethical-political subjectivity. To begin with, Aristotle wisely refuses to accept any sort of hard-and-fast nature-versus-nurture dichotomy when it comes to being virtuous. Although "none of the virtues of character arises in us naturally" (and, for Aristotle, courage is a virtue of character), "the virtues arise in us neither by nature nor against nature. Rather, we are by nature able to acquire them, and we are completed through habit."[49] As is well known, the account of "habituation" is crucial to Aristotle's picture of ethical character-formation. When operating in fashions conducive to the acquisition of various virtues, habit sets up a virtuous circle in which repeatedly performed actions of a specific sort (for example, behaving bravely even when one does not feel brave) lead, over time, to an arousal, heightening, and intensification of tendencies to have feelings of a corresponding sort. In the case of courage, the more often one performs courageous actions, the more likely one is to feel courageous in future situations where such actions would be appropriate (18–20). These thus-cultivated feelings incline a person to perform additional actions corresponding to these feelings, which then further fortify those feelings from which these actions flow.

Badiou's virtue ethics could be said to presuppose-yet-disavow several crucial features of Aristotle's virtue ethics. First of all, while Aristotle and Badiou are in agreement that virtues properly speaking are not present in and automatically given by (human) nature, the former, by contrast with the latter, openly admits the explanatory necessity of positing that this same nature harbors within itself the possibilities and potentials for the accession to a second nature (whether this be Aristotelian character or Badiouian subjectivity, which are two very different concepts) other and more than one's first nature. It is tempting to claim that Badiou, in the noticeable absence of such an admission, cannot account for eventental subjectification in terms other than

49. Aristotle, *Nicomachean Ethics*, trans. Terrence Irwin (Indianapolis: Hackett Publishing Company, Inc., 1999), 18.

pseudo-explanatory, quasi-religious language in which the miracle of evental "grace" magically transubstantiates all-too-human animals into inhuman, denaturalized subjects.[50] Furthermore, Aristotle's definition of virtue, unlike Badiou's, does not restrictively and problematically oppose it to affect as something utterly separate and distinct. For Aristotle, a virtue takes shape through the back-and-forth interactions between states of feeling and modes of doing. Aristotelian virtues aren't equivalent or reducible to affects; nevertheless, virtues are not without their affects. Insofar as Badiou has trouble doing without affects—his repeated employments of affect-language (including the word "affect") despite his sidelining of all things affective is symptomatic of this—he might plant himself on philosophically firmer soil by adopting an Aristotelian definition of virtue encompassing both the affective and the practical within a dialectical relation of co-dependency.

Moreover, through juxtaposing the unlikely odd couple of Aristotle and Badiou while simultaneously playing them off against each other, a Badiou-inspired virtue ethics crucially different from that of Aristotle (one struggling to respond to today's social and political challenges) can be outlined rapidly here. First, instead of counseling moderation, the golden rule of Aristotle's ethics,[51] militancy on behalf of truths held to in the teeth of indifferent and/or hostile surroundings requires at least a touch of excessive immoderation, as per Badiou's stipulation that "There is only extremist truth."[52] Second, whereas Aristotle places the entire weight of his emphasis on a lifetime of continuous, calculated education and training from earliest youth onward[53]—as befits an aristocratic ethics, much is left to the accidents of birth—Badiouian practical philosophy, in a thoroughly egalitarian manner, stresses the importance of disruptive, incalculable occurrences (i.e., events) that could happen to anybody, anywhere, at any time. Third—this point relates to the previous one—Badiouian virtue ethics begins not with the building up of character, as Aristotle's does, but with the tearing down of character, with the shattering of one's recognizable selfhood and quotidian personality by a confrontation

50. Adrian Johnston, "What Matter(s) in Ontology: Alain Badiou, the Hebb-Event, and Materialism Split from Within," *Angelaki: Journal of the Theoretical Humanities* 13/1 (2008): 34–35, 38–40.
   51. Aristotle, *Nicomachean Ethics*, 24–25, 29–30.
   52. Badiou, *Petit panthéon portatif*, 98.
   53. Aristotle, *Nicomachean Ethics*, 19.

with pointed impasses at which one's prior life-world promises to collapse. As Badiou enjoins, "Do all that you can to persevere in that which exceeds your perseverance. Persevere in the interruption. Seize in your being that which has seized and broken you."[54]

Interpreted from a particular slanted angle, a passing moment in the *Nicomachean Ethics* allows a link between the otherwise inversely opposed visions of virtue ethics propounded at length by Aristotle and preliminarily traced by Badiou. The third chapter of the third book of Aristotle's treatise on the good life addresses what he terms "deliberation." Aristotle describes the individual's cognition and comportment as usually steered, in the vast majority of cases, by the auto-pilot of an ethico-moral second nature (i.e., character as formed through habituation). However, there inevitably will be exceptional contexts in which none of the general rules of this established nature are able to adjudicate decisively in relation to a decision to be made (or, in the terms of the conceptual language of Badiou's *Logiques des mondes*, a "point" to be resolved in a confrontation that requires courage[55]). Aristotle discerns an intimate link between unusual, unforeseen circumstances and the palpable awareness of being a volitional agent; this awareness can be starkly contrasted with that accompanying (or, rather, not accompanying) obedience to the second nature of habit-induced character. For Aristotle, deliberation tends to occur only in instances when the predictable-yet-unthematized circuits connecting the second nature of acquired habits and this nature's normal environment break down and cease to function as usual (*Nicomachean Ethics*, 34–36). When aporias, conflicts, deadlocks, and dilemmas arise within and between the spheres of obligations and systems of principles tacitly or unconsciously shaping people at the level of standard fashions of being and doing, persons are hurled into vortices of groundless-but-potentially-ground-giving autonomy (and, for Badiou, processes of subjectification entail giving incarnate shape to and drawing out over time what becomes uniquely possible with the surfacing of these vortices).

From a perspective informed by Badiou's philosophy, these events of structural breakdown, as critical moments of dysfunction or indecision in the socio-symbolic order and the second natures it helps to produce, suddenly present a chance for the individual (the Aristotelian

54. Badiou, *Ethics*, 47.
55. Badiou, *Logiques des mondes*, 96, 322, 459; Badiou, *De quoi Sarkozy est-il le nom?*, 46, 54–55, 99; Johnston, *Badiou, Žižek, and Political Transformations*.

creature of habit) to become a proper subject (as per Badiou's strict distinction between human individuality and more-than-human subjectivity[56]) by directly identifying with the voids of indeterminacy opened up through temporary short-circuiting disruptions to the usual ebb-and-flow of things. These glitches generated within and between the mediating matrices of determination shaping ordinary forms of individuality are the vanishing mediators, the ephemeral windows of opportunity and fleeting disposable ladders, occasionally offering the opportunity for ascension to forms of subjectivity that, however briefly, separate from reified constructions of selfhood subjugating human beings to identities dictated, in large part, by enveloping milieus. This sort of subject is, one could say, a SNAFU subject, a transient set of dynamics able to emerge within being when something goes wrong, when events transpire stemming from the occurrence of peculiar sorts of potentially momentous malfunctions.[57] In terms of ethico-practical subjectivity, what is in Aristotle's practical philosophy an exception (the varieties of unusual circumstances prompting deliberation) becomes the rule in Badiou's virtue ethics. Of course, one of the factors prompting this reversal of an exception into a rule is the glaringly obvious world of differences between the ancient city-state of Athens circa 400 B.C.E. and the internationalized market-societies of today.

Additionally, the formation of the subjects of a Badiouian virtue ethics can be depicted through a one-hundred-eighty degree twist on Althusser's well-known concept of "interpellation."[58] The genesis of an evental subject, as delineated by Badiou, is an occurrence of what could be called "inverse interpellation."[59] If Althusserian interpellation involves a fully functional trans-individual structure thoroughly subjecting/subjugating those it molds and hails, then inverse interpellation involves a somewhat dysfunctional structure plagued by inner inconsistencies summoning into existence subjects not entirely subjected to structure thanks to the possibilities presented by these openings of structural incompleteness, possibilities pointing to incal-

56. Badiou, *Ethics*, 41; Badiou, *De quoi Sarkozy est-il le nom?*, 99; Johnston, *Badiou, Žižek, and Political Transformations*.

57. Johnston, "What Matter(s) in Ontology," 42.

58. Louis Althusser, "Ideology and Ideological State Apparatuses (Notes Towards an Investigation)," in *Mapping Ideology*, ed. Slavoj Žižek (London: Verso, 1994), 130–31, 135–36.

59. Johnston, *Žižek's Ontology: A Transcendental Materialist Theory of Subjectivity* (Evanston: Northwestern University Press, 2008), 112–113.

culable alternatives to the repetitious reproduction of *status quo* situations and everything tied up with them. Furthermore, the subject of inverse interpellation remains a subject in both senses of the term (i.e., as determined *qua* subjected and free *qua* non-subjected). On the one hand, this subject's very chance for arising is conditioned by the sites, situations, and worlds forming localized regions of structurally configured being; on the other hand, once arisen, its paths and pursuits are not directly dictated by any given order of the *"il y a."*[60]

What does the preceding rough caricature of the rudiments of a Badiouian virtue ethics indicate apropos courage, politics, and conservatism as regards his philosophy? On a number of occasions and in connection with observations of various phenomena, Badiou emphasizes that contemporary socio-political circumstances present instances of (non-evental) newness escaping comprehension according to prior categories and definitions.[61] These shifts and changes are aspects of the "global disorientation"—this phrase can be understood as designating, among other things, the uncertainties and tumultuousness of the post-Cold War, post-9/11 world—to which he refers when proclaiming that, "courage locally orients in global disorientation" (*Sarkozy,* 101). In Badiou's view, attempts to plot this new geopolitical terrain on the grids of conceptual coordinates remaining from the politics of the past two centuries betray an absence of courage—namely, a lack of the bravery needed to pass through the dissolution of these earlier cognitive maps (*Sarkozy,* 99). Faced with the urgent, vexing enigmas and problems of a world convulsed right down to its smallest daily details by the manic frenzies of late-capitalist globalization (with its accompanying discontents), the now rigidified individual and collective characters of the personas and practices of nineteenth- and twentieth-century modalities of politics must be allowed to dissipate, however disconcerting and anxiety-provoking this may be. The time has come to dare to discard the old habits of stale political identities, identities dictated primarily by ever more obsolete configurations of the Left-Right divide, in favor of new ones still to be formed. Those who, like Badiou, are brave enough to take some of the first steps in this direction are bound to appear to others still invested

---

60. Badiou, *"La volonté: Cours d'agrégation d'Alain Badiou, 2002–2003,"* notes by François Nicolas (http://www.entretemps.asso.fr/Badiou/02–03.2.htm).

61. Badiou, "Pour une politique illimitée," in *De la limite,* ed. Spyros Théodorou (Marseilles: Éditions Parenthèses, 2006), 151; Badiou, "Interview with Alain Badiou (with Diana George and Nic Veroli)."

in established, settled political selves as strange, irresponsible, or even malevolent. No wonder those of both deeply engrained center-Left and center-Right sensibilities share a suspicion regarding Badiou's apparently rightist leftism. For Badiou, his leftism is "right" strictly in the sense of "correct" or "true."

Two conjoined questions routinely surface in response to Badiou's invocations of courage and related notions (such as discipline, fidelity, and terror). First, how does one distinguish the laudable subjective bravery of aggressively pursuing an event-disclosed truth-cause from deplorable fanaticisms unleashing the evils of irrational violence? Second and more specifically, given its conservative-sounding resonances with very traditional, time-worn discourses on ethico-political virtues such as heroic militancy, does Badiouian philosophy not risk encouraging an anti-progressive return to a past entangled with the twin nightmares of Nazism and Stalinism? Addressing these two concerns in reverse order, a perspective informed by psychoanalysis might maintain that the fear of a historical reversion, at least in select contemporary instances, serves as a screening conversion-into-its-opposite of another very different fear: not worries about a past that is not really past (i.e., history's known devils, as it were), but, instead, profound anxieties that the present and future will not allow for a wholesale reversion to prior forms, that the re-enactment of old roles on the shifting stages of the current and changing theater of political history is untenable folly and farce. Expressed in the parlance of *Logiques des mondes*, even if fragments of the past are "resurrected" (74–75), these resurrections will not amount to pure and simple repetitions easily recognizable and manageable according to the reassuringly familiar political protocols of the pasts from which certain among the (presumed) dead return.

In response to the first concern about the difference, or lack thereof, between evental militancy and authoritarian fanaticism, it must be confessed with blunt frankness: there is no guarantee in advance, at any given point in time, of a clear-cut, self-evident distinction between the violence of justified evental daring and the violence of unjustified non-evental foolishness or barbarity (*à la* the cliché about the fine line between bravery and stupidity). An assurance of this sort is impossible for several reasons, including the incredibly complex multiple temporal dynamics of histories and events.[62] More to the point, to ask for such an *a priori* guarantee about courage is pre-

---

62. Johnston, *Badiou, Žižek, and Political Transformations.*

cisely to lack courage (i.e., the courage for courage, in line with Badiou's contention that confidence and fidelity, as concrete embodiments of courage, are always the "confidence in confidence"[63] and "faithfulness to fidelity"[64]—that is, inherently dialectical doublings involving both doings and feelings to alternating extents[65]). Courage means being brave enough to risk being stupid, or worse. Although difficult to define with precision, a negative definition of Badiouian courage has come into view at this juncture: Courage is that which those who ask for advance guarantees of its justness just do not have.

63. Badiou, *Théorie du sujet,* 339, 341.
64. Badiou, *Ethics,* 47.
65. Johnston, *Badiou, Žižek, and Political Transformations.*

BÉNÉDICTE COSTE

Against the Grain: Michéa's Radical Philosophy and Its Discontents

Jean-Claude Michéa stands apart in the media, in philosophy, and in French contemporary politics. A philosopher and essayist fighting liberal politics, he is praised by right-wing thinkers while the Left seems to ignore him. As Serge Audier writes:

> Michéa's viewpoint has the peculiarity of appearing as antiprogressive, populist, and staunchly hostile to the "Left" in the name of community values of an original socialism that indeed appears more imaginary than real. Using working class rhetoric to comment on "simple people," this fashionable essayist of anti-liberal rhetoric appears as a disciple of the "Tory" anarchist George Orwell.[1]

Antiprogressive, populist, original socialism, working class, anti-liberal rhetoric, fashionable essayist: those derogatory terms qualify a philsopher as well as challenge readers to give a stable definition of their meaning. Indeed they are themselves at stake as the products of ongoing debates regarding their shifting meanings. What follows deals both with the difficulty of defining them[2] and aims at presenting the writings of a philosopher who challenges political categories and affiliations when he co-authors a book such as *Les valeurs de l'homme contemporain* with Alain Finkielkraut, the producer of the talk-show "Répliques" on France Culture, who has repeatedly invited him on the show, and with Pascal Bruckner, who declared himself a supporter of French President Nicolas Sarkozy. Claiming to embrace left-wing values, Michéa has in fact been pegged as a conservative or a right-

---

1. Serge Audier, *La pensée anti-68* (Paris: La Découverte, 2008), 46.
2. In what follows, "liberal" will be used according to Michéa's definition and designates both free-market policies and political neoliberalism.

YFS 116/117, *Turns to the Right?* ed. Johnson and Schehr, © 2009 by Yale University.

wing thinker because of his critique of contemporary morality. Such a presentation is questionable because of its reductionism and its bias, but it illustrates the common representation of a radical thinker who can still appear as reactionary when his ideas are reduced to fragments of sentences sometimes unfairly taken out of context or seen from a viewpoint where the political world is split between Left and Right, a division that Michéa has himself criticized. What follows aims at presenting his ideas before discussing how they may fit into the contemporary landscape as defined by its "*droitisation*," to use the word made popular by the journalist Eric Dupin. In his 2007 essay,[3] *À droite toute,* "*droitisation*," that is, the turn to the Right in politics, designates the political recomposition of the last two decades along a divide between societal issues such as security and immigration, rather than economic ones. The "*droitisation*" found its latest expression when Sarkozy was elected.[4]

The effect of readings that turn Michéa into a reactionary or a conservative in the current context must be acknowledged, and there is no denying that he is a media-hyped writer with ambiguous ideas regarding mores and individual psychology. Still, it would be a mistake to classify him as a right-wing thinker or a reactionary, as I shall show in what follows; in fact, he presents himself as an anarchist in the vein of the George Orwell of *Animal Farm*.[5] My aim is thus twofold: to show that his theses denounce the traditional political French Left/Right divide, and to discuss their aporias in order to understand how they may be harnessed in the current context of the return of the Right. Only if a redistribution of positions in the political spectrum occurred could Michéa be termed "reactionary," but that redistribution might also affect the positions of thinkers who currently claim to write from a left-wing perspective.

The mainstream French press enjoys interviewing such a relaxed and "cool" philosopher who, besides being very photogenic and writing with flair, plays the part of the essayist explaining contemporary anxieties about education, the fate or future of the Left, the status of minorities, and economic growth, among other subjects, to a wide

---

3. Eric Dupin, *À droite toute* (Paris: Fayard, 2007).

4. Ignacio Ramonet, "Populisme français," *Le monde diplomatique* (June 2007) http://www.monde-diplomatique.fr/2007/06/RAMONET/14842. For a more detailed study, see Etienne Schweisguth, "Le trompe-l'œil de la droitisation," *Revue française de science politique* 573–74 (2007): 393–410.

5. "Conversation avec Jean-Claude Michéa," *À contretemps* 31 (July 2008).

readership. In 2007, the French weeklies *Le point*[6] and *Le nouvel observateur*[7] devoted articles to his latest book, *L'empire du moindre mal* [The Empire of the Lesser Evil] and the center-leaning *Marianne* published excerpts from it.[8] These articles generally reformulate Michéa's radicality in political terms as an opposition between liberalism and conservatism and between modernity and anti-progressivism. Critics usually note his denunciation of the damage of free-market policies that is part of his sustained critique of capitalism and productivism. What he wrote about Orwell in 1995 also applies to Michéa himself: "What these times refuse to take into consideration is that someone may be . . . willing to change the way we live without getting rid of the past and, at the same time, a faithful friend of the working-classes."[9] Both a progressive and a conservative, Michéa has shown the solidarity of moral and economic issues in his 2002 *Impasse Adam Smith* [The Adam Smith Dead-end], and all his writings aim at highlighting the unity of liberalism in its anthropological and philosophical aspects, more than in its political or economic dimensions, while criticizing its logic, rather than attacking some hypothetical essence, through a thorough study of the dialectics between liberal ideas and their materialization in history.

In *Orwell anarchiste tory* [Orwell, Anarchist and Tory], his first book (1995), Michéa studied Orwell's political critique of English socialism, and portrayed a radical socialist *cum* conservative writer whom the Establishment could not assimilate. He saw Orwell's socialism as predicated on "those ethical and psychological positions

6. "Jean-Claude Michéa et la servitude libérale. Entretien intégral avec Elisabeth Lévy," *Le point* 1825 (6 September 2007). The interview is introduced in this way: "A disciple of Orwell, the philosopher Jean-Claude Michéa is a favorite author for all proponents of 'critical thought.' An acid detractor of capitalism, tirelessly advocating an egalitarian society, he does not spare the Left he deems guilty of having broken from the human values of original socialism. In *L'empire du moindre mal*, he strikes at the heart of both the liberal system and the 'religion of economics.' All liberals need urgently to read it." See http://www.lepoint.fr/content/debats/article?id=199481.

7. Aude Lancelin, "Y a-t-il une vie après le libéralisme? Entretien avec Jean-Claude Michéa," http://bibliobs.nouvelobs.com/2007/09/27/ya-t-il-une-vie-apres-le-liberalisme. The foreword to the interview reads: "An anticapitalist and antilibertarian, the philosopher strikes back with *L'empire du moindre mal*. . . . A radical attack on the liberal way of living."

8. "Quand Jean-Claude Michéa taquine la droite libérale . . . et la gauche bien pensante," in http://www.marianne2.fr/Quand-Jean-Claude-Michea-taquine-la-droite-liberale-et-la-gauche-bien pensante_a78775.html.

9. Jean-Claude Michéa, *Orwell anarchiste tory suivi de À propos de 1984* (Castelnau le Lez: Climats, 2000), 118.

without which the functioning of a socialist society *on a daily basis* is doomed to remain a utopia or an instance of *wishful thinking.*"[10] Such positions partake of what Orwell called "common decency," which he did not theorize but which designates a reality that almost everyone feels intuitively: "it is a code of conduct that almost everyone can understand although it is never stated as such."[11] Functioning as a point of resistance to any kind of oppression, Orwell's "common decency" is a constant reference for Michéa.

In 1998, in *Les intellectuels, le peuple et le ballon rond* [The Intellectuals, the People, and the Soccerball], Michéa criticized French intellectuals' scorn for soccer, and highlighted the fact that their analyses turn it into a sport for underpriviledged youngsters; in so doing, he positions himself against the analyses of Jean-Marie Brohm and Marc Perelman[12] who emphasize the social and economic damage the game causes. Published when the World Cup championship was taking place in France, the book enjoyed only a limited success. Media recognition for Michéa came in 1999 with the acid theses of his third essay, *L'enseignement de l'ignorance* [Teaching Ignorance]. Michéa analyzed education issues by examing the shift from schools transmitting knowledge in the name of freedom to becoming institutions that train individuals to participate in the twenty-first-century global economic war. In spite of its iconoclastic theses mainly directed against Bourdieu's theory of social reproduction, *L'enseignement de l'ignorance* underlines the importance of educational issues in democracies, but it does not appear to offer a solution. His lack of solution, however, does not derive from political nihilism. He does in fact mention Orwell's notion of "common sense" with which every citizen is endowed and that may helm an individual act without any help from a guide or savior. At the same time, however, it soon becomes clear that there have been reactions to the current educational crisis, and numerous conservative essays and pamphlets, such as Brighelli's *La fabrique du crétin* [Manufacturing idiots]. This 2005 volume calls for the restoration of old-fashioned teaching methods, and it blames governments on the Left for having lowered educational standards.

Wider in scope and aims is *Impasse Adam Smith,* in which Michéa denounces "the impossibility of overtaking capitalism on its left." This

10. Michéa, *Orwell anarchiste tory,* 93.
11. George Orwell cited in Michéa, *Orwell anarchiste tory,* 171.
12. Jean-Marie Brohm and Marc Perelman, *Le football, une peste émotionelle* (Paris: Gallimard, 1998).

book targets the French Socialist Party which had just suffered a humiliating defeat in the first round of the 2002 presidential elections, and it does so in an ironic tone that would become the philosopher's trademark. Michéa examines the birth of political and economic liberalism in order to show that any criticism of liberalism limited to its economic dimension is doomed to electoral failure. The Socialist Party, which embraced the cause of free-market economics after having embraced political neoliberalism, will always be outperformed by the real proponents of capitalism. As for anti-globalization movements sticking to a criticism of neoliberal economic policies, according to Michéa, they have strayed from the real struggle. He argues that there is a unity within both veins of liberalism, which demands a radical critique "analyzing the ill *at its roots* and undertaking to cure it as such."[13]

Michéa sees contemporary neoliberalism and socialism as predicated on the worship of progress and modernity. As an heir to Enlightenment thought, the French Left is grounded in a metaphysics of progress, a feature it shares with the economic and political neoliberalism of the Right, as both were born from the unstable compromise between Proudhonian socialism and the republican refusal of any return to the *Ancien Régime* in the nineteenth-century. Such a compromise, he argues, functioned until 1945, but since then, the Left has unwittingly become the political machine for legitimizing free-market policies in the name of the modernization of mores, that is, of social liberalism. It is this liberal-libertarian modern Left that should be radically criticized, and Michéa pleads for a return to the nineteenth-century criticism of modernity and to working-class socialism as well as to anarchism. Such a critique also ought to come back to Orwell's "common decency," now defined as "this subtle and complex interplay founding both our benevolent relations to others, our respect for Nature, and more generally, our intuitive sense of what is owed to each of us" (71), in order to universalize it so as to set up a new society based on moral values such as solidarity, civility, liberty, and equality. Michéa's common decency has an ethical and anthropological dimension that also corresponds to the values of the popular and working classes, of the "common men" who do not take part in the domination of their fellow-citizens and who steer clear of the lure of power and individual success. For Orwell, common decency was a decisive point of resistance to totalitarianism on both the Right and the

---

13. Michéa, *Impasse Adam Smith* (Castelnau le Lez: Climats, 2002), 12.

Left, and for Michéa, it is the *"essential starting point* of all *socialist* critique in the original meaning of the term"* (97). It is precisely this type of ethical reference that political neoliberalism, under the guise of the liberalization of mores, makes impossible; hence the necessity of a radical break from the imaginary of the Left if one wishes not to return to the socialist failures of the twentieth century.

In *L'empire du moindre mal*, published after the 2007 presidential election, a slightly less optimistic Michéa offers a deeper genealogy of European liberalism seen as a historical contingency, from the Renaissance to the twenty-first century, in which he deliberately simplifies matters and chooses specific ideological slants: political neoliberalism is called the "Law," and its economic avatar, the "Market." Contrary to common assumptions, neoliberalism cannot be reduced to political reaction or conservative ideas but is "a political ideal" referring to the "radical [and permanent] project of a radical transformation of the human order."[14] It is predicated on the idea that all attempts at instituting Goodness and Virtue lead to evil, with the result that neoliberalism is doomed to wish for the least evil society, thus precluding the possibility of all (or any) collective, moral standards.

Michéa pits peaceful and open-minded sixteenth-century humanists against seventeenth-century politicians (*"Politiques"*), who, confronted with the Wars of Religion, sought a means of ensuring the peaceful coexistence of nations and individuals. Their solution involved a compromise grounded in the neutralization and the privatization of moral standards under a layer of "tolerance." Thereafter, the only possible war would be one of mankind against nature, and it would use science and technology. This "war of substitution" (28), channelling mankind's energy toward work and industry, found welcome support in the physical sciences of the time, founded on notions of equilibrium. At the same time, Hobbes's bleak description of human nature underlies all subsequent political thought (31). The philosophical necessity of thinking about people as they are and not as they ought to be led to an "anthropology of weariness" (32) in which an individual is considered to be a pedestrian and harmless member of society, rather than a hero. At the same time, the idea of a common Good was discarded for the sake of the pursuit of each individual's possessions and private pleasures. Politics was defined as the conception

---

14. Michéa, *L'empire du moindre mal. Essai sur la civilisation libérale* (Paris: Flammarion-Climats, 2007), 17. All references are to this edition.

and application of a system of weights and counterweights able to generate political order and harmony, "without any need to ever make an appeal to the virtue of the subjects" (33). According to Michéa, the basic axiom of liberalism is that power must be philosophically neutral. It is an agency in charge of harmonizing competing liberties by limiting their range of action and by establishing the primacy of the Just over the Good. The liberal State is axiologically neutral.

Having defined the archeology of liberalism, Michéa embarks on showing the "double and parallel movement leading philosophical liberalism to offer the utopia of a rational society grounding its pacification in the mere dynamics of the Market and the Law" (33). He recognizes the difference between economic and political liberalism, but links them together, as each seeks the means of escaping its antinomies in its counterpart: the Law in order to fight the Market and conversely. He recognizes that notions relating to what would become free trade and free-market capitalism first appeared in an economic form in the eighteenth century, as Adam Smith's theory of "doux commerce" that would give rise to free trade, before finding its best political expression a century later in the writings of Benjamin Constant, who sought a minimal State and maximal private freedoms. Those two constitutive dimensions were fused in the writings of Frédéric Bastiat, an opponent of both working-class socialists and Saint-Simon's heirs. Bastiat argued that only complete freedom of all economic exchanges could ensure a peaceful society, as that would allow individual charity to remedy economic inequalities. Michéa observes cunningly that this "structural necessity" became Margaret Thatcher's "trickle-down effect," before he comments on the solidarity of the Law and the Market. And the latter can bring happiness to all through the substitute religion of consumption. Conversely, the Law becomes a substitute religion as well as the fight against all discrimination, with the exception, of course, of economic discrimination.

Michéa does not list the damage wrought by economic liberalism[15] as such, as a list has been drawn by Marxists and opponents of globalization of whom he steers clear in order to concentrate on the effects of political liberalism. Deprived of any collective moral standards on which to stand , the liberal Law is reduced to recording the changes in the equilibrium between contending groups. This has somewhat sur-

15. However, he calls for the end of oil-driven economies and capitalist exploitation and argues that such a radical societal change may be brought by climate changes.

prising effects, as Michéa offers the example of the simultaneous fight *against* tobacco and *for* the decriminalization of drug use in France. If both these events come to pass, a strange situation would arise in which everyone was free to consume drugs, a position adopted by self-confessed political libertarians such as Alain Madelin, without being able to smoke in public places, a position usually held by the orthodox Left. Facing societal issues, the Law obeys its natural bent, which necessarily leads to "a *massive regularization* of all kinds of possible and unlikely behaviors" (39), even if they are self-contradictory, with the effect, Michéa observes, of foreclosing all limit and marginality.

Continuing his anthropological analysis of the liberal condition, Michéa explains that the thesis that the Law and the Market may socially integrate whoever comes in their sphere, and that this aptitude is natural, is "psychological naivete," for both can only provide "secondary" forms of socialization (135). The liberal contract depends on trust, which in turn depends on what sociologist Alain Caillé calls the "primary sociality" at the basis of all society as defined by Marcel Mauss's concept of the gift, theorized in Mauss's 1920 essay on "giving, taking, and giving back" in contrast with Beaumarchais' "asking, receiving, and taking," which illustrates the liberal gift. Indeed, the scholars of MAUSS (Mouvement anti-utilitariste dans les sciences sociales [Anti-Utilitarian Movement in the Social Sciences]), of whom Caillé is one of the key players, are one of Michéa's favorite references. The cycle of the gift sets debt as the essence of sociality. It also gives a relevant place to Orwellian common decency, as decency defines our capacity to enact it and allows us to "implant *basic human virtues* at the deepest level of the socialist practice" (139). Opposed to the free-market contract whose value rests on the possibility of defaulting (as the international banking crisis of fall 2008 amply demonstrates), Mauss's cycle of the gift can be both universal and locally translated, according to the specificity of each society. Were Mauss's cycle of the gift internalized with an aim of being used to non-mimetic and emancipatory ends, it would provide the basis on which to build resistance and revolt. These in turn would enable the subjective autonomy defined by Cornelius Castoriadis as the capacity to govern and be governed. Castoriadis is another fundamental Michean reference along with the Internationale situationniste and Guy Debord, whose *Commentaires sur la société du spectacle*[16] he cites. Like

16. Guy Debord, *Commentaires sur la société du Spectacle* (1988) *Œuvres* (Paris: Gallimard, Quarto, 2006), 1593–1646.

those ultra-leftist thinkers, Michéa decries the specialization of tasks and the increasing role played by "experts," whom he sees as depriving citizens of the possibility of political action and as turning economic growth and moral evolution into natural processes before which individuals are impotent. If libertarian modernity is defined by the foreclosure of all collective and common moral standards, it becomes necessary to reappropriate them in order to be able to resist the dominant world order. If libertarian modernity is defined as an ever-increasing specialization, mankind needs to reappropriate its own history. Castoriadis's autonomization process leads to a newfound common decency that Michéa offers as set of moral rules grounded in the daily sphere and in the variety of human experience.

The society Michéa calls for is predicated on already existing possibilities, such as civility, that must be radicalized, interiorized, and universalized. In this light, Michéa also relies on an anarchist analysis of mankind and society. For him, anarchism is not only the institution of a free, equal, and decent society by formerly dominated classes, it is also the vehicle of a "fundamental lucidity" (167). Within the political field, it introduces the effects of a subject's individual history, including his or her relation to the unconscious, and does so by acknowledging, for instance, the existence of a "will to power" permeating all human relations, even in the most egalitarian societies, although this will to power also stems from particular social and historical conditions. The emphasis placed by anarchists on the issues of family and school education makes anarchy the *"moral foundation* of all possible revolution"* (172). Conversely, the repression of these issues is at the origin of the failure or bureaucratization of all revolutionary movements.

Michéa appears thus to be situated within a radical tradition for which both the Left and the Right are equivalent because both are grounded in the same eighteenth-century anthropology. When he is viewed on a Right-Left axis, it becomes difficult not to turn him into a renegade of the Left or even a conservative. This is what the mainstream press does. According to *Le Figaro:* "Try as he might to be an 'anarchist,' Jean-Claude Michéa is indeed the kind of 'conservative' that H[annah] Arendt defined when she wrote that a world abandoned to the power of ideology or to the sole concern of the economy is dangerous for human liberty."[17]Accusing him of simplifications con-

17. Paul-François Paoli, "Jean-Claude Michéa, l'incorruptible," in http://www.lefigaro.fr/livres/2006/07/20/03005–20060720ARTFIG90283-jean_claude_michea_l_incorruptible.php.

cerning the French liberal tradition, Jacques de Saint-Victor turns him into "an unwitting liberal"[18]; conversely, for *Le monde*, he is "a socialist conservative."[19] Indeed those contradictory and oxymoronic definitions fail to grasp his radicality and have the effect of re-inscribing him within an opposition he himself has deconstructed. Still, Michéa cannot be said to embrace the anti-globalization movement, which he blames for seeking some adjustments in the concept of the market, without, however, abandoning notions relating to the metaphysics of progress. He also distances himself from the extreme Left, which he calls the "advanced spearhead of the Spectacle," and which appears to be seeking a common cause uniting all popular classes. But does he embrace conservatism? Can the Right annex him for a philosophical legitimation to strengthen the will that emerged during the last French presidential campaign to bury the supposed values of May '68—permissiveness and moral relativism—and enact a genuine political reaction? Is Michéa a reactionary?

Beyond a certain reductivism often found in media sound-bites and beyond some uses of his positions by others for political ends, there are some aporias and short-cuts in his analyses that could make him seem ambiguous or ambivalent. To avoid such a conclusion, it is necessary for the reader to unpack these aporias and short-cuts, to read the authors to whom he refers, and to follow the rhetoric and deontology of his references. Moreover, this route is the necessary and obvious one, given the fact that Michéa avoids all political affiliations and intervenes in public debates only as a philosopher. Michéa's position on "same-sex marriage," for example, is aporetic. One might argue that this position should be consonant with the liberal Law he describes, and if that Law remains neutral as it should, it is difficult to understand why same-sex marriage has not in fact become legal wherever that Law obtains. Interviewed about it,[20] Michéa declared himself hostile to such a law, preferring to rely on the common sense of individuals, associations, and groups. However, opinion polls show that common sense is far from sufficient for extending the right to marry to all individuals regardless of gender, since, as we know, a majority of the

18. Jacques de Saint Victor, "Un libéral qui s'ignore," in http://www.lefigaro.fr/livres/2007/09/13/03005–20070913ARTFIG90242-un_liberal_qui_s_ignore.php.

19. Philippe Raynaud, "Jean-Claude Michéa: les dilemmes du libéralisme," *Le monde des livres* (7 September 2007). *Le monde des livres* had asked P. Allies, Professor of Political Science at the Law School in Montpellier and member of the Socialist Party to review *Impasse Adam Smith* in 2002.

20. Michéa, personal interview, 12 December 2007.

French populace rejects a law in favor of same-sex marriage. Common decency seems to be finding its limits, although Michéa argues that the role of the State, whatever its form, is to encourage such fair claims by supporting progressive values as society matures, for example. But when it comes to this issue, it seems clear that family or societal values today do not allow for such a possibility. Michéa responds to this dilemma, or aporia, by referring to the philosopher François Julien on the art of indirect action in Chinese culture that recommends feeding the plant rather than the flowers. He also proposes returning to the Situationists' notion of the "construction of situations,"[21] which may help cultivate ontological dispositions to ordinary civility and decency against a conservative reaction. However, he does not ignore the difficulty of changing values or constructing situations, nor does he downplay the naivety that often exists in attempts to raise the popular classes to a state of (moral) exemplarity. Similarly, he recognizes the ambiguities of moral standards likely to morph into moralism.[22]

It is undoubtedly on societal and moral issues that Michéa may appear conservative to some. In this light, it is worth noting that a great number of reactionaries in matters of rights and societal issues claim him as an inspiration. The psychoanalysts Charles Melman and Jean-Pierre Lebrun quote his essays in support of their refusal to question the heteropatriarchal order within the context of a psychoanalysis called upon to ridicule the French civil union (PACS), as well as feminist and gay struggles.[23] Ironically, Michéa quotes them when he comments upon the inconsistencies of the liberal Law or the liberalization of mores. He also quotes Michel Schneider, the proponent of free-market economics and moral conservatism who calls for less of a welfare state and more heterocracy in *Big Mother* (2002).[24] Michéa is keen to acknowledge the ambiguities of Schneider's gendering of the political sphere in order to attack the welfare state, which he compares to an intrusive mother whom one has to fend off. But if he rejects Schneider's economic liberalism, he adopts his genderization of poli-

21. Debord, *Rapport sur la construction de situations* (1957) *Œuvres* (Paris: Gallimard, Quarto, 2006), 309–28.

22. Sylvain Dzimira, "Jean-Claude Michéa avec le MAUSS. Compte-rendu," *Revue du MAUSS permanente*, March 20, 2008.

23. Charles Melman et Jean-Pierre Lebrun, *L'homme sans gravité* (2002; Paris: Gallimard, Folio Essais, 2005).

24. Michel Schneider, *Big Mother: Psychopathologie de la vie politique* (Paris: Odile Jacob, 2002).

tics. Scrutinizing liberal domination, he notices that its patriarchal dimension gave rise to fruitful analyses but that there is no equivalent when it comes to the subjection and manipulation by others who "find their unconscious model within the *maternal ascendancy*" (173). Although it is rarely discussed, the "maternal ascendancy" appears when the Symbolic law vanishes, resulting not in increased personal liberty but in a liberation of the superego assuming, for the occasion, the aspect of the "possessive and castratrating 'bad mother'" (175), Michéa explains, refering this time to Slavoj Žižek. The father commands that the Law be obeyed and insists on the submission of the subject to the Law insofar as external behavior is concerned, whereas the Mother stands for unconditional love predicated on emotional blackmail. She wields limitless power, and subjects contract a debt they cannot ever pay back. The invisible hand of patriarchal domination can thus be said to have shielded the no less invisible hand of matriarchal domination, which appears when free-market liberalism and its attendant ideologies have destroyed the Symbolic order in the name of the Market and the Law. As a result, a new type of normativity anchored in the subject's imaginary is created and refered to the "power of mothers." Through such an unorthodox psychoanalytical analysis predicated on the yoking of such politically and psychoanatically different authors as Žižek and Lebrun, it becomes difficult to frame liberalism, which now appears as the return of the "immemorial [repression] of the *empire of the Mothers*" (177). The liberal destruction of Castoriadis's heteronomic societies and their replacement by societies of control subjected to the increasing authority of experts replacing adults are said to express the return of the repressed.

Even though Michéa makes it clear that the "feminist struggle" needs to be waged, now more than ever (192), and that both genders may exert domination, it is still surprising to see him genderize ascendancy in derogatory terms for women, and, in so doing, seem to follow the highly reactionary writings of a minority of French-speaking psychoanalysts. Forgotten are the writings of Castoriadis, himself a psychoanalyst, which paid tribute to sexual liberation movements, conceived the possibility of an autonomy without any father figure, and hailed the advent of minority movements. Gone too are the situationist writings that rejected all sexual, and therefore, mercantile identities.[25] Michéa ap-

___

25. Jean-Pierre Voyer, *Lettre ouverte aux citoyens du FHAR* (Paris: Institut de Préhistoire Contemporaine, 1971).

pears to be joining the latest products of the current French return of the Right.

The liberal infantilization he contrasts with psychic maturity or personal and collective autonomy has its origin in the work of another scholar, Christopher Lasch. An important reference for Michéa, the American academic enjoys an ambiguous status in France where he is sometimes presented as reactionary[26] and sometimes hailed for his anti-capitalist stance. Hence, there is a need to distinguish between his American and French reception, as both rely on different political traditions and history. Michéa had Lasch's *The Culture of Narcissism* republished in France in 2000. The prefaces he wrote to this and Lasch's other essays describe the historian as a radical, anti-progressive thinker, a populist opposed to the liberal American Left.[27] Michéa also values Lasch's critique of capitalism which led him to denounce those cultural changes that occurred in the twentieth-century and gave rise to a youth-oriented culture, culminating in 1960s counter-culture. We may however wonder if we can transpose Lasch's theses to France whose political tradition is quite different. Serge Halimi[28] reminds us that American populism cannot be equated to its French version, for, in France the term is derogatory and used to describe the National Front's agenda. For Serge Audier, Lasch is a reactionary and a conservative who contributed to what he calls "anti-May-68 thought." For Michéa, Lasch's radicality locates him in the tradition of working-class socialism, as well as in the denunciation of the anthropological effects of capitalism. The different reception of Lasch in France and in the United States is parallel to Michéa's often contradictory reception in France. It is perhaps moot to eschew a simple Right/Left opposition in this case and see his work instead through the lens of an opposition between political and economic anti-liberal radicalism and liberalism. And it is this position that will finally tell us whether Michéa is an adversary to or a proponent of the (re) turn to the Right.

26. Audier, *La pensée anti-68*, 319–20.

27. Christopher Lasch, *La culture du narcissisme. La vie américaine à un âge de déclin des espérances. Traduction de Michel L. Landa. Précédée de Pour en finir avec le XXIe siècle de Jean-Claude Michéa.* (Castelnau-le-Lez: Climats, 2000). The first French edition was in 1981. The original edition was *The Culture of Narcissism: American Life in an Age of Diminished Expectations.* (New York: Norton, 1978).

28. Serge Halimi, "Le populisme, voilà l'ennemi!" *Le monde diplomatique* (April 1996): 10.

RICHARD J. GOLSAN

Pascal Bruckner and the Politics of the *Moraliste:* Realism or Reaction?

By any measure, describing the political outlook of a figure as complex and often as paradoxical as Pascal Bruckner, and then placing the writer squarely on the "Left" or the "Right" in France today, is no easy task. As Bruckner himself states in a 2005 interview, when it comes to his politics as well as his *engagements* of the past and present, he can appear ambivalent and even deliberately contradictory, and some might argue, self-contradictory. For example, speaking of his role in the events of May 1968, Bruckner acknowledges his ambivalence, stating that, while his sympathies tended toward "a libertarian extreme Left position," he never joined any group, and he considers himself in the final analysis to have been more of an "onlooker" than an "activist."[1] Discussing his current political allegiance, Bruckner asserts that he belongs to the socialist Left, but adds that his socialism is a "decaffeinated one." And even within that "decaffeinated socialist Left" Bruckner considers it "important to circulate ideas that are considered right-wing or reactionary." In some instances, this is precisely what he has done. Bruckner concludes: "In this way you benefit from listeners you would not otherwise be able to reach" (16).

In Bruckner's essays and novels, the writer's *esprit de contradiction* —and not just his ambivalence—is readily apparent, most obviously in the divergent ways in which he approaches fiction and non-fiction writing. For while some of Bruckner's better-known essays and editorials are frequently overtly political and polemical—his caustic attack on the *tiermondisme* or "Third Worldism" of the sixties and seventies

---

1. "Interview with Pascal Bruckner," *South Central Review* 22/2 (Summer 2005), 13.

YFS 116/117, *Turns to the Right?* ed. Johnson and Schehr, © 2009 by Yale University.

92

in *Le sanglot de l'homme blanc* (1983), and its inheritors in the last decade or so in *La tyrannie de la pénitence* (2006) are cases in point— his fiction is deliberately "apolitical." As he notes, novel writing "frees [him] from reality"; it affords him the opportunity to "search for extremes and an exaltation and an indulgence of erotic and amorous exaltation pushed to the limit." By contrast, the writing of non-fiction, especially in the form of the essay, "leads . . . back to reality" (16).

But even if Bruckner's essays seem to offer fertile ground for accurately assessing his political outlook, the above-mentioned *esprit de contradiction*, coupled with a taste for paradox and irony, makes the task more difficult, as does his ambivalence about intellectual *engagement* in general. In stark opposition to intellectuals of earlier generations, Bruckner takes a cautious, indeed a "conservative" view as to when and under precisely what circumstances it is appropriate for the intellectual to intervene in the public debate: "The intellectual should, ordinarily, only engage himself in the area in which he has acquired real competence." Moreover, he continues, "[t]aking an active part in society's politics is justified only when the politicians and the media fail us and speak untruths" (16).

Bruckner's apparent conservatism on the subject of intellectual commitment might point to a broader conservatism, in that it hardly bespeaks a revolutionary fervor or a radical distrust of the status quo. It would seem to imply that, for him, governments and the media—presumably in democratic societies—are generally reliable, and need to be taken on only occasionally and under unusual circumstances. But to conclude from this that he is best characterized as a "conservative" *intellectuel engagé* is also misleading, in that, as André Glucksmann has recently pointed out, he is first and foremost not a "committed intellectual" at all, but rather a *moraliste*.[2] As such, his primary objective is not to stir his readership to take specific political actions or to embrace particular causes. Instead, Bruckner is motivated more fundamentally by a desire to carefully observe and diagnose the ills of modern society as well as the failings and hypocrisies of his fellow human beings, especially of the French and other Europeans. Given this approach, it is no surprise that the titles of many of his essays begin precisely with words that underscore or allude strongly to these ills and failings: *Misère de la prospérité, Tyrannie de la pénitence, Le sanglot de l'homme blanc,*

2. André Glucksmann, "On Pascal Bruckner," *South Central Review* 24/2 (Summer 2007), 26.

Mélancolie démocratique, Le vertige de Babel, and so on. Bruckner is a masterful observer in his analyses of contemporary society and the foibles of Europeans today. According to Tzvetan Todorov, he possesses a real gift for observing and describing *l'actualité,* a gift matched by very few in France today.[3] And as Paul Berman has asserted recently, in his essays, Bruckner's talent for identifying modern and above all contemporary European cultural neuroses—especially the expressions and subterfuges of Western self-hatred—is unmatched. For Berman, he is essentially an "anti-theorist" very much in touch with reality.[4]

Be that as it may, it would be naive and misleading to suggest that Pascal Bruckner is fundamentally "apolitical," or that he has not taken strongly partisan stands that, in some instances, lend credence to the claims of some that he is "on the Right." His attacks on *tiermondisme* certainly targeted earlier generations of France's left-wing intelligentsia and luminaries like Jean-Paul Sartre, among others. In the 1990s, Bruckner's outspoken opposition to Serb aggression in Croatia and Bosnia, and later his support for the NATO bombings of Kosovo, even though shared by many on the French Left, put him at odds both with the likes of the socialist president François Mitterrand in the first instance (for whom Serbia had always been one of France's "friends") and in the second, with figures like Régis Debray, who publicly excoriated Jacques Chirac for his support of the bombing of Kosovo in 1999.[5] Moreover, Bruckner's positions with regard to Bosnia and Kosovo re-established his close proximity, not only with Alain Finkielkraut (his former co-author) whom many on the Left had come to view with suspicion largely because of his pro-Israel stance, but also with André Glucksmann, the former Maoist whose own right-wing credentials, at least for some, would later be confirmed by his staunch and even fanatical support of George Bush and the American invasion of Iraq.[6] While Bruckner's "culpability" here was largely "guilt by association," which also put him at odds with the remnants of an old guard Stalinist Left, his support of the bombing of Kosovo linked him (and others) to the one of the true *bêtes noires* of many on the

3. Conversation with the author.

4. Paul Berman, "Pascal Bruckner," *South Central Review* 24/2 (Summer 2007), 47.

5. For a discussion of Debray and Kosovo, see "The Debray Affair" in my *French Writers and the Politics of Complicity: Crises of Democracy in the 1940s and 1990s* (Baltimore: The Johns Hopkins University Press, 2006), 123–42.

6. For a discussion of André Glucksmann's support of the war in Iraq and President George W. Bush, see my "Preliminary Reflections on *Anti-antiaméricanisme:* André Glucksmann *et compagnie,*" in *Contemporary French and Francophone Studies (Sites)* 8/4 (Fall 2004), 391–404.

French intellectual Left, *l'ennemi américain* (to invoke the title of Philippe Roger's well-known recent study.) The fact that Bruckner had repeatedly skewered French anti-Americanism and delighted in exposing its hypocrisies and excesses has only confirmed his reputation, for some, as a "reactionary."

But the major "charge" against Pascal Bruckner is that, both in the context of his *anti-antiaméricanisme* and, more centrally in his belief, exemplified in his positions relative to Bosnia and Serbia, that the Western democracies have the right and even the *obligation* to intervene in countries where tyrants are oppressing their own people, he initially supported the U.S. invasion of Iraq. In an editorial in *Le monde* (3 March 2003), co-signed with Glucksmann, Romain Goupil, and Bernard Kouchner, Bruckner affirmed, as the title of the piece stated, that "Saddam must go, either way" [Saddam doit partir, de gré ou de force]. Moreover, in subsequent interviews in *Le Figaro, L'express*, and elsewhere, he condemned his fellow Europeans and Europe's leaders (especially in the wake of the Madrid train bombings) for their failure to understand or to deal appropriately with Islamic terrorism. More recently, Bruckner's close association with Olivier Rubinstein's new review, *Le meilleur des mondes*, one of whose issues has already been attacked in *Le monde* of 22 November 2007 as supporting the United States and especially American neo-conservatism, is further circumstantial evidence of his supposedly rightist sympathies, of his French brand of pro-American "neo-conservatism." Finally, his occasional sympathy for and even support of Nicholas Sarkozy, himself considered pro-American at least up to the economic "crash" in the fall of 2008, is considered very telling.

For those who wish to characterize Bruckner as being a pro-American reactionary in essence, it does not matter that, in 2005, he had already changed his views about the U.S. intervention in Iraq: he condemned the war as unjustified and denounced the horrors of Abu Graib and Guantánamo, both of which he attributed to the "democratic Messianism and stainless-steel consciences" of the Bush administration. Nor does it matter that, decades earlier, he had been involved in denouncing American support of the Pol Pot regime in Cambodia as well as the brutal excesses of war in Vietnam.[7]

7. For Bruckner's criticism of the US in Vietnam, see *Tears of the White Man: Passion as Contempt*, translated with an Introduction by William Beer (New York: The Free Press, 1986), 15–17. All future references to *Le sanglot de l'homme blanc* are taken from this translation.

But even though it is possible to draw up a laundry list of Bruckner's *engagements* "on the Right," his strongest political pronouncements and *partis pris* generally emerge in relation to broader concerns and perspectives that are themselves those of the *moraliste* more than they are those of the narrowly partisan *intellectuel engagé.* Moreover, in giving voice to specific political positions within the larger frame of a dissection of the ills besetting Western modernity, Bruckner also articulates these positions in such a way that the motivations and sympathies behind these engagements appear to be those of someone with essentially *leftist* rather than rightist sensibilities. This may well be a good example of his strategy of circulating right-wing ideas in left-wing circles. But, more importantly, the approach itself is characteristic of his most powerful and polemical essays. In order to test this claim and to assess more comprehensively his politics both in relation to his vision as *moraliste* and his perspective on French, European, and global realities, I should like to turn to a discussion of two of his most ambitious, provocative, and representative works: *Le sanglot de l'homme blanc* and its "sequel," *La tyrannie de la pénitence.*

That Bruckner's stinging critique of *tiermondisme* in *Le sanglot de l'homme blanc* appealed to right-wing, conservative, and certainly anti-communist sensibilities in Europe and outside is evident in the blurbs on the dust jacket of the American translation of the book published, not coincidentally, in the heyday of Reaganism in 1986 by the then right-wing Free Press. One blurb, by Jeanne Kirkpatrick, Reagan's Ambassador to the United Nations, praises it as "a powerful antidote to fashionable self-deceptions." The other, by Jean-François Revel, lauds Bruckner for having exposed "one of the greatest political and moral hoaxes of our century."

In the broadest terms, the "Third Worldism" denounced in *Le sanglot de l'homme blanc* grew out of the Bandung Conference held in Indonesia in 1955. According to William Beer, the conference, which brought together representatives from twenty-nine African and Asian countries, was strongly influenced from the outset by China, and was the "direct consequence of the Sino-Soviet split." The main purpose of Bandung was to consolidate opposition to colonialism. According to Beer, it was intended to create a "third power block" distinct from the two others: "the capitalist industrial world (the United States, Western Europe, Australia, New Zealand, and Japan) and the communist industrial world (the Soviet Union and its Eastern European allies)."[8] For many leftist intellectuals in the West, and especially those disillusioned with the excesses of Stalinism, support for this anti-colonialist "Third World" offered a new source of hope as well as revolutionary idealism and fervor.

There is also a specifically French and francophone target for Bruckner's acerbic critique of *tiermondisme*, embodied in Frantz Fanon's pronouncements in *Les damnés de la terre* and especially Jean-Paul Sartre's stunning and violent apology for Fanon and his ideas in his famous 1961 preface to Fanon's work. In a lengthy footnote in *Le sanglot*, Bruckner derides Sartre's hypocrisy in repeatedly pronouncing his outspoken support for Third Worldism, while in reality feeling nothing but "indifference" for the people of the Third World. Bruckner also dismisses Fanon's work as a "treasure-trove of theoretical nothingness, historical falsehood, and hateful demagoguery" (184–85). While the harshness of Bruckner's own rhetoric is evident in these lines, it is important to recall the violence of the writings of Fanon and Sartre to which he is reacting. For Sartre, *all* French and Europeans are complicit in, and guilty of, the crimes of colonialism, even if they are unaware of it or even denounce colonialism itself. It was these very same French and Europeans, after all, who sent the colonists off to colonize in the first place. And the violence directed by the colonized against the colonizers is really the latter's violence *turned back against them*, except that, as opposed to the colonizers' violence, the violence of the colonized is a purifying, liberating, profoundly justified, and even sacred violence that in its accomplishment attaches or roots the alienated colonized back to his own native, national soil:

> For, at the outset of the revolt, it is necessary to kill: to bring down a European is to kill two birds with one stone, it is to wipe out an oppressor and an oppressed in one fell swoop: what is left behind is a dead man and a free man. The free man, the survivor feels his *national* soil beneath him for the first time. In this moment the nation no longer moves away from him. It is there where he goes, there where he is: never far off, the nation merges with his freedom.[9]

Moreover, in attacking the European, in chasing him out by force of arms, the colonized rid themselves of what Sartre calls "the colonial neurosis" and, in the process, recover their "lost transparency."

8. See William Beer's Introduction, "Third Worldism in France and the United States," in *Tears of the White Man*, x.

9. Jean-Paul Sartre, "Les damnés de la terre," in *Situations, V, colonialisme et néocolonialisme* (Paris: Gallimard, 1964),183.

If the violence of the colonized purifies, liberates, ennobles them, and makes them whole, while rooting them in their national soil and making the once colonized nation come to life, the reverse occurs for the European colonizers. The latter's corruption revealed and exposed, their nation disintegrates as the new community and nation of the formerly colonized emerges. With regard to Algeria, Sartre writes: "The union of the Algerian people produces the disintegration of the French people." He continues: "The colonized recomposes himself, and we, the ultras and liberals, colonists and 'metropolitans,' we are in the process of decomposing" (190). In 1961, Sartre concludes, the word "France" itself, which now and in the past has signified a country, is in the near future in danger of signifying nothing more than a "neurosis" (192).

The extreme nature of Sartre's remarks and the attitudes they reveal conform to and justify Bruckner's critique of *tiermondisme*. But it is important not to lose sight of the essential positions of Fanon's work, which stakes out extreme positions and justifies violence in many instances. For example, in *The Morals of History*, Tzvetan Todorov notes that Fanon is given to disturbing characterizations of violence. In Fanon's view, for the colonized, violence "is a cleansing force" that "frees the native from his inferiority complex and from his despair" and makes him "fearless and restores his self-respect."[10] The enemy to be rejected and destroyed, moreover, is not just the *colon*, but Western culture itself. In this regard, Todorov quotes Fanon to the effect that: "When the native hears a speech about Western culture, he pulls out his knife—or at least makes sure it is within reach" (43). Todorov wonders what real difference there is between the colonizer's knife and Goebbels's famous pistol. Todorov concludes that in their own legitimate struggle against colonialism "nationalist anticolonialists" like Fanon essentially compromise their own cause *not* by completely rejecting European traditions and culture but by embracing the "dark side" of those traditions and that culture, the violence and intolerance of the likes of Sorel and Barrès. In this way, colonialism and its ideology are not defeated. Rather, according to Todorov, they win "a dark victory over their adversaries, since the latter have decided to worship the same demons as the former" (58–59).

While Todorov is concerned essentially with the destructive con-

---

10. Quoted in Tzvetan Todorov, *The Morals of History*, trans. Alyson Waters (Minneapolis: University of Minnesota Press, 1995), 57.

sequences of "nationalist anticolonialism" on the outlook and psychology of the colonized and formerly colonized, in *Le sanglot de l'homme blanc* Bruckner focuses on the destructive implications of *tiermondisme* for the *European* outlook and psyche. Not only does *tiermondisme* encourage a false sense of history and distort the realities of the present, it encourages, at least in its most overt and superficial manifestations, a Manichaean vision of humanity according to which Third World peoples are pure and unsullied—modern embodiments of Rousseau's noble savage—and Europeans are corrupt and evil. Yet his analysis of *tiermondisme* probes more deeply and exposes the more nefarious motivations, sentiments, and subterfuges at its core. In the first place, to idealize—to idolize, in some instances—the peoples of the Third World, to make them the embodiment of what is best and purest in man, while at first glance a laudable and charitable impulse, is for Bruckner the expression of much less admirable attitudes and motivations. Idealizing "others" turns them into abstractions: it dehumanizes them and is, ironically, an expression of one's indifference to them as fellow human beings: in their fundamental indifference and ignorance of the colonized, Europeans "cannot recognize that the 'other' [the colonized] is really another person"; they idealize him, "just as their predecessors devalued him" (*Sanglot*, 128). Either way, the result is the same: "Third World worship" has been, and will always be, about the "militant ignorance" of and indifference to others (121).

If *tiermondisme* reveals itself to be indifference and arrogance parading as charity and admiration, it exposes the hypocrisy of the European in other ways as well. For those who embrace *tiermondisme* through the imitation of the colonized and formerly colonized peoples they profess to admire—for Bruckner, this imitation of the Other is one privileged mode of expressing one's *tiermondisme*—, there is the vicarious pleasure of sharing in the latter's triumphs and accomplishments: "If I pretend to be the other, his victories become my victories"(27). More nefarious and disturbing than falsely claiming the success of others, however, is the *tiermondiste*'s tendency implicitly to reject his own culture by justifying and even defending the right of Third World peoples to ignore and even destroy precisely those principles and practices that are most admirable in the European and Western traditions. For example, *tiermondistes* "glorify the same behavior in the Third World peoples that they always criticize in themselves and their fellow Europeans: excessive xenophobia, cultural narcissism, and relentless ethnocentrism"

(109). At the same time, for the *tiermondiste,* because the virtues and advantages of Western cultures and societies—"intellectual rigor, logic, and education"—are considered the "exclusive property of wealthy countries," their imposition on Third World countries is dismissed as a "diabolical imperialist ploy" (22).

If *tiermondisme* appears to generate and to countenance a cultural self-loathing on the part of the European, it is also responsible for a kind of perverse and self-serving arrogance that not only allows its proponents to feel a secret disdain for Third World peoples but to treat them and their cultures as disposable—and misunderstood—commodities. Adopting a kind of Dostoyevskian psychology, Bruckner argues that Europeans' commiseration with—and self-avowed sense of guilt over—the sufferings of Third World peoples (another privileged mode of expressing *tiermondiste* sympathies) does not in fact bring the former closer to the latter. Rather, it creates a disdainful distance between the two: the "overblown conscience" of the *tiermondiste* that commiserates with all the sufferings of the downtrodden peoples of Africa, Asia, and Latin America is ultimately an "empty conscience" (69). Moreover, the sense of guilt of the commiserating European constitutes not a commitment to better the lot of Third World peoples but rather a disavowal of responsibility. Finally, concern for and lamentations over the sufferings of all the untold millions of downtrodden and suffering in Asia, Africa, and Latin America maintains them in the status of unfortunate masses, while, in contrast, the commiserating Europeans are real individuals. Once again, the basic humanity—the individual existence and reality—of Third World peoples is stripped from them. Along these lines, Bruckner notes caustically that the lives of starving children in Africa and Asia are "sacred" to the *tiermondiste,* not because they are children and fellow human beings, but because they are starving. Otherwise, they would not exist for him.

Bruckner's indictment of the *tiermondiste* and of Europeans as well would appear to be ubiquitous in *Le sanglot de l'homme blanc.* Insofar as the European is concerned, his language slides deliberately from a distancing third person to the use of first-person plural that underscores "our" complicity: "we"—Europeans (and other Westerners)—are guilty of indifference, disdain, and a destructive self-loathing that serves no one. When Bruckner affirms in *Le sanglot* that, by turning toward the Third World, Westerners are not looking for a different, "real" world but are in fact only seeking "the negation of their own [world]," he would appear to bear out Berman's claim that the central theme of the book, along with many recent essays, is European and Western self-hatred.

As subsequent works make clear, Bruckner's real objective is as much a probing of the spiritual and psychological malaise and destructive self-disdain of the modern European as it is a debunking of the dubious ideology of *tiermondisme*, which, for him, is but one symptom or manifestation of this more deep-seated and chronic malaise. As he argues in *La tyrannie de la pénitence*, contemporary Europe's morbid, ongoing obsession with the dark, criminal moments of its recent past—the *devoir de mémoire*—is also part of the same self-hatred, and is its most recent avatar. Like *tiermondisme* before it, the "duty to memory" allows for the same perverse combination of arrogance coupled with a fundamental indifference to others. In becoming in recent years what Bruckner derisively refers to as "athlètes de la pénitence," Europeans ignore the obligation to act in the present, for they seem to focus exclusively on the past. Culpability, after all, is easier than responsibility: the former is "a lighter burden to bear, and one gets along well with one's own conscience."[11]

The "duty to memory" also encourages a kind of cultural narcissism or solipsism that leads not to an openness toward others but rather to a narrow, selfish focus on oneself. One's guilt, moreover, also becomes the sign of one's "election." Europeans take a perverse and secret pride in the fact that they are the sole proprietors of the most unspeakable crimes in history, against which all other crimes are measured. As Bruckner writes, to be "the king of infamy" is to "remain at the crest of history" (*Tyrannie*, 50). Like their crimes, moreover, Europeans are "exceptional," and their experience of horror allows them to give lessons to the world, without being willing to intervene to prevent comparable crimes from happening.

Finally, the "duty to memory" has allowed for and even encouraged a dubious and often dangerous rewriting of history. For Bruckner, "memory" in this context is the polar opposite of history, and he asserts that the opposite of "memory" is not forgetfulness (*l'oubli*), as is commonly assumed, but in fact history itself (*Tyrannie*, 183). Whereas history requires an honest and objective accounting of, and responsibility toward, the past, memory distorts and even perverts the past in the name of the political and ideological purposes of the present. For

11. Pascal Bruckner, *La tyrannie de la pénitence* (Paris: Grasset, 2006), 118. All further references are to this edition.

example, he argues that the accurate, historical understanding of the crimes of Nazism has been seriously and dangerously distorted through the equation of these crimes with those of other "European" crimes, and the crimes associated with colonialism in particular. The misguided aim, of course, is to underscore the horror of the latter, but the result is that the former, along with Nazism itself, loses its historical and moral specificity and significance. According to this perspective, "Nazism began on the day when the white man—Portuguese, Spanish, Dutch—set foot on the shores of Africa or America and began sowing death, chaos, and destruction around him" (147). Along similar lines, the (deliberate) misunderstanding and distortion of Nazism allows for the criminalization of its victims and their legacy in the form of denunciations of Israel and the Israeli people, and thus, for some apologists, according to Bruckner, "when the [Israeli] Jew oppresses or colonizes, he transforms himself immediately into a Nazi —there is no middle ground" (85). Or when Gilles Deleuze wishes to denounce Zionist "genocide," he compares it to the massacre of Oradour (86).

In France, the list of crimes to whose victims a "duty to memory" is owed includes Vichy and the Holocaust, along with the Algerian war: *la guerre sans nom.* But more recently the list has lengthened to include the horrors of trench warfare during World War I and even the brutalities of the Napoleonic era. In effect, both history and memory or, more accurately, history *as memory,* have become grist for the mill of French self-hatred and guilt, and the unrelenting focus on the darker moments of the past only prolongs and perpetuates the malaise. The choice of epigraph for *La tyrannie de la pénitence,* taken from Camus's *Actuelles* of 1948, starkly sums up this state of mind and the impasse in which the French find themselves: "We are living in a time when men . . . have become accustomed to being ashamed of everything. Ashamed of themselves, ashamed of being happy, of loving, of creating. . . . It is therefore necessary to feel guilty. So we are now dragged before the secular confessional, the worst of all."

In political terms, what are the implications of Bruckner's dissection and condemnation of *tiermondisme* and of his denunciation of Europe's morbid obsession with its past, viewed as a kind of "Jurassic Park" of horrors, to invoke Jacques Julliard's colorful phrase?[12] In the earlier book, there can be no doubt that the author's principal target is

12. Jacques Julliard, *L'année des fantômes* (Paris: Grasset, 1998), 341.

"bien pensant" leftists for whom Third Worldism offered a new way and inspiration in the face of a decline of faith in Marxism. As he writes, "Anticolonialism serves as a substitute Marxism for an entire Left with no means of understanding the world" (*Tears of the White Man*, 152). In the later volume, his political targets are somewhat more scattershot, but they certainly include a pro-Palestinian and anti-Israel French Left that, through condemnations of Israel, wishes to lump Jews together with their erstwhile persecutors. They also include fervent *anti-américains* like Jean Baudrillard, who, in Bruckner's eyes, displayed a "pornographic jubilation" in his description of the collapse of the World Trade Center. For Bruckner, Baudrillard's applause for the hijackers was less an expression of true sympathy for the global victims of U.S. policies than it was a manifestation of one of the darkest features of *tiermondisme*, that is, the tendency to dehumanize others through a condescending display of solidarity. In the end, Bruckner notes, even the hijackers were dehumanized in being lauded as no more than "simple human projectiles" (95). Most centrally, Bruckner's political targets would include all those who would distort the past not only for their own political demands of the moment but also so as to ceaselessly denigrate Europe and France itself in such a way as to maintain both in a state of paralysis and helplessness in the face of the dangers of the present. A very recent example of this tendency, which occurred after the writing of *La tyrannie de la pénitence*, would be Alain Badiou's denunciation of contemporary France as a rebirth of Vichy in *De quoi Sarkozy est-il le nom?*, after the election of Nicolas Sarkozy as president in the spring of 2006.[13]

Given the objects of Bruckner's criticisms as well as the vehemence of his rhetoric in both volumes, it is possible to situate Bruckner on the political Right as it is currently construed. But here again, this would be, first, to ignore one of the more striking features of *La tyrannie de la pénitence:* the book's thoroughgoing condemnation of Bush's policies and contemporary U.S. democracy. More significantly, it would be to ignore both the fundamental—and global—lessons the author draws from his analyses of *tiermondisme* in *Le sanglot de l'homme blanc*, the *devoir de mémoire* in *La tyrannie de la pénitence*, and his recent effort to sum up the lessons of both books in a lecture given in 2008 at Texas A&M University and the Univer-

---

13. Alain Badiou, *De quoi Sarkozy est-il le nom?* (*Circonstances, 4*) (Paris: Lignes, 2007).

sity of North Carolina-Chapel Hill entitled "The Provincialization of the West."

For those comfortable in linking Bruckner with *anti-anti-américanisme* and thus with a largely uncritical adulation of American dynamism and hegemony, passages dealing with the America of the Iraq war and George W. Bush in *La tyrannie de la pénitence* must have come as a surprise, to say the least. In a section entitled "The Blustering Colossus," Bruckner chastises the United States as a country obsessed with its sense of "election" and its own superiority. It is this sense of superiority, moreover, that allows many Americans to believe that they can "remove themselves from the duties that fall on the shoulders of all humanity." (234). They can—and often do—ignore what he describes as *les lois communes* (shared laws) that would compel everyone (in the sense of the categorical imperative) to work in concert and in good faith with the United Nations and the International Court of Justice in the Hague, for example. In docilely going along with the Bush administration by tacitly accepting and thus condoning the horrors of Abu Ghraib and Guantánamo, as well as accepting the continued use of torture by the American military and intelligence, many Americans, for Bruckner, allow the very principles on which American democracy was built to be undermined. Moreover, the same is true when they allow themselves to be spied on by their own government. And if this were not enough, the same people cheered on the Bush administration's "crazy dream, in the second Gulf War, of remodeling . . . the entire face of the Middle East" (235). In so doing, these supporters accepted on faith the dangerous "wisdom" of Bush's neo-conservatives, whom Bruckner characterizes as "Bolsheviks who have moved to the Right and who have borrowed from the Trotskyists, their former brothers, a Promethetian voluntarism and willingness to casually ignore the facts" (235). The lead-up to Iraq and the success of the neo-conservatives was the first time in modern U.S. history that the elite of Washington truly put themselves under the sway of Ideology, which he labels a "European illness" (235).

Bruckner's comprehensive critique not only of the Bush administration but of the profound arrogance and irresponsibility of U.S. people today in *La tyrannie de la pénitence* tends to challenge the claim, perhaps definitively, that he is on the Right primarily because of a pro-U.S. bias. At the same time—and coupled with his critique of European self-hatred in both volumes—it raises a more troubling and broader series of questions that bear not only on the present but also on the future, and the possibility of constructive action in both. First, if both the U.S. and Europe are seriously and egregiously compromised by their own blindness and arrogance, what does this say about the future of democracy and its Western champions? What role, if any, should the latter play on the global stage when faced with new dangers and fanaticism? Finally, can Europe and the United States help each other overcome their respective shortcomings for the betterment of both and in the name of cooperation and even solidarity?

Already, in *Le sanglot de l'homme blanc*, Bruckner envisages a first step, albeit a "philosophical" and not a political one, that moves beyond Western blindness and solipsism and prepares the ground for positive and guardedly optimistic answers to the questions just raised. He argues that a first step toward "curing" the disease of *tiermondisme*, to escape the trap of European self-hatred is, as he puts it, truly "to accept the outlandish fact of 'otherness'—and to set it on a new course that is no longer based on deprecation or idealization" (153). In a section entitled "In Defense of Eurocentrism," he also asserts that Europeans need to recognize and acknowledge their "attraction" to their own "native land"—their need for a "home." If one can successfully accomplish these two goals, one can move beyond the pitfalls of *tiermondisme* and aspire to becoming truly "cosmopolitan," a worthy ideal in Bruckner's view. However, if one fails in one's quest to achieve an authentic cultural openness, one is doomed, at best, to remain a "Don Juan" of other cultures, who picks them up and discards them just as quickly without truly understanding them. Conversely, without a profound attachment to one's native soil, one risks losing, among other things, the ability to truly appreciate cultural contrasts: "having only one national culture is deadening, but not having a national culture is, too" (155). In the end, in *Le sanglot de l'homme blanc*, the author seems to advocate a kind of psychological and cultural *juste milieu* in which the extremes of the false idealization of other cultures and the excessive deprecation of one's own are eliminated in the name of a new receptivity and tolerance of one's own culture as well as the cultures of others. This call to understand and respect the dignity of others as well as oneself, and in essence to treat both equally, does not jive with a left-wing *tiermondisme*, especially at its most militant and doctrinaire. But it can hardly be considered right-wing or reactionary. If the first step toward coming to terms with the ills besetting Western democracies involves embracing on an individual level a true "cosmopolitanism" of cultural openness and self-acceptance, a second step involves true reconciliation between Europe and the United States and the creation of a new trans-Atlantic pact whose aim is to temper the failings and excesses of both parties and to foster the growth of democracy globally. How is this to be accomplished? As he explains at the end of *La tyrannie de la pénitence* and in his recent lecture on "The Provincialization of the West," Europe and the United States must learn from each other. In many ways, the two are polar, but also complementary, opposites, and this latter fact facilitates the task. While Europe embodies one conception of the Enlightenment based on a profound "skepticism and art of living," America embodies another one, based on "optimism and religiosity" (*Tyrannie,* 216). Where Europe rejects History in the name of the horrors of its own recent past, the United States embraces it in its headlong rush to change and reshape the world. Where Europe is consumed by self-hatred, the U.S. indulges in excessive, and often self-blinding, pride, patriotism, and even jingoism. Finally, and paradoxically, where Europe's extraordinary intellectual and cultural accomplishments have led to "mass graves, gas chambers, and the Gulag," the militant "defense" and promulgation of "democracy" by the United States have resulted in the destruction of democracy and democratic principles at home and abroad.

What can the two learn from each other? According to Bruckner, the United States, in its zealousness and overconfidence, which have lately resulted in reckless and tragic adventurism abroad, can learn modesty and caution from a Europe chastened by the excesses and horrors of its own recent past. Europe can benefit from U.S. optimism and its "can-do" spirit in order to overcome a paralyzing obsession with the traumas of memory. Together, both can forward the aims of democracy worldwide by benefiting from the respective wisdom of each. For a belligerent and recently bellicose United States, Europe's preference for understanding and negotiating with one's enemies would be salutary, whereas for Europe—overly docile and passive in Bruckner's view—the U.S. recognition of the need for military preparedness is a lesson that must be learned.

For Bruckner, this happy trans-Atlantic reconciliation is not simply a dream, it is a necessity. In a world increasingly threatened by extremism and fanaticism—and Islamic extremism in particular—the seeds of democracy must be planted and nurtured by the United States and Europe working together. But both must accept the (old) lessons of the new millennium: democracy cannot be exported at gun point, nor can it spring full-blown out of despotism. As he notes in his lecture, "The Provincialization of the West," democracy is "a historical journey that calls for a slow process of maturation," something that Europe and the United States often forget at their peril.

Pascal Bruckner's championing of a new "cosmopolitanism" and trans-Atlantic reconciliation to forward the aims of democracy continues to put him occasionally at odds with newer (as well as traditionally) leftist principles and ideals in Europe and the United States. His insistence, for example, on true cultural openness in the conclusion of works like *Le sanglot de l'homme blanc* underscores his disagreement with "identity politics" on both continents, expressed in the form of *communautarisme* in France and "multiculturalism" in the United States. With characteristically provocative flair, Bruckner characterizes the latter as "at heart . . . a legal apartheid" (*Tyrannie*, 175).

Bruckner's championing of democracy, and especially of a trans-Atlantic alliance to spread it worldwide, also runs afoul of many on the Left who view attempts at global democratization, especially by the United States, simply as disguised efforts to create an American Empire. In France, not long after the events of September 11, 2001 and during the initial stages of the Iraq war, numerous books and articles denouncing U.S. imperial ambitions were published by well-known *gauchistes* including Jean Baudrillard, Ignazio Ramonet, Étienne Balibar, and Emmanuel Todd, among others. (This occurred, of course, in the United States as well, with works by Chomsky among many others). And even if the rhetoric has cooled somewhat, very recent works such as Amy Chua's *Day of Empire* warn that America "would be far truer to its own history and principles in striving to be an exemplar to the world—a 'city on the hill'—rather than arrogating to itself the Sisyphean task of remaking societies around the world in its own image."[14] Of course, the fact that Bruckner is advocating a collaborative effort by the United States and Europe, and a kind of reasoned and reasonable "velvet revolution" of global democratization, gets lost in the face of the harsh political realities and deep divisions left by the "war on terror" in its global manifestations.

Finally, a residual and deep distrust by many on the Left of any form of nationalism, especially in Europe, would make them suspicious of Bruckner's call for an acceptance of cultural "rootedness." They would also likely take offense at his call to acknowledge and

14. Amy Chua, *Day of Empire: How Hyperpowers Rise to Global Dominance—and Why They Fall* (New York: Doubleday, 2007), 336.

commemorate the finer moments of the nation's past rather than its crimes. On the latter score, his call to "oppose a duty to remember our past glories" (*Tyrannie*, 248) to the duty to remember Europe's crimes might strike some as deliberately provocative, and even dangerous. Be that as it may, the debate over the uses and abuses of the nation's past in France is a long-term and highly vexing issue. It can and does blur facile distinctions between Right and Left.

In the final analysis, Bruckner would, in all likelihood, argue that any accusation of right-wing or reactionary sympathies on his part is ultimately inconsequential and unimportant for several reasons. First, as he has written recently, in France, at least, "it has become very difficult to distinguish Right from Left, given how much they resemble each other and overlap." Moreover, most individuals are given to politically contradictory impulses. One can be "at the same time a socialist, a conservative, and a liberal," and one can also at the same time "believe in free enterprise, desire to reign in inequalities, and respect traditions."[15] Finally, even "hot button" issues like *anti-américanisme* and the hatred of Israel are not the exclusive domain of the Right or the Left. They are in fact shared most visibly by the extreme Left and the extreme Right in France today.

More importantly, given a global perspective, focusing intensely on these traditional divisions within Western democracies can serve, in Bruckner's view, as a distraction from the larger matter at hand: the necessity and duty of Europe and America to join together to spread democracy, with all its imperfections, peacefully and carefully to a troubled world. Given these imperatives, he has spoken favorably of and voted for political figures who recognize the need of cooperation between Europe and the United States and the necessity for Western democracies to recognize their shortcomings and to change for the better, one would hope. For these reasons, Bruckner acknowledges having voted for Nicholas Sarkozy in the second round of the 2006 French presidential election and, before the 2008 presidential elections in the United States, he voiced his support for Barack Obama in the United States.

Ultimately, these brief remarks on Bruckner's political outlook today bring us full circle, and more specifically back to his ideas on engagement in general and his role as *moraliste* in particular. In effect, his engagements are not born out a specific ideology but arise from

15. Letter to the author, 9 October 2008.

his dissection and analyses of the ills besetting contemporary Western democracies as well as global crises. These analyses expose problems, contradictions, and paradoxes that for him defy simplistic—and ideologically driven—solutions and explanations. This is essentially a pragmatic position, of which Bruckner is thoroughly aware. If this is the case, then this explains why he is reluctant to align himself comfortably or completely on the Left or Right. Hence his "allegiance" to a "decaffeinated Left" or his predilection for circulating "right-wing ideas" in "left-wing circles." But these witty expressions of apparent political ambivalence should not hide his very real commitment to a form of "realism" that acknowledges simultaneously both the limitations of the past and the present and the need for, and possibility of, positive change in the future. In this commitment, Pascal Bruckner reveals himself to be not an *homme de droite* or a reactionary, but a "realist" in the positive sense of the term, and perhaps a *progressiste* in spite of himself.

III. The Political Self

NACIRA GUÉNIF-SOUILAMAS

The Inflated Ego and New Games of Belonging

"I would prefer not to."
—Herman Melville, "Bartleby the Scrivener"

The late modern era has erected a singular landmark that can be defined as the invention of the "inflated ego," which, in order to be molded, requires from any human being willing to get on board for this journey to the core of oneself an ability to develop various skills. One of them is a strong will to comply to the autonomous human norm shaped and conceptualized since the eighteenth century by German *Bildung* literature and philosophy and the French Enlightenment, both of which designed a particular kind of behavior that today translates into the obligation to be free from any belongings and bonds considered detrimental to one's own fulfillment. Since that time, self-fulfillment has become such a strong beacon that it should not (in the Kantian sense) be limited by any concerns, and certainly not by mutual consideration. In order to secure such goals, the ego, once strongly tied to structures of kinship, has to morph into a self-sustainable individual by reducing and, ideally, erasing dependence and altruistic considerations. The self-sufficient individual thus obtained undergoes a strange process of inflation, both metaphorically and intellectually, that leaves him or her with the strong belief that not only does the individual own himself or herself, but also that many things, along with other humans, are submitted to his or her will and must serve the specific goals attached thereto. All ties cut, such humans may become convinced of their own importance, which is displayed in arrogant behaviors that, viewed from below or at a distance, quickly become humorous if not grotesque.

In this article, I sketch out patterns of such "inflated egos" and give them flesh and speech in order to locate them and their influence on the contemporary postcolonial French stage. The centerpiece of

YFS 116/117, *Turns to the Right?* ed. Johnson and Schehr, © 2009 by Yale University.

113

this narrative will be the current French president, Nicolas Sarkozy, as I examine how he highlights and embodies this phenomenon to such an extreme that it results almost in caricature. Not only does he ex-emplify the "egotization" process but, in so doing, he recalls and re-news the status of "strange bedfellows" he shares with the most stig-matized figures of the French public scene in the four past decades: the black and Arab youngsters from segregated underclass neighbor-hoods. Hence, as they proliferate at all levels and in various locations of French society, inflated egos appear to be the gatekeepers of the au-thenticity of a nation-state deeply changed by its newcomers and the "new" French: many come from corners of the former empire, and yet some "old" French seem reluctant to acknowledge the tremendous contributions the newcomers are making. To understand the rules of the game one needs to have in mind its central character as well as its necessary reverse figure: the failed ego.

PRIVATE MEMORIES OF
INFLATED EGO ENCOUNTERS

Each of us has personal and social experiences that relate to the concept of an inflated ego. Some of them transcend the everyday social world from which they have emerged and unabashedly underline their own unusual status. A tall, white man is talking to his friend above your head and, despite, or because of, your short, insignificant presence, he makes you wonder if you really exist. A sophisticated woman stands in front of a door and she does not realize that she prevents someone else from going through, as if her body image exceeded her physical imprint and required a much larger space than the one she fills. You find a col-league's scrawlings on the blackboard when entering the room for your next class, and they make you wonder whether he/she rushed out and forgot to wipe them off or if he/she meant to share powerful insights with you and your students. Or consider people who leave the scraps of a meal on the table at which you subsequently sit down or drivers who do not stop at a crosswalk as they forget all too easily their erst-while pedestrian status. There are arrogant minds that say what they believe their interlocutor will say, because "they" know better, or in-versely, the same brilliant minds urge you to end your sentence, as you have already used up your time, and you are just filling it with empty, useless statements. Or consider journalists (usually men dressed in black) who take on inquisitorial tones that allow them to try to condemn the disgraceful stepmother, culprit of the day, the veiled French student, culprit of the month, or the violent Arab youngster, culprit of the year, who slings hate speech at the police.

And we should mention the philosopher's podium, from which "he" reigns, speaks for others, and brings to our attention others' numerous, considerable, and insightful statements we could not otherwise understand, and, in so doing, reconfirms the eternal knowledge of the Western, heterosexual, white man. However, ironically, he forgets that one thing puts the hypnotized audience on the track of his blatant truth; quietly attending all the meetings he holds, his hat seems to be silently whispering to them: "you should know better." One should add the philosopher's alter ego, the female thinker of the twentieth century who has recently disenfranchised herself from patriarchal power, and yet, while entering the next century, inadvertently reinstates it when imposing a local feminist blend on subaltern women, one that fits the hegemonic, republican, universalist regime with its compulsory ways of behaving and speaking. These are the same domesticated women who wind up having to give vibrant and dramatic testimony of oppression against their male kin in the trial over "civilization." Last but not least, there is the *immortel* of the *Académie Française* who has raised himself to the status of a "*lieu de mémoire,*" which, in its plural form, he contributed to instate as the locus of national identity production and reproduction, as the vital geography of a civil religion molded in the same old sacred rituals of preservation and regeneration once built for autochthonous purposes.

Such endless lists bring many other memories to each individual's mind and stress the unavoidability of the inflated ego as a potential side-effect of individualization itself. The dilation observed in mundane, as well as formal, occasions subsumes all versions of the common dynamic and thus underlines the notion that the progressist figure of the individualized citizen of modern times ended up ruining them. Thus, the mystery of this enduring and expanding persona is to be traced back to ways of becoming a "self" as the main prescription of the Western civilizing process with which we must engage. However, such an ego-compatible prescription comes with its political, cultural, racial, and gender preconditions, restrictions, and retentions, so it needs to be contextualized in order to develop both its nuances and its failures.

A BLINDING ENLIGHTENMENT STILL ON TRACK

Since the Enlightenment, modernity in France has been marked by the question of how to become an autonomous human being, namely an individual locally embodied by the citizen as political being. More than in other European countries or in the USA, citizenship in France has always been the ultimate standard for measuring the achievement of a modern Frenchman. Thus, not being a citizen meant that the human being was incomplete and hardly a human according to an enriched ancient Greek definition: children, women, slaves, people without property, Jews, and natives. Or it meant that he/she did not meet the requirements for becoming virtuous and consequently deserving to be a citizen. This latter case applies to all sorts of people who got their status without any of the pre-requisites defined by state law and the French cultural frame: foreigners, refugees, outcasts, the poor, strangers, defectors, or queers. These individuals are not acknowledged as such, since they have a hard time escaping their label and the "natural" category to which they are assigned by the dominant views of the majority. Hence, when finally succeeding in mimicking some standard, individualized traits, they are instantly failed by their judges who condemn them for dullness or lack of veracity. This first civilizing step of imitating an unprecedented model, scarcely explained to newcomers, and which, by itself, was an achievement, is still mandatory for becoming the site of invention of oneself as a subject. Hence, until recently, subjectivity remained a reserved feature that not all individuals could experience or claim. In order to become an ego able to express all kinds of feelings and invest in a large range of behaviors and belongings, one has to provide the proof of having undergone a subjectivation process, and this, in order to not be sent back to the indistinctive insignificance of unachieved essence. "Be anything but obvious" says an advertisement for an expensive watch. Such an invitation attracts and convinces consumers who want to become individuals through buying and displaying signs of exception that others do not have. Accessories are not the only items individuals must possess and display; manners and behaviors, names and titles, and material choices and opinions are part of the panoply put under the scrutiny of others. But some with certain complexions and genders are more entitled to embody the legitimate ego and to provide the measure of its accomplishment than others. Those who declare themselves to be the true offspring of the genuine French *gentilhomme* turned *honnête homme,* once invented by philosophers and vetted by their citizen-disciples now show signs of personality dilation. Henceforth, those who arose from this accumulative and intensive march toward the current individualized standard are likely to be inflated with notions of self-sufficiency, and are consequently incapable of responding to any criteria of open-mindedness or of curiosity. All other kinds of humans who claim to be the site of such curiosity must provide the proof of the metamorphosis they have undergone. Thus, the games of belonging that have become mandatory skills are to be played according to the rules of the majority. These games must adhere to the majority's main goal of preserving the French species in an era of a provincialized France that had been a central figure of civilization. If those who belong to the circle of equals, namely French citizens of French descent, must be the rule providers, they are experiencing an ever stronger challenge in defining how to belong to France and behave as French. Inflated egos precisely come into play when Frenchness is supposedly threatened by uncivilized new French individuals who must be denied such privilege. They intervene as a defense battalion scattered all over the scenes of contact between the real French and the others: the fake French, whose proliferation and contamination may lead to the exhaustion of French essence with the licensed copyright of abstract, universalist, and egalitarian republicanism. The legitimate upper class that once called itself the aristocracy and saw itself as the salt of the earth, if not necessarily its blood, has been replaced, by virtue of the Revolution, by the former commoners become the bourgeoisie. This configuration was sustained through the rhetoric of egalitarian fiction by eliding the enduring components of the aristocratic regime inherited by the bourgeoisie and the current middle class through a process of renaming or relabeling that did not quite succeed in exhausting its powerful influence and cutting its deep roots. The *beauf, bobo, bling-bling,* and other local types of modern individuals all belong to the multi-secular, autochthonous category of the commoner (*roturier*). The renamed protagonists of the autonomous/autochthonous individual's long-lasting drama act to protect the core of the precious entity and express its quintessence through body language and a cultivated version of the mother tongue that raises French, both as a language and a culture, and France, both as a nation and a notion, to the level of a luxury that is so hard to decipher that it is rarely shared. As usual, the core of the highly valuable entity is probably empty as is the treasure box and the throne of the king. Nevertheless, unlike a squad of bodyguards, meant to remain gathered in a visibly powerful formation, inflated egos act from where they stand, from their daily base and through a daily routine that keeps them unnoticed, yet fiercely effective when promoting the preservation of the French entity through its multiple figures, be they casual, popular, intellectual, or ritual. This diffuse and suave unknown repressive ideological paradigm activates the turn of the screw that morphed and moved far from its pre-68 configuration in an appeal to individualization and, simultaneously, in an attempt to record its deviant suspicious sites. Inflated egos stand as sentinels at the crossroads; they are not yet totally assimilated to the aristocratic, blue-blooded model, and thus still crave recognition; they are rooted in various *terroirs* that convey the flavor of fake treasures both past and present.

LE PRÉSIDENT DE LA RÉPUBLIQUE

Surprisingly or not, the mythic French figure of *l'honnête homme* as the defender of the essence of Frenchness, has recently morphed, and is currently embodied by personae like Nicolas Sarkozy, dressed in smart "bling-bling"street attire out of courtesy to the ideals of the Fifth Republic once accustomed to the military uniform of its founder, Général de Gaulle. When exercising the powers of his position, the President borrows attributes and accessories that do not easily circulate, such as the suit as a disguise for the military mindset deep in his mind, the Elysée palace that he has transformed into a Jacksonian kitchen cabinet for corporate and media strategies, the gorgeous first lady of highly educated, cosmopolitan, and bourgeois extraction, whom he marries after a second divorce. In so doing, he illustrates the anthropological version of the royal alliance as an arranged marriage, with his friends as matchmakers. One should also add his stature, elevated by all kinds of body techniques, hard jogging, face-mastering desperate attempts, rolled up sleeves to indicate "hard work" *à l'américaine,* all of which are intended to show how willing he is to embody contemporary received ideas about status —although not quite equipped in the first place—, the vision falsely genuine and authentic, the verb, picked from a drastically shrunk lexicon meant to strike his listeners' minds and leave them speechless. Not only does he act as an imposter, but he also intends to redefine the perimeter of power by confusing the profile of the *roturier*—subject of the king without rights, property, and/or legitimacy when making his way to a higher position—with that of the *honnête homme*—sovereign subject of Reason and citizen of the Republic. All these attributes are meant to give credentials to the changes over time he intends to embody; as

Lampedusa's Prince Don Fabrizio of Salina in *Il Gattopardo* soberly noted, all should change so that nothing would change. Hence, the position holder is replete with a large set of ideas and slogans systematically and meticulously stolen from leftist writers and thinkers and retooled to the post-68 criticizing rhetoric about too loose a society longing for the return of authority and straight behavior. Thus did the self-proclaimed hero declare without a blink during his campaign that he was "born heterosexual." Thus, for all French people, he falsely comes out with a virulent critique of the culture of May '68, while he simultaneously practices all its contradictions behind closed doors. The misleading analysis allows that he despises such culture and considers it harmful to French greatness. More likely than not, he uses it as a privilege, and, in order to maintain it as such, he distills various statements so as to divert ordinary French people from it, especially the new multicultural French. One of the most striking effects of his rhetorical and political stance is that, like the inflated ego, he abolishes the separation between public and private spheres, a cornerstone of republican rhetoric, and endlessly displays his life in ways that facilitate our assessment of his rhetorical double bind. He gives voyeuristic access to his way of life, as if he had invented the life of a docile tycoon in quest of recognition, and yet he pretends that it cannot be imitated by the common man. This kleptomaniacal and exhibitionistic tendency combined with a self-confident mindset finds neither limits nor opponents. Hence, it easily spreads and penetrates psyches ready to confess their freedom/sin. Noticeably striking is the psychologization and individualization of political issues, such as the abuse and concentration of power he enacts through the media and public commentary. Such intellectual surrender prevents a majority of political actors from addressing the threats he represents to democracy, freedom of speech, and his rare opponents. The President thus provides the nation, as well as the larger (inter)continental scene, with a parody not so much of the power he undoubtedly and excessively exercises, but of the legitimacy of its holder. He thus renews the gesture or imposture historically assigned to the *roturier* under absolute monarchy, from the parvenu in a bourgeois hierarchical society to, more recently, the new French who do not resemble a multisecular reinvented Frenchness.

THE NEW FRENCH ENMITY'S DOMESTIC SITES

The brand of power initiated by the President with particular skills and needs is highlighted in events such as the belated and already obsolete imitation of American neo-liberal stances bound to exhaust themselves soon, the dramatized unfolding of an alternately threatened and arrogant national identity fiction, the increasing rate of illegal immigrants' expulsions, the spectacularly entertaining six months of French European presidency, the criminalization of large categories of racialized French and non-French residents, and the nonchalant militarization of public spaces and of everyday life's physical and psychical territories. The citizenry and its tentative minorities owe it all to a president who took seriously and literally the question of restoring French prestige under a patched-up banner and who dedicated all his energy and his unsophisticated mind to raising it high against the new enemies of the Republic. One could object to such a critical stance by saying that, for many opponents of the *intégrisme républicain,* Sarkozy, as leader of the Right, and the country, as well as an individual, has been a blessing for his opponents. Indeed, he feeds the conversation to excess when he simultaneously endorses the defensive discourse of the French nation and values—for example by fighting in Afghanistan (to protect the values "over there" that may be endangered *hic et ubique*)—, but also by fighting and vilifying "dangerous" and "violent" heterosexuals such as Arab and African boys who supposedly frighten all the girls with whom they interact. And, without any transition, he disrupts the basis of a fictional Republicanism by expressing his religious beliefs in public, placing the priest higher in the hierarchical standards of moral education—Durkheim wake up!— than the teacher, and by displaying in an ambiguous manner his religious/ethnic background as the Catholic son of a mother with a Jewish father: once by outsourcing the comment to close friends and another time by putting the allusion in the mouth of his glamorous decoy, his wife. The games of belonging played by the President and his crew are predictable, as they blend superficiality and arrogance, mystification and awkwardness, and moral values and so-called offensive action. The show must go on, at the expense of the extras, compelled to endorse identities necessary to the plot, and of the political landscape behind them that offers proto-fascist soft discrimination and covert repression.

THE CLOSED GATES OF PROMISED FRENCHNESS

In such a light, the turn of the screw imposed on certain human beings, ranging from the children of the formerly colonized who do not comply with the new standard of Frenchness to potential immigrants still beyond the numerous boundaries raised against their vulnerable mobility, reeks of humiliation, destruction, and death. The number of real deaths of individuals trying to escape expulsion from society has risen in the past few years. Far from being merely performative, suicides and risky attempts to cross borders embody the very way in which playing the individualized game of existing has had high costs for those exposed to the imposition of arbitrary criteria, as they attempt to fulfill their dreams, often without success, or as they try, sometimes in vain, to avoid their worst nightmares. Such an extreme regime of individualization is noticeable in the way gendered performances are allowed or forbidden, when they are marked by race, ethnicity, or perceived sexual ambiguity. In such cases, they may be perceived, at least potentially, to have a risk of contamination. In a wide range of being, belonging, and behaving games, "gay" Arabs stand at the forefront of a plural scene where all signs and markers are not equal, and where they require adjustments in order to be tolerated, if not to say accepted. The very way they are labeled—*jeunes homosexuels des quartiers*—is supposed to mirror the condition of the other group pictured as always harassed in the multiethnic underclass suburbs: *les filles des quartiers*. Thus, both groups embody the ultimate pattern white French moral entrepreneurs have imagined, as the latter offer a pasteurized kind of fight for freedom for so-called gay and women's rights that ends up being a renewed version of the colonialist and Orientalist civilizing mission. These moral entrepreneurs champion statements confusing both sets of rights and take a stance against ethnic and racial minorities living in appalling housing projects in order to chastise them and hold them responsible for the failure of their essentialized culture that purportedly kept the younger generation from integration into mainstream France. But such stigmatization forgets to mention—or deliberately eludes—the social tensions and the dismissal encountered by three generations of immigrants' offspring and the gradual racialization of social-class relations. This scapegoating process makes it more difficult for any such individual to become a reflexive individual who would meet the requirements of the dominant, white, male, French standard that has assimilated republican values associated with equality between the sexes.

Under such a standard, there is no viable subjectivation process for those who try to avoid the dominant definition and its specific requirements about giving up family and group ties in favor of uncertain individualized and challenging allegiances. The imposed pattern of being, belonging, and becoming ends up weakening the agency of the new French—immigrants or the children of immigrants—and places them in the position of the suspect requested to justify proper behavior and opinions. The inflated egos described above play a key role in dismissing the applications of those who would aspire to the new blend of Frenchness. This is a substantive departure from the concept of Frenchness of imperial times, a notion that was meant to draw the line between French, republican, white citizens, and the colonized who were to remain beyond this "Mohamed" or "Mamadou" racial line. The current standard draws the line between those who comply with up-to-date, market-oriented ways of individualizing themselves and those who try to escape the web of compliance with a "Frenchness" that insists on rendering invisible inappropriate markers. The list of such inappropriate markers includes the mother tongue, if it belongs to the lower strata of the hierarchic linguistic cartography of the territories of the Empire, such as Arabic and African languages; the exotic pieces of clothing when they smack of the local, such as the Islamic headscarf or the veil, both very French ways to designate the hidjab and its variants labeled as submissive signs; and finally, the sexual behavior of visibly different men and women who show resistance to entering the local market of love and marriage. Speech, dress, and sex become three major beacons on the way to Frenchness and once "the happy few" arrive, these are the tokens of their successful admittance to the circle of equals. Yet, once this step is fulfilled, standards are erected as a totem, always noticeable wherever the permanent applicants stand and reminding them that they have invisibly to behave as French citizens, but with somewhat of an ethnic twist that has become so fashionable recently with the promotion, for example, of symbols of integration like the "women of the president." Gender is a powerful tool in domesticating the new French, as shown by the three women—two Arabs and one black—appointed in Sarkozy's government, people chosen not so much for their agency and political competence, as for their Westernized look, their deliberate choice of surrendering their beliefs in favor of communication skills, and for the obvious, consensual symbol of diversity they embody. Even the sign of unease or revolt they may show is part of the device put in place in order to argue that integration is not only possible but is also desirable, as sexy ways of being demonstrate. The latest episode of the French government soap opera does not have to be imagined by television writers; it has been displayed and widely commented on, when the Minister of Justice, Rachida Dati, of Algerian-Moroccan parents, became pregnant, and subsequently announced that she would not disclose the name of the father with whom she does not live. Hence, when, on 2 January 2009, the girl was born, Dati disclosed her name, Zohra, but remained silent on whether the child would be declared to have a father's name and/or be raised by her alone. Such a decision, which is wholly compatible with a republican deontology relative to one's personal life is in ironic contradiction to the unstated obligation that minorities are supposed to cut allegiances with some of their ties and traditions—but which ones specifically?—in order to be welcome in the brave new world of individualization.

CLANDESTINE SUBJECTIVATION

As noted above, the inflated ego requires a total lack of a sense of relativity, a high capacity to place oneself at the center of the world, and an equivalent penchant for ignoring external reality so as always to be able to focus on oneself. This ability to include the world—to the extent of being the world—itself requires skills in order to abolish the external reality worth noticing. It also means a constant focus on oneself and an inability to lose sight of oneself. Such mandatory skills have become widespread in the market of self-design; nevertheless, they are not accessible to all customers. Those who are tagged as unable to reach the requirements of self-building are usually kept outside of this common market where recipes and tricks are exchanged by hard-nosed self-designers.

The turn of the screw is noticeable in the suppression of freedom of speech, especially when it comes from/to the subaltern, new French trying to imagine ways to exist, speak, and write without the imprint of the dominant character: the reasonable white male, the *honnête homme.* To utter a word, make a statement, or raise an issue, and thus cross the line of silence that, since the return of the imperial color line —racial and ethnic—"made in France," has merged with the enduring class and gender line, the new French of immigrant and colonial descent have to convince themselves of some intrinsic value outside the everyday and the normative. The narrow path often trod by Arabs, Jews, and blacks, is one of humor, and they conveniently often play the roles of buffoons in the media and elsewhere, denizens of an underworld controlled by the powers that be. Although recently expanded, the place of humorous topics is fraught with danger, and those who do not understand the extent and limits of French humor can easily fall victim to those powers. And for some, in all camps, irony has become a strong antidote to internalized racism and unnoticed discrimination. Irony becomes both the incarnation of an ancient mode of healing and that of a contemporary way of becoming oneself.

More than ever, inventing oneself has become a national game and a democratized matter of conversation in France. This implies not only being skilled in—and acculturated to—the trends of Frenchness, but also having supposedly (and happily) escaped from primary belongings, in order to construct, between artificiality and authenticity, a sophisticated way of being free. This not only spreads the deceptive image of a possible world where imagination and subjectivation can be recognized; it also dooms all individuals, whatever position and capital they have, to keep up with the game, remain in it whatever the cost, and contribute to fuel its worst tendencies: elimination and erosion as side effects of inflation. Ultimately, such excesses of self should be considered cautiously, as they bring back to the forefront the symmetrical process of identity fragmentation versus identity reunification that has remained unnoticed in "mediatic" and political scenography: the establishment of a so-called "decent" society in times of renewed colonization.

BRUNO CHAOUAT

Moroseness in Post-Cold-War France

In 1813, Adelbert von Chamisso, a French aristocrat exiled in Prussia, published *Peter Schlemiel's Remarkable Story*, an intriguing parable in which the main character sells his shadow. Later refusing to redeem his shadow at the price of his soul, Schlemiel spends the rest of his life wandering. A geographer and botanist, he toils on a volume of natural history that will remain incomplete, adding his stone to the edifice of knowledge.[1] This novella, appearing at the twilight of the Napoleonic Empire and among the ruins of Europe, suggests that one cannot give up one's shadow with impunity in exchange for a material benefit. The reference to Jewish folklore notwithstanding,[2] it is a cautionary tale nurtured by Christian ethics, intimating that no material value can be placed on one's soul. If the devil (*diabolos*) carries within his name the act of separation (*diaballein*),[3] the tempter of Chamisso's fable separates the subject from his image, the self from his shadow. Without a shadow, human subjectivity collapses. For the shadow—the clothing of the self —is a metaphysical veil without which the pudenda would be displayed to everyone's eyes. Obscene and impudent is shadowless man, triggering reactions of fear and aversion. Having agreed to the devil's bargain, the wanderer deprived of his shadow carries and spreads his curse. The man without a shadow is a self without his other, a solipsistic subject. The *Remarkable Story of Peter Schlemiel*, a metaphysical and moral fable, hovers over the following reflections as an allegory of the intellectual history of the present sketched below.

1. Adelbert von Chamisso, *Peter Schlemiel, The Man Who Sold His Shadow*, trans. Peter Wortsman (New York: Fromm International, 1993).
2. On Yiddish literature and Chamisso's novella, see Ruth R. Wisse, *The Schlemiel as Modern Hero* (Chicago: University of Chicago Press, 1971).
3. Claude Reichler, *La diabolie* (Paris: Edition de Minuit, 1979).

YFS 116/117, *Turns to the Right?* ed. Johnson and Schehr, © 2009 by Yale University.

Although its literature and philosophy have long valued discontent and malaise, France now holds "the dubious distinction of being the world leader in the per capita consumption of psychotropic medications."[4] Assuming that an antidepressant such as Prozac is effective despite recent studies that seem to invalidate that claim,[5] the French may thus be happier; and if so—a non-verifiable assumption, even for social engineers and governance experts—, it would be to the extent that medical politics has launched a deadly assault against the death drive. Moroseness, negativity, and metaphysical affliction must be alleviated for a liberal democratic society to "function" and for France to be competitive in the new world order. And precisely because malaise is now depreciated and even deemed a disease, because melancholy has deserted the realm of normalcy, some grumpy French writers and essayists are reacting, irritated with what Pascal Bruckner recently called the "obligation to be happy."[6]

To suggest that France has a long tradition of valuing discontent and moroseness may seem counter-intuitive. Is not France the country of lightness, of belief in progress, and of frivolity? Consider Renaissance Epicureanism; Grand Siècle exuberance; the pagan "frivolity" of the sans-culottes,[7] as a paradigm for later spontaneous upheavals. Consider nineteenth-century utopianism, scientism, and positivism and their promises of knowledge and happiness. Consider Georges Bataille's exaltation of idleness and waste, the May '68 motto, "*jouir sans entraves*" ("Enjoy without restraint"—a "carpe diem" redesigned for revolutionary and anti-state purposes). Consider post-'68, neopagan French thought and its glorification of intensities and the unrestrained libido (Deleuze, Guattari, Lyotard).[8] Consider Jean Genet's celebration of anti-state terrorism as a festive if tragic endeavor.[9] Fi-

4. Jennifer Willging, "Another Prozac Nation: The Problem of Psychotropic Medication Consumption in Contemporary France," forthcoming in *Contemporary French Civilization* 33:1 (2009).

5. Sarah Boseley, "Prozac, Used by 40m People, Does Not Work, Say Scientists," *The Guardian*, February 26, 2008.

6. Pascal Bruckner, *L'Euphorie perpétuelle: Essai sur le devoir de Bonheur* (Paris: Grasset, 2000).

7. Jean-François Lyotard, "Frivolité en Révolution," in *Rudiments païens: Genre dissertatif* (Paris: Unions générale d'éditions, 1977).

8. See *Nietzsche aujourd'hui? 1. Intensités* (Paris: Unions générale d'éditions, 1973).

9. See my forthcoming essay, "Out of Palestine: Jean Genet's Shooting Stars," in *Israeli-Palestinian Conflict in the Francophone World*, ed. Nathalie Debrauwere-Miller (London: Routledge, 2009).

nally, consider sociologist Michel Maffesoli, enthralled by the giddy communities born of our postmodern world: his *Contemplation du monde* reads like a Nietzschean song of praise to the Dionysian principle written, not on the Zarathustrian heights of Engadin, but on the shores of what would soon become *"Paris-plage."*[10] And while these are very different kinds of "frivolities," all have their pagan, festive, hedonistic moment, even when they drift into the tragic, as is the case with Bataille and Genet. As Fragonard's pastoral swings, Rousseau's fusional fête, and Diderot's epicurean materialism demonstrate, France has enjoyed a long tradition of challenging the unbearable gravity of being.

Yet a powerful countercurrent has always accompanied those hedonistic forces. This shadow—metaphysical moroseness—may bear some relation to the spirit of the counter-revolution. More broadly, a culture of moroseness can be ascribed to a less easily dateable intellectual and literary phenomenon charted by Antoine Compagnon in *Les antimodernes.*[11] Although the authors Compagnon studies often come after the Revolution and react to its ideology of progress, the antimodern ethos precedes the buoyant beginnings of the Enlightenment and, a fortiori, the post-revolutionary hangover.

As Compagnon has shown, antimodern rhetoric finds a source of inspiration in Pascal, founder of existentialism and messenger of the tragic condition of dereliction.[12] Pascal's gloomy aphorism, "A king without diversion is a man full of misery,"[13] does not suggest that one is happy when entertained. Rather, entertainment—and, closer to us readers of the Frankfurt School and of Guy Debord, the culture and industry of entertainment—diverts even the most fortunate humans from their ontological wretchedness. Entertainment is, as the French would have it, a *cache-misère.*

Thus, from Pascal to the Schopenhauerian novelist Michel Houellebecq and other contemporary moralists whom I call, using Alain Fin-

10. See Michel Maffesoli, *La contemplation du monde: Figures du style communautaire* (Paris: Grasset, 1993). "Paris plage" is a summertime operation initiated by the mayor of Paris, Bertrand Delanoë, in 2002. Beaches are set up along the Seine river during that season.

11. Antoine Compagnon, *Les antimodernes: de Joseph de Maistre à Roland Barthes* (Paris: Gallimard, 2005).

12. Lucien Goldmann, *Le Dieu caché: Étude sur la vision tragique dans les* Pensées *de Pascal et dans le théâtre de Racine* (Paris: Gallimard, 1955).

13. Blaise Pascal, *Pensées* (Paris: Gallimard, Bibliothèque de la Pléiade, 1935), line 1144.

kielkaut's witticism, "*mécontemporains*,"[14] France has its share of morose literati. This moroseness is found in the counter-revolutionary *Stimmung* traversing the nineteenth century, and expressed in critiques of the plague of modernity and democratization by Joseph de Maistre, Baudelaire, Flaubert, the Goncourt Brothers, Charles Péguy, Georges Duhamel, Georges Bernanos, Céline, and even Roland Barthes. As Compagnon argues, the more antimodern they are, the more modern they reveal themselves to be: "Without the antimodern, the modern would soon be lost, since the antimoderns are the moderns' freedom, or moderns plus freedom" (*Les antimodernes*, 447).

If Nietzsche bred a current of neo-paganism and an odd, mystic atheism in France starting in the 1930s,[15] the gleeful messenger of the death of God also inspired more somber, Schopenhauerian and radically morose appropriations, such as those of E. M. Cioran, author of *Précis de décomposition*[16] or *De l'inconvénient d'être né*,[17] and Maurice Blanchot. In the 1920s and '30s, Heidegger radicalized the Nietzschean deconstruction of metaphysics. Gravity, according to the Christian ascetic ideal or to the atheistic sense of tragedy and dereliction, allegedly fosters an authentic relation to one's finitude. Heidegger's new *Cogito* goes—*I am unhappy, therefore I think,* or *I think, because I am unhappy.* Thought—or *Dasein*'s relation to itself (*Dasein* being the only being for which Being is a question)—is triggered by anxiety, which comes from the imagined experience of the withdrawal of all beings. Without malaise, man is reduced to a *res extensa*, matter without thought, body without soul, to retranslate Heidegger into metaphysical or theological categories to which he surely would have objected.

Heidegger's philosophy was tailored to fit three French political and intellectual expectations. First, progress. Seeing in Heidegger an opportunity to revive humanism, Sartre harnessed Heidegger to his own revolutionary purposes. In France, as Jacques Derrida showed, existential ontology became a humanistic doctrine.[18] Second, antihumanism. Where Nietzsche heralded the death of God, Heidegger an-

14. Alain Finkielkraut, *Le mécontemporain, Péguy lecteur du monde moderne* (Paris: Gallimard, 1991).

15. The *Collège de Sociologie,* especially the journal *Acéphale* (1936–1939), founded by Georges Bataille.

16. E. M. Cioran, *Précis de decomposition* (Paris: Gallimard, 1949).

17. Cioran, *De l'inconvénient d'être né* (Paris: Gallimard, 1973).

18. Jacques Derrida, "Les fins de l'homme," in *Marges de la philosophie* (Paris: Minuit, 1972).

nounced the end of anthropocentrism. Although goals and means differ, structuralism and post-structuralism—postmodernism—used Heidegger for a critique of humanism and human agency.[19] Third, Heidegger provided material that would nurture a French inclination toward the critique of technology and modernization, thereby promoting the reduction of liberal democracy and its beacon, America, to a form of survival in a concentration camp.[20] *Reductio ad Hitlerum*[21] became a French specialty. Heidegger (in)famously declared: "Agriculture is now a motorized food-industry—as to its essence, the same as the manufacturing of corpses in the gas chambers and the extermination camps, the same as the blockade and starvation of countries, the same as the production of the hydrogen bombs."[22] This provocative diagnosis, which likens the rationalization of society and nature to modern war, concentration camps, and even extermination camps, had enthusiastic followers—for example, Jean Baudrillard or Giorgio Agamben.[23] To the influence of Nietzsche and Heidegger on French thought, one should add that of the Frankfurt School, its critique of Enlightenment and of instrumental rationality.

Within the last ten years, another German critic of modernity and technology has enjoyed growing influence, especially as the heir to Guy Debord and the Situationist International. Günther Anders, who died in 1992, was a radical opponent of nuclear energy and nuclear weapons. In 1957 he published a voluminous work entitled *Die Antiquiertheit des Menschen* [The Obsolescence of the Human Being].[24]

19. See Vincent Descombes, *Le même et l'autre, quarante-cinq ans de philosophie française (1933–78)* (Paris: Éditions de Minuit, 1979).

20. On Heidegger and the critique of America, see Michael Ermarth, "Heidegger on Americanism: *Ruinanz* and the End of Modernity," in *Modernism/Modernity* 7/3 (2000), 379–400.

21. To borrow Leo Strauss's bon mot: "we must avoid the fallacy that in the last decades has frequently been used as a substitute for the *reductio ad absurdum:* the *reductio ad Hitlerum*. A view is not refuted by the fact that it happens to have been shared by Hitler." *Natural Right and History* (Chicago: University of Chicago Press, 1953).

22. Quoted in Victor Farias, *Heidegger and Nazism* (Philadelphia: Temple University Press, 1989), 287.

23. Giorgio Agamben, *Homo Sacer: Sovereign Power and Bare Life* (Stanford, CA: Stanford University Press, 1998), trans. Daniel Heller-Roazen. The concentration camp is described as the "nomos" of modernity. On the striking contamination of the critique of postmodern experience by the vocabulary of the Holocaust, see Jean Baudrillard, *Passwords* (London: Verso, 2003).

24. Günther Anders, *L'obsolescence de l'homme: sur l'âme à l'époque de la deuxième revolution industrielle*, trans. Christophe David (Paris: Edition de l'Encyclopédie des Nuisances, 2002). Original title: *Die Antiquiertheit des Menschen; über die Seele im Zeitalter der zweiten industriellen Revolution.*

Modern man traded his soul for technological advancement, and experience for expertise. Powerless and ontologically inferior to his machines, man pales in comparison to them. Robots are more efficient, do not make mistakes, and, should they break, are replaceable. The book was first translated into French in 2002, at the initiative of the *Éditions de l'Encyclopédie des Nuisances*, a marginal publisher who hosts post- and para-Situationists, Guy Debord's *enfants terribles.*

Not a cheerful philosopher, Anders, in the late fifties, using phenomenology and social critique mixed with allegories, poems, and the personal experience of a Central European Jew exiled in Hollywood, predicted the death of man, buried under his prostheses. While Heidegger lamented the mastery of man over Being,[25] Anders, contemptuous of Heideggerian jargon,[26] argued that man had become the slave of his instruments. In the name of anti-humanism, Heidegger launched his attack on technology, deemed anthropocentric. Conversely, in the name of a desperate humanism, Anders lamented the anthropological mutations birthed by the second industrial revolution.

It is difficult to decide whether the writers, texts, and ideas examined here belong to progressive, conservative, or reactionary thought. I have mentioned the influence of the Frankfurt School and of Günther Anders, but also of Nietzsche and Heidegger. Are we facing a "turn to the Right"? I would be hard-pressed to distinguish, in some of the texts under scrutiny, between the conservative or even reactionary yearning, and the opposition to the neoliberal, capitalistic status quo, an opposition endorsed by the new global Left. Yet we can establish an ideological and intellectual distinction between the French writers I am considering and the new "New Left," despite their similar diagnosis of and shared discontent regarding the global market and advanced liberal democracy. Some favor a return to order based on limits—sexual difference, borders, syntax, unity as opposed to democratic multiplicity and formlessness. Such a choice may be characterized as reactionary, a right-wing avatar of Nietzscheism, aristocratic, even antidemocratic—at least if one considers democracy in its most advanced, neoliberal phase.

25. On the concept of "Gestellen," or "En-framing," or "arraisonnement," see Martin Heidegger, *The Question Concerning Technology and Other Essays*, trans. William Lovitt (New York: Harper and Row, 1977).

26. Günther Anders, "On the Pseudo-Concreteness of Heidegger's Philosophy," in *Philosophy and Phenomenological Research* 8/3 (New York: University of Buffalo, 1948).

By contrast, the new "New Left" claims to use the potential of the neoliberal order—collapse of borders, virtual reality and cyberspace, deconstruction of sexual difference, blurring of class, racial, and ethnic differences, erosion of the patriarchal family—, harnessing these mutations to its revolutionary ends and to the promotion of direct or "absolute democracy."[27] This is the option of the "*altermondialistes*," the global anti-globalization movement or "movement of movements,"[28] represented by Toni Negri and Michael Hardt. In France, *Le monde diplomatique* has done much to popularize this tendency.

The writers discussed here share rhetorical and ethical features with those who were stigmatized in 2002 by intellectual historian Daniel Lindenberg as "new reactionaries," nostalgic for a heroic, even fascist order. It is my conviction, contrary to Lindenberg's normative pamphlet,[29] that these authors undermine the borders between reaction and progress. This collapse may be a symptom of our post-Cold War, post-ideological reality.

Indeed, the corpus surveyed here bears witness to disillusion. Hopes grounded in the vague remnants of communist ideology and revolutionary dreams collapsed alongside the Berlin Wall, generating disenchantment, "*misère de la philosophie*," to use the title of Lyotard's posthumous work.[30] I will chart this intellectual and ideological disillusionment through vignettes from different discourses and genres—literature, literary theory, philosophy, polemics, and psychoanalysis.

*   *   *   *   *

Richard Millet, novelist, essayist, and reader for Gallimard, has written on silence, music, and the decline of the French language as well as of European culture and literature in general. An outstanding stylist, he sometimes displays a precious classicism combined with the tradition of libertinage. His fictions are traversed by a rural, mythological, chthonic vein à la Giono, colored with Proust's and Claude Simon's predilection for verbal meanderings and interminable sentences. In *Désenchantement de la littérature*,[31] Millet attributes lit-

27. Phrase used by Toni Negri after Spinoza and Marx, in "Un mouvement social inédit: Refonder la gauche italienne," *Le monde diplomatique* (August 2002).

28. Expression found, for example, in Michael Hardt and Toni Negri, *Multitude, War and Democracy in the Age of Empire* (New York: Penguin Press, 2004).

29. Daniel Lindenberg, *Le rappel à l'ordre: Enquête sur les nouveaux réactionnaires* (Paris: Seuil, 2002).

30. Jean-François Lyotard, *Misère de la philosophie* (Paris: Galilée, 2000).

31. Richard Millet, *Désenchantement de la littérature* (Paris: Gallimard, 2007).

erature's decline to globalization, Americanization, the collapse of borders and ensuing miscegenation. The epigraph is a quotation from Nietzsche that targets democratic globalization: "Democracy is the historical form of the decay of the state."[32]

Though half-Lebanese (Christian) and half-"*Français de souche,*" and bilingual in French and Arabic, Millet is vehemently opposed to Creolization, being, rather, "euronostalgic." In an aphoristic pamphlet à la Cioran, entitled *L'opprobre. Essai de démonologie [Dishonor: Essay in Demonology],* that triggered a mini-scandal for its alleged racism,[33] Millet provides this chimeric, Janus-like, schizophrenic, and politically incorrect self-portrait: "Provincial, Catholic, white, heterosexual, and in search of purity in all things: perfect half-breed, even Levantine, with some features of Asian cruelty and indifference toward my fellow humans."[34]

Ironically, Millet does not see cultural hybridization or migration as contributing to the progress of literature and culture, contrary to progressivist, multicultural currents represented by the Deleuzian poet Edouard Glissant and writers such as Raphael Confiant and Patrick Chamoiseau.[35] He professes, genuinely or as a form of provocation, a return to cultural and linguistic integrity. But while Cioran's targets were the demons of existence, in *L'opprobre* Millet dispels rivals in the literary world. Something petty in Millet's pamphlet distinguishes it from Cioran's desperate attempts at exorcising the demons of being, but to be fair, one does not find such pettiness in Millet's novels—complex narratives written in sumptuous style, open to endless interpretation.

The "last writer," predictably, is Millet himself. His voice, reminiscent of Chateaubriand's *Mémoires d'outre-tombe,* as is often the case among morose and contrarian writers, is posthumous. His "rural" novels stage a tragic chorus or a bard—the swan of the village with the biblical name of "Siom" (Zion),[36] an Atlantis in the heart of Corrèze drowned by the tidal wave of modernity. Millet claims to be the survivor of an extinct world: "We float in the language of the Late Em-

32. Friedrich Nietzsche, *Human, All Too Human: A Book for Free Spirits,* section 8: paragraph 472 (1878).

33. "Richard Millet: généalogie d'un malaise," *Le monde* (June 6, 2008).

34. Millet, *L'opprobre, Essai de démonologie* (Paris: Gallimard, 2008), 75.

35. Jean Bernabé, Patrick Chamoiseau, and Raphaël Confiant, *Eloge de la créolité* (Paris: Gallimard, 1993).

36. This is not the place to discuss Millet's spelling of "Siom" with an "m" instead of an "n."

pire, whose arrogant orality, in a few short years, rendered centuries of rhetoric obsolete and the monuments of language obscure; we wander in the ruins of a great civilization whose Greeks and Romans we are becoming" (*Désenchantement* 51). Millet lives a literary post-life in a post-literary world, claiming to be the last witness to a civilization that has reached its twilight. Chateaubriand is not far off, but neither is another "posthumous" writer, Jacques Derrida, who wrote, "I am the last defender and illustrator of the French language,"[37] as well as the untranslatable *"Je posthume comme je respire,"*[38] several decades after having endlessly glossed Monsieur Valdemar's "I am dead."[39] Indeed, Millet's ideological stance appears as a strange mix of the postmodern literary absolute à la Blanchot or Derrida and of nostalgic and reactionary yearning.

In 2002, novelist and essayist Pierre Jourde, an admirer of Millet and author of a "rural," naturalistic, autobiographical novel,[40] published *La littérature sans estomac*,[41] a pamphlet that, despite or because of its iconoclastic tone, was awarded a prize by the Académie Française. The title winks at Julien Gracq's 1950 *La littérature à l'estomac*[42] in which Gracq lamented the then-contemporary crisis in literary judgment. *La littérature sans estomac* is a fitting title for a book by a novelist who would later publish a voluminous, somber, and superbly written if literally indigestible novel entitled *Festins secrets*,[43] in which the provincial bourgeoisie plots with the local immigrant *Lumpenproletariat* to hunt and consume human flesh. *La littérature sans estomac* is a gastronomic metaphor suggesting that French literature has become anorexic and lacks guts. The book targets the literary business represented by the so-called *"rentrée littéraire"* (a comical phrase that intimates that literature, like the French people themselves, takes summer vacations), literary salons, and literary awards. All these public events betray, for Jourde, a general crisis in literary judgment.

Jourde's main targets are telegenic icons such as Christine Angot,

37. Derrida, *Le monolinguisme de l'autre* (Paris: Galilée, 1996), 79.
38. See Geoffrey Bennington and Jacques Derrida, *Jacques Derrida* (Paris: Seuil, 1991), 28.
39. Derrida, *La voix et le phénomène. Introduction au problème du signe dans la phénoménologie de Husserl* (Paris: Presses Universitaires de France, 1967).
40. Pierre Jourde, *Pays perdu* (Paris: Pocket, 2004).
41. Jourde, *La littérature sans estomac* (Paris: Esprit des péninsules, 2002).
42. Julien Gracq, *La littérature à l'estomac* (Paris: José Corti, 1950).
43. Jourde, *Festins secrets* (Paris: Esprit des péninsules, 2005).

Philippe Sollers, Michel Houellebecq, and François Beigbeider. Especially robust is his charge against auto-fiction and egotism or *angotism,* a form of literary narcissism clothed as aesthetic, political, and moral radicality. The reader of Jourde's book is led to wonder what it means to challenge the social order today and what it means to be a radical in the fields of literature and politics. The opening of the chapter devoted to Angot suggests that, far from threatening it, the critique of the social order fosters the neo-liberal system, today's dominant world order. What Angot displays as her radical difference, in this case her incestuous penchants, merely nurtures a system based on the reduction of all differences—the free market. Thus, the allegedly obscene exhibition of one's radical difference enhances a system that values all differences—gender, race, sexual orientation, perversions, and so on—as potential products that can be exchanged in the market of cultural goods. If difference can be exchanged, it loses its untradeable and intractable essence. What passes for resistance (in art, literature, ideas) plays into the hand of the cultural market.

Furthermore, Jourde suggests that Angot formulates her critique of the social order a little late, insofar as the patriarchal family has been under fire for several decades. To reveal one's incestuous inclinations, and even to act them out, hardly amounts to transgression—quite the opposite. Our age of intimate exposure is that of the normalization of all forms of transgression of the Law. Hence radical transgression and resistance, paradoxically, would consist in the reaffirmation of the Law—in this case, the incest taboo—and in the limitation of *jouissance.* Today, transgression, rather than constituting a revolutionary behavior or a form of resistance, merely perpetuates the norm, as Jourde expresses it in the following ironic antiphrasis:

> Incest constitutes a strikingly original topic. Christine Angot's text falls like a meteorite on fire on the purring comfort of our culture. Who could have predicted that this pamphlet would trigger public curiosity? Who could have predicted that a conspiracy of silence would not surround a book that undermines the very foundations of family and the social order? (*La littérature sans estomac,* 84–85)

Jourde is in tune with another satirist, literary critic and polemicist, the late Philippe Muray, who coined the bon mot *"mutins de Panurge"* (after Rabelais's *"moutons de Panurge"*) to mock the conformity of transgression that he identified as a feature of our hedonistic societies. Social and cultural conservatism would be the only form of resistance in an age that has turned personal or even collective transgression into the norm, and self-exposure into art and literature. The tendency to denounce the conformity of transgression and the urge to find a genuinely critical anchorage at the risk of being accused of reactionary thought is common to the writers I am examining. For Millet and Muray, this nonconformist conservatism is expressed, for example, in an apology of Christianity, sexual difference, and heterosexuality.

In accordance with Ian Buruma and Avishai Margalit's analysis of anti-western metaphysics,[44] Millet expresses his paradoxical agreement with Islamic extremism in the name of an Islam-free Europe and of a return to the authentic values of Western civilization threatened by the Americanization of the world. His resentment leads him to embrace conspiracy theory about the attacks of September 11, 2001, and to share the condemnation of Western nihilism with Muslim fundamentalists:

> Although I abhor Islamism, I also reject the same things it does. But I will not be an apostate. It is not impossible to believe that the attacks of September 11, 2001 were staged by the U.S. with Saudi money. Likewise, one can doubt that Americans have really walked on the Moon. The Spectacle prevails, and with it the new economy of war. (*L'opprobre* 52)

For the irreversible decline of Western civilization and aesthetics, Millet blames democracy: "Language has, from the perspective of style, collapsed in democracy" (*Désenchantement* 38). Furthermore, like Guy Debord but without the revolutionary aspirations, he reclaims the critique of virtual reality and commodity as spectacle and of new technologies, as well as the general process of the disembodiment of human experience and its replacement with simulacra. The darkening of our world, he writes, is the "sign of a sham cloaked as general revaluation, truth traded for its shadow, the proliferation of doubles, replicas, clones, the defeat of the One, post-metaphysical ecstasy, belief according to which an analogical world, a virtual reality is preferable to the very flesh of this world" (*Désenchantement* 62).

Jaime Semprun, a neo-situationist whose work is published by the *Encyclopédie des Nuisances*, while far removed from Millet's Christian ideology, contests neo-leftist optimism. The following quotation from Günther Anders, which Semprun invokes in his latest book, gives a glimpse of Semprun's radical pessimism, accompanied by a strident call for inertia: "Whatever we do or whatever we do not do, our going on

44. Ian Buruma and Avishai Margalit, *Occidentalism: The West in the Eyes of Its Enemies* (New York: Penguin Press, 2004).

strike personally does not change anything, since we live now among a human kind for which the "world" and the experience of the world have lost all value: nothing henceforth has any interest, except for the phantom world and the consumption of this phantom."[45] For Semprun, fifty years after Anders's sinister remarks on the second industrial revolution, it is impossible to believe that the forces of production can be harnessed so as to implement direct democracy. A threshold was crossed in the twentieth century when the forces of production became lethal. After Hiroshima and Chernobyl, once technology and science are harnessed to total war and dehumanization, production equals destruction (*Catastrophisme*, 127). Semprun, though faithful to materialist analysis, especially in his analysis of cultural and social mutations, rejects, not unlike Lyotard, the redemptive beacon of Marxism.

The fall of the Berlin Wall and the collapse of communism, instead of inaugurating an age of hope for global democracy, heralded the transmogrification of man into a hedonistic machine: a post-historical, Nietzschean last man. The following description of techno music is reminiscent of Adorno's and Anders's critique of jazz and of mass culture in the 1950s: "Techno music is mechanical music; the one who listens to it (the raver) is a man-machine, an agitated nervous system, that lets itself be enthused by music until he experiences a feeling of joy which he is the only one to believe in. The lovers of techno music are the authentic children of German reunification."[46]

I conclude by returning to my initial allegory of the alienated shadow. Over the past five years, several works of different genres have alleged that, in the wake of the disappearance of the real, as Jean Baudrillard would have it, the Other has also disappeared. This disappearance is consistently attributed to the new world order, characterized as a process of globalization, Americanization, unrestrained individualism, hedonism, and advanced consumer culture. This process is indefinite and limitless, having no *telos* beyond its own perpetuation. Our postmodern submission to process has replaced the modern faith in progress.

To describe the disappearance of the Other, the young essayist Dominique Quessada has forged the concept of "*altéricide*."[47] Quessada

45. René Riesel and Jaime Semprun, *Catastrophisme, administration du désastre et soumission durable* (Paris: Éditions de l'Encyclopédie des Nuisances, 2008), 126.

46. Semprun, *L'abîme se repeuple* (Paris: Éditions de l'Encyclopédie des Nuisances, 1997), 12.

47. Dominique Quessada, *Court traité d'altéricide* (Paris: Verticales, Gallimard, 2007).

argues that while claims for difference increase everywhere, the Other fades away, as in Monty Python's *Life of Brian,* in which the pseudo-Messiah exhorts the crowd to resist conformity—an exhortation to which the galvanized crowd responds by shouting in one voice: "We are all different!" Thus, "the Other is excluded through the most radical exclusion: integration. It is excluded through inclusion" (*Court traité,* 58). The West, according to Quessada's argument, has entered its post-dialectic phase. Exit Hegelian history as the work of the negative.

From a clinical, Lacanian perspective, psychoanalyst Charles Melman reaches an uncannily similar conclusion.[48] Melman diagnoses a radical mutation of psychic and libidinal economy. For him, unrestrained hedonism enhanced by the neoliberal order has led to the loss of the lost object and undermined the very structure of desire grounded on the split subject as a result of the entry into the Symbolic. Total accessibility, presence, and unmediated satisfaction have taken over lack, delay, and representation. Desire is an old memory: "It is no longer a psychic economy centered on the lost object and its representatives that is being legitimized [by our society]. Quite the opposite —it's a psychic economy organized by the presentation of an accessible object and by the ultimate accomplishment of *jouissance*" (*L'homme sans gravité,* 224). Exit the gravity of neurosis.

In his pamphlet, *L'obscénité démocratique,*[49] Régis Debray laments the transition from democracy to "*egocracy*": "the Republic's stage . . . must be rescued from obscenity, when politics becomes the '*tout-à-l'ego*'[50] of a country which has fallen prey to the tyranny of Nielsen ratings, emotion, and intimacy."[51] The essayist promotes a return to civil religion to counter the "current idea of a happiness coterminous with the immediate fulfillment of desires."[52] The tradition of transcendence and decorum is threatened by the Americanization of the French Republic. The theater of the Republic, rooted in the distinction between the body in the literal sense and the symbolic body of the civil servant, has become obsolete. For Debray, the chasm between the "resident in

48. Charles Melman and Jean-Pierre Lebrun, *L'homme sans gravité: Jouir à tout prix* (Paris: Denoël, 2002).

49. Régis Debray, *L'obscénité démocratique* (Paris: Flammarion, 2007).

50. Literally the "everything-to-the-sewer" is the pipe running from a house to the sewer. Debray plays with the homophony between "ego" and "égout" (sewer.)

51. Debray, *L'obscénité,* back cover.

52. Interview with Régis Debray in the Christian daily *La Croix,* "L'échelle des revenus est devenue l'échelle des valeurs," November 8, 2008, http://www.la-croix .com/article/index.jsp?docId=2346234&rubId=786.

flesh and blood of the Elysée and this abstraction called the presidency of the Republic" ought to be restored, lest civilization collapse: "Function transcends the individual . . . [W]ill this legacy of civilization become obsolete?" (*L'obscénité*, 26). The mystical, immortal body of the civil servant has fallen into the obscene and narcissistic formlessness of immanence. The grandiose, solemn, mysterious spectacle of Republican power has become specular presence on the TV screen—a mirror of the vile instincts of the crowd. Exit politics as theater.

I submit the following hypothesis that may apply at least to Debray's discontent if not to other "*mécontemporains.*" In 1979, Claude Lefort analyzed the conditions of possibility for the emergence of totalitarianism.[53] For Lefort, totalitarianism is the dialectic counterpart of the democratization process, democracy being the process by which the social order becomes immanent. Resorting to Ernst Kantorowicz's theory in *The King's Two Bodies*, Lefort argues that the transition from transcendence to immanence rests on the abolition of the symbolic, mystical body of the king. Once this body has been abolished through regicide and its traumatic memory and repetition in postrevolutionary France, the place remains vacant. The *demos* fills this vacuum, but this filling remains indeterminate and immanent. The transcendent Other, in democracy, is replaced with the immanent other—"*tout autre,*" anyone, or, as Giorgio Agamben would have it, "whatever singularity."[54] Totalitarianism, Lefort suggests, is a pathological reaction to the anxiety triggered by this vacuum. The totalitarian regime provides the illusion of plenitude—the State, its bureaucratic apparatus, its pompousness—yet this plenitude is bereft of the transcendence that characterized the metaphysics of the Old Regime.

French contemporary moroseness may be the symptom of the fading away of an anthropological regime grounded on the shadow of the transcendent Other—the nation, the Republic, the state—and the emergence of forms of communities yet to be determined. The receding of this shadow has conjured up an anxiety of formlessness—the multitude, the people, the "obscene."

53. Claude Lefort, "L'image du corps et le totalitarisme," in *L'invention démocratique* (Paris: Fayard, 1981), 159–76.

54. Giorgio Agamben, *La communauté qui vient, Théorie de la singularité quelconque* (Paris: Le Seuil, 1990). See also Jacques Rancière, *La haine de la démocratie* (Paris: Fabrique, 2005).

IV. Literary Plaints

DOUGLAS MORREY

Sex and the Single Male: Houellebecq, Feminism, and Hegemonic Masculinity

The astonishing international success of the novels of Michel Houellebecq may be explained in large part by the presence of graphic, if not to say salacious, descriptions of sexual activity and by the key role that sexuality plays in the unfolding of the novels' plots. This, in any case, is what the marketing of Houellebecq's books would apparently have us believe, and possibly even more so in those countries where he is published in translation than in his native France. All of the British editions of Houellebecq's novels since *Les particules élémentaires* (1998), translated as *Atomised* (2000), have featured on the cover a photographic image of a young woman in underclothes or swimwear, sometimes with her back to the camera, sometimes gazing demurely at the prospective reader. Houellebecq's reputation as a writer concerned with sex above all was created by this book with its numerous racy scenes set in nudist campsites and swingers' clubs and the voyeuristic adventures of the hapless Bruno bringing himself off with more or less discretion to the sights of schoolgirls on trains, naked teenagers in communal showers, and couples canoodling in a jacuzzi. The multiplication of fantasy scenes culled directly from the repertoire of pornography in Houellebecq's next major novel *Plateforme* (2001) served only to consolidate this impression of a particularly single-minded author. However, anyone who has actually read a book by Michel Houellebecq will know that in fact he describes a world in which the majority of people spend most of their time deprived of sex. It would be no exaggeration to say that all of the heroes and narrators of Houellebecq's novels, at one stage or another of their narrative,

YFS 116/117, *Turns to the Right?* ed. Johnson and Schehr, © 2009 by Yale University.

abandon all hope of ever knowing a happy and fulfilled sex life. This article will concentrate on the absence or impossibility of sex in Houellebecq's work, focusing in particular on the first two novels (*Atomised* and its predecessor, *Extension du domaine de la lutte*, from 1994, translated as *Whatever* in 1998). It will seek to bring out the political conclusions from Houellebecq's analysis of sexuality which can sometimes be obscured by the author's hasty and ill-informed rejection of feminism.

In some ways, then, it would be more accurate to say that the world of Houellebecq is a world without sex. In this sense, the opening paragraph of *Extension du domaine de la lutte* stands in a neatly metonymical relation to all the rest of Houellebecq's oeuvre. At a party among work colleagues, a young woman gradually removes her clothes while dancing, before finally getting dressed again when she realizes that no one is paying any attention: "She's a girl, what's more," Houellebecq notes, "who doesn't sleep with anyone."[1] Houellebecq seems to suggest that what the French critic Jean-Claude Guillebaud has called "le tapage sexuel"—the constant background racket of sexual representation and solicitation in our society[2]—may be less interesting to people than is commonly assumed. Approaching forty, Bruno in *Atomised* discovers that women of his age "aren't really into sex any more," although they may pretend otherwise.[3] The narrator's priest friend in *Whatever* concludes: "we need to hear ourselves repeat that life is marvellous and exciting; and it's abundantly clear that we rather doubt this" (*Whatever*, 30). Houellebecq's world is populated by the single, the frustrated, and the reluctantly virginal; it is a world in which sex is certainly very visible but remains inaccessible to the vast majority.

In a context where the market value of sexuality is clearly displayed, sexual relations no longer appear as a natural extension of emotional attachment; nor is it even really physical pleasure that is most important in finding a sexual partner, but rather—and this is one of Houellebecq's key insights—the narcissistic gratification that accrues to the individual as a function of the desirability of the partner. Sexuality, "liberated" though it may be, no longer figures as the object of a "free" choice, but appears instead, to quote Jean-Claude Guillebaud, as

---

1. Michel Houellebecq, *Whatever*, trans. Paul Hammond (London: Serpent's Tail, 1998), 3.

2. Jean-Claude Guillebaud, *La tyrannie du plaisir* (Paris: Seuil, 1998), 16.

3. Michel Houellebecq, *Atomised*, trans. Frank Wynne (London: Vintage, 2000), 239.

"a constitutive injunction of our era," a kind of ordinance of accepted modern behavior (Guillebaud, 136). The ruthless competition and demand for excellence that drive the labor market and economic relations have gradually encroached upon the private sphere in such a way that personal relationships and sexual practices are now subject to the same pressure. But, to paraphrase Georges Bataille, the orgy can lead only to disappointment. The sex clubs described in *Atomised* are anything but fun, marked rather by the stress and exertion of an erotic tournament:

> Gaping from multiple penetrations and brutal fingering (often using several fingers, or indeed the whole hand), their cunts had all the sensitivity of blocks of lard. Imitating the frenetic rhythm of porn actresses, they brutally jerked his cock in a ridiculous piston motion as though it was a piece of dead meat. . . . He came quickly, with no real pleasure. (*Atomised*, 294)

As I mentioned above and as should already have been clear from my title, Houellebecq's heroes are all single men. Now, as Jean-Claude Bologne has pointed out, if single people make up most of the protagonists throughout literary history, it is only because literature has traditionally described a more or less teleological trajectory toward the formation of the happy couple.[4] And, although social and sexual habits and mores may have altered a great deal in recent decades, the priorities and the destiny of single people—in particular single women— have arguably changed very little in contemporary popular fiction and cultural production. In the recent vogue of Anglo-American novels produced about, by, and for single women—the so-called "chick lit" publishing phenomenon—, some critics have maintained that as much attention is given to the heroine's career and to conspicuous consumption as to the male mate. It nonetheless remains the case that in most of these novels the encounter with the "right" man, even if it doesn't provide the expected conclusion to the narrative, has a crucial role to play in defining the heroine's aspirational psyche. In any case, even where marriage or its equivalent is no longer prioritized, as in works by contemporary French women writers such as Virginie Despentes's portraits of unapologetic, unrepentant sex workers, or Catherine Millet's memoir of a copious sexuality lived out with numerous anonymous partners, the focus is on women making the most of their single status.

4. Jean-Claude Bologne, *Histoire du célibat et des célibataires* (Paris: Fayard, 2004), 7.

Yet the history of single people, as Bologne's study has amply demonstrated, is above all a history of discrimination and marginalization: unable to find their place in a society increasingly centered around the family, single people were derided as being unfit for marriage, hit with punitive taxes to correct their apparently selfish lack of contribution to society, and always the first to be sent to war. Indeed, until very recently, the single life has been a largely thankless one. The true originality of Michel Houellebecq in contemporary literature, I want to argue, lies in portraying the single life as unenjoyable and unwanted, even as it becomes increasingly unavoidable. So, for all of the high-profile sex in Houellebecq, most of his characters spend most of their time alone. For instance, the relationship between Bruno and Christiane in *Atomised* lasts for around a hundred of the novel's three hundred pages, but much of that is taken up with retrospective accounts of Bruno's miserable student years. Even at the height of his relationship with Christiane, Bruno cannot help but suspect that it might just be "a bad farce, one last sordid joke that life had played on him" (*Atomised*, 295). The same would be true of *Platform* and *The Possibility of an Island* (2005): brief, if sometimes ecstatic, sexual relationships appear only as short-lived anomalies in the endless plain of monotony and disappointment that characterizes these men's lives. Houellebecq's single male perhaps finds his hideous apogee in the character of Raphaël Tisserand in *Whatever*. Cursed with "the exact appearance of a buffalo toad" (*Whatever*, 54) and further lacking in charm or social graces, Tisserand provokes an involuntary disgust among women, and is condemned to live as though "protected from the world by a transparent film, inviolable and perfect," feeling increasingly like "a shrink-wrapped chicken leg on a supermarket shelf" (98). To Houellebecq's credit, we are a very long way here from what R. W. Connell has called "hegemonic masculinity," that which occupies a position of power within a given order of gender relations and which "embodies the currently accepted answer to the problem of the legitimacy of patriarchy, which guarantees (or is taken to guarantee) the dominant position of men and the subordination of women."[5] Even if hegemonic masculinity in the West today relies less on paternalistic authority and more on a physical beauty that borrows from characteristics once reserved for femininity, it continues to be the capacity to attract sexual partners that shores up masculine power.

5. R. W. Connell, *Masculinities*, 2nd edition (Cambridge: Polity, 2006), 77.

The novels of Michel Houellebecq are above all narratives of sexual frustration. The single man may live alone, but his solitude is crowded by an unwelcome double of himself. This is clearly the experience of Raphaël Tisserand, as it is cruelly summed up by the narrator: "The sexual failure you've known since your adolescence . . . , the frustration that has followed you since the age of thirteen, will leave their indelible mark. . . . You will always be an orphan to those adolescent loves you never knew" (*Whatever*, 116). On several occasions in Houellebecq's work, sexual frustration threatens to spill over into physical violence toward other people. The narrator of *Whatever* encourages Tisserand, admittedly without success, to take out his disappointment in murdering a young stud and his beautiful girlfriend. Brigitte Bardot, the heroine of one of the embedded narratives within this novel, and whose corpulent physique lends a cruel irony to her given name, experiences a similar welling of anger: "She could only assist, in silent hatred, at the liberation of others; witness the boys pressing themselves like crabs against others' bodies . . . ; live to the full a silent self-destruction when faced with the flaunted pleasure of others. . . . Jealousy and frustration fermented slowly to become a swelling of paroxystic hatred" (*Whatever*, 90). In this way, the over-riding feeling in our leisure society becomes one of "an immense and inconceivable bitterness"(148). Such is also the diagnosis of the future narrator of *Atomised:* describing the era in which Michel Djerzinski lived, he concludes that "the men of his generation lived out . . . lonely, bitter lives" (*Atomised*, 3). There is, I will insist, a properly political dimension to this identification of bitterness as the main result of today's social relations.

Houellebecq's most crucial political insight, the one that provides the foundations for his entire novelistic structure, can be found in the well known thesis of *Extension du domaine de la lutte:* it states that there exists a system of social hierarchy, parallel to that of personal wealth, but based on sex and, in a context where free rein is given to market logic, "sexual liberalism produces phenomena of *absolute pauperization*" among the undesirable, equivalent to long-term unemployment and economic and social exclusion (*Whatever*, 99). Indeed, *Les particules élémentaires* suggests that sexual success became the *main* criterion of social superiority some time during the 1970s, before being matched by renewed economic competition with the arrival of globalization. The discourses of work and sexuality appear increasingly inseparable, each borrowing and re-employing the key terms of the other. Houellebecq notes that sexuality is sold, in a culture of marketing, as a kind of adventure, necessitating "originality, passion and individual creativity (all qualities also required of employees in their professional capacities)" (*Atomised*, 293). Meanwhile for Bruno, who more often than not has to pay for sex, the state of his love life is almost entirely determined by fluctuations in the market: the arrival of immigrants from Eastern Europe drives down the cost of prostitution in Paris, but he is forced to cut back when he has to pay for repairs to his car. Also commenting on the parallel evolution of economic and sexual development, Jean-Claude Bologne has suggested that our era of economic insecurity might equally be characterized as one of emotional casualization: just as workers no longer expect a job for life and are obliged to refine their personal qualities in order to be re-employable, so too marriage or long-term relationships might be seen as a sort of "active life" of the feelings, marked by periods of unemployment, changes in management and, ultimately, retirement (Bologne, 375).

For Houellebecq, sexuality in the modern world has become altogether impossible or at least unbearable. Consumer society constantly seeks to arouse desire without providing any satisfactory outlets for it, this task continuing to fall to the private sphere which is itself increasingly uncongenial. "Human relationships [are becoming] progressively impossible" (*Whatever*, 14), the fluidity of the labor market and the multiplication of leisure options meaning that "people rarely *see each other again* these days" (40). It is precisely the proliferation of choice that diminishes the possibility of meaningful relations. Meanwhile, love has become an outmoded sentiment, structurally incompatible with a free sexual marketplace based around narcissistic competition: "Love as a kind of innocence and as a capacity for illusion, as an aptitude for epitomizing the whole of the other sex in a single loved being rarely resists a year of sexual immorality, and never two" (113).[6] This is already Aldous Huxley's *Brave New World:* Bruno and Michel remark upon the accuracy of Huxley's science fictional predictions in which reproduction is increasingly regulated but ever more detached from sexuality; there is a diminished importance of the family as well as a reduction of the difference between ages and chemically balanced moods. Although it is hypocritically decried as a totalitarian nightmare, this is precisely the ideal world we are currently

6. The explicitly judgmental sense of "sexual immorality" is not present in the original French: "vagabondage sexuel," which merely implies non-committal promiscuity.

trying to create. Huxley was wrong on only one point according to Houellebecq: sexual competition cannot be eradicated by scientific rationalism alone, since its counterpart, individualism, leads to an increased drive for narcissistic differentiation.

With no real possibility of love in this society, there is no room for family life either. For Houellebecq, sexual liberation marked "another stage in the rise of the individual," which the family was powerless to resist. The family was "the last unit separating the individual from the market" (*Atomised*, 135–36), and, in these novels, this membrane protecting us from the brutal reality of economic relations has been definitively torn. Bologne suggests that it is the single person, rather than the married couple, that has become the key point of reference in our society, such that many couples continue to behave as though they were single, enjoying separate homes, separate cars, separate hobbies, and separate holidays in a kind of "*égoïsme à deux*," or juxtaposition of two single lives (Bologne, 371–72). In this context, then, marriage, and especially children, can appear as an obstacle to self-realization. In Houellebecq's world, certainly, parental responsibility is met with negligence, or indifference at best. Bruno's father "wanted to do his best for the boy, as long as it did not take up too much of his time" (*Atomised*, 53). Bruno and Michel will both be brought up by their grandparents. Bruno has a son of his own, who merits no more than one or two offhand remarks in the course of the novel and who really comes to his father's notice only when he becomes old enough to be considered a rival in the sexual marketplace.

This apparent condemnation of a society in which family ties are severed and filial relations give way to bitter sexual contest could perhaps be interpreted as a retreat into reactionary values. That would, however, be too hasty a judgment, since one would search in vain, in Houellebecq's writing, for any nostalgia attached to the image of the family. If he describes the collapse of the family, it is seemingly without regret and without any illusions regarding an idealized family life that might have existed in another era. Houellebecq can have Bruno insist that Pope John Paul II "was the only person—the only person— who really understood what was happening in the West" in the 1980s (*Atomised*, 216), but does that necessarily mean he approves of the Vatican's sexual politics? If it remains difficult to circumscribe Houellebecq's political stance with precision, it is perhaps because the sexual arena is particularly open to ambiguous political interpretation. For instance, both Bologne and Guillebaud cite the rise of a "new chastity" movement in the USA, with organizations such as True Love Waits, which, although easily associated with the Christian right, are sometimes understood by their adherents to be a deliberate rejection of sexual consumerism, often with an explicitly asserted post-feminist agenda (Bologne, 337; Guillebaud, 137–38). In his first novel, Houellebecq borrows a vocabulary of "struggle" familiar from Marxist politics. The title *Extension du domaine de la lutte* is drawn from the key paragraph in which the narrator sets out his theory of the parallel system of sexual hierarchy: "Sexual liberalism is an extension of the domain of the struggle, its extension to all ages and all classes of society" (*Whatever*, 99). Should we then interpret this sexual struggle as an extension of that most unfashionable of concepts in our would-be post-political age, the *class struggle*? Or is this struggle rather a kind of evolutionary survival of the fittest and thereby stripped of any explicitly political meaning?[7] We shall return to this question below, but for now, we might simply share Guillebaud's concerns about an opposition between a clamoring permissiveness, on one hand, and a nostalgic moralism on the other: the simplistic division of sexual politics into a legislatory prudishness versus an irresponsible libertarianism is a false opposition that we must be willing to resist (Guillebaud, 9).

For Houellebecq, it is the so-called "sexual revolution" of the 1960s and '70s that must bear a large part of responsibility for our current sexual malaise. In Houellebecq's interpretation, this sexual revolution was essentially the invention of middle-aged men who thereby came up with a way of sleeping with a lot of much younger women. The veterans of May '68 who set up the hippie campsite called the "Lieu du Changement" ("Place of Change") in *Atomised* conceive of it according to "the principles of self-government, respect for individual freedom and true democracy"; still, the site's main purpose is "to provide an opportunity to 'get your rocks off'" (*Atomised*, 114). Houellebecq's critique of the sexual revolution finds an unexpected echo in feminist writing where it has been interpreted as an extension to the whole of society of sexual values coded as highly masculine—promiscuity, emotional detachment, objectification of the body, genital sexuality. The radical feminist critic Sheila Jeffreys accuses the sexual revolution of marking the moment when sexual activity became

---

7. In any case, the bizarre rendering of the title in the English translation as the dismissively postmodern *Whatever* tends to cut short the very possibility of debate.

mandatory, necessitating a certain erotic efficiency and ostracizing those who would not or could not take part.[8] With his customary dose of exaggeration, Houellebecq too condemns a culture in which the bodies of other people are so many props to be used in the individual pursuit of novel sensations: *Atomised* relates the dark trajectory of David di Meola, failed rock star and son of a hippy patriarch, who makes a career for himself in Satanic murder:

> Having exhausted the possibilities of sexual pleasure, it was reasonable that individuals, liberated from the constraints of ordinary morality, should turn their attentions to the wider pleasures of cruelty. . . . From this point of view, Charles Manson was not some monstrous aberration in the hippie movement, but its logical conclusion. (*Atomised*, 252–53)

It would, in fact, be possible to draw striking parallels between feminist discourse and Houellebecq's analyses if he were not so stubborn and misinformed in his resistance to feminism. Houellebecq actually tends to blame feminism for many of the cultural calamities he describes. Where men and sex are concerned, it seems, "feminism has hit them harder than they like to admit" (*Atomised*, 166). Houellebecq's portraits of feminists from the '68 generation are breathtaking in their cruelty, and the fact of placing such libellous words in the mouth of Christiane, herself a woman of the same generation, seems a rather facile device to evade responsibilty (though it is one that Houellebecq employs frequently throughout his novels). Thus feminists, apparently, "could never shut up about the washing up" and once they had "managed to turn every man they knew into an impotent whinging neurotic. . . . They usually ended up ditching their boyfriends for a quick fuck with some macho idiot before getting someone to give them a baby and settling down to make jam" (*Atomised*, 173–74). Houellebecq is disingenuous, not to say deliberately misleading when he delightedly recounts the unhappy fate that awaited these women: "As their flesh began to age, the cult of the body, which they had done so much to promote, simply filled them with disgust for their own bodies—a disgust they could see mirrored in the gaze of others" (125). But this "cult of the body" has nothing to do with feminism—which, on the contrary, has always been responsible for its most sustained and committed criticism; nor does it have much to do with the hippie

8. Sheila Jeffreys, *Anticlimax: A Feminist Perspective on the Sexual Revolution* (London: The Women's Press, 1990), 110.

movement satirized throughout *Atomised;* the "cult of the body" belongs, rather, to liberal, free-market capitalism for which it figures both as a marketing device and as an aspirational model, whose attainment, needless to say, necessitates the purchase of numerous products, from sports equipment and cosmetics to surgical enhancement. While accusing feminism of responsibility for phenomena that it has itself combated, Houellebecq also allows the real victories of women's liberation to be tarred with the same satirical brush. Thus the free indirect speech used by Houellebecq in his portrait of an abortion doctor attached to the hippie community (*Atomised,* 86–87) contains a silent but pernicious irony that risks consigning women's control of their own reproductive systems to the rubbish heap of historical bad ideas, along with free love and flared trousers.

From time to time, in Houellebecq's trenchant analyses of the sexual arena, there may be a passing recognition of the kind of unthinking objectification to which women's bodies are subjected in everyday social intercourse. In an Italian restaurant, the narrator of *Whatever* complains about the waiter's lack of attention: "Ah, if we'd been wearing slit skirts that would have been different!" (*Whatever,* 108). But Houellebecq's own descriptions quite systematically reproduce this objectification. Observing a young woman in a nightclub, the narrator notes, "The wide hips, the firm and smooth buttocks; the suppleness of the waist which leads the hands up to a pair of round, ample and soft breasts; the hands which rest confidently on the waist, espousing the noble rotundity of the hips" (*Whatever,* 111–12). Here, then, a visual description immediately passes over into a physical, erotic appropriation. The same effect is produced, in a rather more vulgar register, when Houellebecq observes that a woman has "blow-job lips" (*Atomised,* 127–8). It is precisely this that provides the focus for one of feminism's most fundamental objections to the patriarchal order—what Carole Pateman has called "the male sex-right"[9]: the demand by men to have access—whether physically, verbally or commercially—to women's bodies displayed in a more or less public manner. Houellebecq's indulgence for prostitution amounts to the same thing: the public availability of women's bodies in order to satisfy male desire (the idea behind *Platform*—that of a generalized sex tourism whereby the inhabitants of developing countries sell their bodies on the open market to the jaded desires of Westerners—though it may be largely

9. Carole Pateman, *The Sexual Contract* (Cambridge: Polity, 1988), 199.

tongue in cheek, carries the same implication). The mercilessness of his descriptions of women—especially of older women, where the horror of flabby skin is reminiscent of Céline—also seems to demand, in much the same way as the consumer society that Houellebecq condemns, that women take a kind of public responsibilty for the physical condition of their bodies.

At the same time, the appeal to a scientific or evolutionary discourse in Houellebecq's work tends to naturalize his presentation of human sexuality. Thus Houellebecq offers a detached, clinical description of the hormonal and anatomical transformations that mark the onset of puberty in teenage girls, but he betrays his own libidinal investment when he evokes, in far from neutral terms, the "round, full, pleasing aspect" of the resulting forms (*Atomised*, 66). The ultimate implication of this pseudo-scientific discourse is that biology is destiny, even if the science-fiction narrative arc of *Atomised*, as well as *The Possibility of an Island*, tend to suggest the opposite, depicting a species that struggles to escape a biological fatalism. In the meantime, though, what this means is that far more dubious assertions, such as the assumption that ugly women will necessarily be ignored while beautiful women are condemned to a tragic sexual destiny by the predatory instincts of men, are lent the spurious authority of science. In the same way, the young Michel Djerzinski, in the very early stages of a reflection on the future of his species, draws conclusions about instinctive male aggression and the nurturing qualities of women based on the observation of wildlife documentaries and his pubescent schoolmates, apparently without considering the vast cultural gulf that separates these two examples. As R. W. Connell has argued, biology today occupies a role previously filled by religion in legitimizing an ideological difference between genders. But the attempt to give a hormonal or evolutionary justification to male dominance of women generally relies on a fictitious biology that ignores the overwhelming evidence of historical and cross-cultural diversity (*Masculinities*, 47–48).

I mentioned above that Houellebecq's heroes are far from representing hegemonic masculinity. This in itself is hardly surprising, since the masculine ideal is only ever incarnated in a very limited number of individuals. However, this does not prevent representatives of more marginalized masculinities from enjoying what Connell calls "the patriarchal dividend," a set of cultural benefits resulting from the subordination of women and that includes material wealth, political power, prestige, privilege, and the right to command. Houellebecq's analyses seem to be blind to these advantages and this is ultimately what limits the usefulness of his demonstration. It is easy to feel sorry for Houellebecq's protagonists, viciously sidelined as they are in the sexual marketplace, constantly confronted with their own sexual worthlessness even as the culture of marketing insistently calls upon them to take part in the erotic adventure, as the only conceivable way of achieving the obligatory personal fulfilment. But even as we pity them, we ought to recognize that these men find themselves in a situation that has been familiar to women for centuries: that of being reduced to an object with an exchange value within a relentless traffic where what is at stake is the right of access to bodies. It is not feminism that is responsible for this situation. On the contrary, it is feminism that allows us—that allows Houellebecq—to identify it in the first place, and to denounce it with such indignation. It is free-market capitalism—which feminism has always understood as playing an integral role in the patriarchal order—that has extended this situation to the whole of society such that men today are equally well-placed to feel its dehumanizing effects. In Houellebecq's novels, beneath the resentment directed at women and the sulks and scowls of sex-starved men, there rumbles a subterranean howl of rage inspired by our consumer society. Listen to the narrator of *Whatever:* "I don't like this world. I definitely do not like it. The society in which I live disgusts me; advertising sickens me; computers make me puke. . . . Bullshit. Pure fucking bullshit" (82). Now, there is a rallying cry we can all unite behind, whether we're getting any or not.

KARL POLLIN

Saint-Maurice of the Saber, Gnostic of Postmodern Times

To evoke Maurice G. Dantec in a volume of a journal questioning a possible ideological shift to the Right of contemporary French intellectuals seems nowadays almost self-evident. Because of his atypical profile, however, Dantec thwarts the great majority of stereotypes commonly associated with the traditional Right. Mostly celebrated for his philosophical thrillers, such as *La sirène rouge* (1993) and *Les racines du mal* (1995), and for his ambitious science fiction novels, including *Babylon Babies* (1999), *Cosmos Incorporated* (2005), and *Grande Jonction* (2006), he disconcerted a large part of his readership by publishing from 2000 to 2006 three imposing volumes of a controversial "metaphysical and polemical diary," entitled chronologically *Le théâtre des opérations*, *Laboratoire de catastrophe générale*, and *American Black Box*. But can we actually call such a monstrous and bulimic text a "diary"? Far from exposing the daily torments and lamentations of the ego, it tends to outstrip the very notion of literary genre, defining itself as an "attempt at a genealogical account of all the ongoing wars, including those that are won or lost at this very moment, or thousands of years ago, or those that have already arisen in the next centuries"?[1] While mixing together a wide range of fields, from anthropology to geopolitics and from cognitive science to religion and philosophy, Dantec rejects both the quiet optimism of the positivist scientist and the consensual neutrality of the cautious intellectual who prefers to keep out of the fray. As a matter of fact, drawing the genealogy of all past, present, and future wars presupposes that

---

1. Maurice G. Dantec, *Le théâtre des opérations* (Paris : Gallimard, 2002), 125–26. Translations in this article are my own unless otherwise specified.

YFS 116/117, *Turns to the Right?* ed. Johnson and Schehr, © 2009 by Yale University.

the writer transform himself literally into a warrior,[2] and turn his text performatively into a "sort of weapon of mass destruction,"[3] a "virus" designed to wipe out the dominant ideologies that, according to him, configured the twentieth century. No sense of moderation is to be expected from this global mode of address, and the writer, at the risk of collapsing into paranoia, must lie constantly in ambush in order to stave off the revived defense mechanisms of his self-proclaimed enemies. To what extent must we then take for granted labels such as "right-wing" or "reactionary" when applied to Dantec's diary? I should like to suggest that these specific labels, more than a convenient way to name, classify, and distance oneself from the writer's political and theoretical views, can rather be understood as the symptomatic expression of a repressed anxiety that takes possession of the French progressive left-wing intellectuals, who must face the primeval instability of their ideological foundations during their reading of Dantec's diary.

Let's be honest: the goal of this article is neither to attempt to circumscribe the guiding lines of Dantec's geopolitical views nor to take sides on the ideological controversy that is taking place in France about his work.[4] Such a perspective would amount to a subordination of the singularity of literary expression to the transmissibility of a political message, whose validity could then be approved or rejected. In other words, it would reduce the writer's sentences to simple tools of communication, designed to carry a whole set of opinions that can be debated rationally in the context of an open discussion. Dantec's latent hostility to journalistic and scholarly discourses can thus be analyzed as a radical opposition to this common perception of language that prevails in our contemporary cultures. According to him, language should initially be represented as "pure sovereignty, pure creative liberty . . . [that] in fact goes against any form of *communication*, any sort of *community*, because it is the specific Agent of Separation."[5] Moreover, the diarist indicates several times that he does not want to be understood by his peers, to such a degree that he has been com-

2. On Dantec's militarist views of both writing and international relations, see Douglas Morrey, "Dr. Schizo: Religion, Reaction and Maurice G. Dantec," *Journal of European Studies* 37 (2007): 295–312.

3. Dantec, *American Black Box* (Paris : Albin Michel, 2007), 14.

4. For a synthetic analysis of these views, I refer to Paul Garapon, "Maurice G. Dantec sur tous les fronts," *Esprit* 279 (November 2001):118–34.

5. Dantec, *Laboratoire de catastrophe générale* (Paris : Gallimard, 2003), 225. Emphasis in original.

pelled sometimes to reframe his work entirely in order to destroy the initial conditions of its unwitting commercial success. Far from searching to establish a consensus, his use of language can therefore be apprehended as an offensive and performative mode of writing aimed at generating crises and ruining the forces of homogenization that run through human societies in general, and French society more specifically.

It appears indeed that the "virus" conveyed in the three volumes of *Le théâtre des operations* is first meant to contaminate the French readership. Coming from a novelist who left his native country in 1998 to settle in Quebec, and who on many occasions praised George W. Bush's foreign policy, this indication is not so much an absolute rejection of French tradition in itself, as it is the rejection of a set of modern values and progressive ideologies shared among citizens of Western countries. Certainly, according to Dantec, France, unlike the United States, has been subjected to a "jacobinic and proto-bolshevist form of Republic" and the country has been therefore "conditioned to hate its monarchic, catholic, absolutist and imperial past" (*American Black Box*, 508). However, beyond its history, France symbolizes above all for Dantec a world power that has progressively lost its political sovereignty, and that is now doomed to remain impotent in the face of the present and future crimes caused by the conflicts of civilizations. In this way, the genocide perpetrated by the Serbs in the former Yugoslavia, and also Saddam Hussein's regime in Iraq, become immediately identified in the diary with borderline situations where France, in partnership with the armed forces of the United Nations, fails to represent a moral authority and contents itself with brandishing the empty rhetoric of human rights, without actually being able to prevent their constant violations. In contrast to France and the European Union, which are portrayed as incapable of bearing a prophetic word or of promising any assumed risk of sacrifice, George W. Bush is identified by the author with "the man of the situation," who supposedly embodies a non-dialectical return of the United States to its "imperial, Christian, spiritually and scientifically advanced roots" (*American Black Box*, 255; 412). Although polemical, Dantec's views about sovereignty seem nonetheless consistent, as they accentuate the fact that this concept presupposes by definition not only the idea of inalienability, but also the unifying power of an absolute sovereign who is placed above the laws in a state of exception. From this starting point, which consists in postulating the political supremacy of the one over the multiple, Dantec can then mock a series of "progressive" notions and propositions—such as cultural relativism, tolerance, gay marriage, or affirmative action—that precisely put forward the acknowledgment of a certain difference or of a certain plurality. No doubt the most violent—and probably the most problematic—expression of this privilege given to the one to the detriment of the multiple, lies in the attacks addressed repeatedly by the author to Islam. After having taken an inventory of the crimes perpetrated in its name, Dantec compares Islam to "a communism of the desert," "a protonazism," before reaching the conclusion that this religion is "a nihilism, if not nihilism par excellence" (*American Black Box*, 279; 364; 278). Presenting himself in his diary as a "Catholic of the future," a "Catholic of the end of time,"[6] he requires Western forces to engage in a new holy war in order to fight this new peril.

This deliberately condensed and simplified sketch of the major ideological orientations of Dantec's diary is first intended to understand why the great majority of French national newspapers, and also an appreciable number of literary critics, have delighted in labeling the author as a "conservative," "right-winger," or even "reactionary." However, applying such labels to Dantec's work is not only an oversimplification. It is also primarily a strategic move by French readers to name and to exorcize in the same gesture a fundamental fear that has been repressed within their predominantly agnostic society.

In his 2002 essay, Daniel Lindenberg was one of the first scholars to denounce the rise of new "reactionary" discourses in both French literature and humanities, discourses that break French republican taboos by openly challenging such values as human rights, equality, freedom of morals, and the mixing of cultures.[7] In terms of pure political tactics, Lindenberg's approach is undeniably clever. Defending positions that correspond in France to those assumed by the moderate Left, Lindenberg enhances his own temperate views by contrasting them with

---

6. Dantec, *American Black Box*, 568. We must underline here that Dantec sets a capital distinction between Islam in itself and actual Arab populations who practice this religion and "experience tragically at the same time the position of the victim and the position of the torturer" (*American Black Box*, 262). Far from advocating of course the physical extermination of the Islamists, Dantec promotes nonetheless their symbolic disappearance, suggesting that "nothing should prevent us from trying to convert them to Christianity, with all the risks that such an operation presupposes (apostasy is punishable by death by the Koranic laws)" (*American Black Box*, 263).

7. Daniel Lindenberg, *Le rappel à l'ordre: Enquête sur les nouveaux réactionnaires* (Paris : Seuil, 2002).

those expressed by more radical and sometimes more demanding left- or right-wing intellectuals, who are categorized in his book under the same providential label. In this fragile and heterogeneous pantheon of reactionary thought, Dantec the Atlanticist[8] takes a first-rate position between the ex-Maoists, Alain Badiou and Jean-Claude Milner, the communist Alain Soral, and the very Kantian philosopher Luc Ferry, who accepted the position of Minister of Education in 2002 under Jean-Pierre Raffarin's conservative government. Accused of defending anti-feminist positions and ridiculing the fundamental principles of the French revolution, Dantec is also portrayed by Lindenberg as an author who "does not flinch . . . from using abstruse philosophical jargon"[9] and who endeavors to bring back writers such as Pierre Drieu La Rochelle, known for his positions in favor of collaboration with Germany during the Occupation, into "official" culture.

How seriously must we take this accusation of being reactionary in regard to Dantec's work? As Jean-Marie Donegani and Marc Sadoun point out, "Right" and "Left" refer to notions that do not have a proper existence themselves.[10] In other words, they are just complementary and relative positions that make sense only as a pair. From this perspective, the figure of the reactionary, as it is used by Lindenberg in relation to Dantec, takes part in a global strategy of distorting mirrors, through which the left-wing intellectual oversimplifies the positions of his adversary in order to legitimate rhetorically both the relevance of his own political sensibility and his claim to represent the conscience of the nation. If we accept looking deeply into the three volumes of the diary, it appears conversely, as I shall try to demonstrate in the pages that follow, that Dantec's work, in constant (r)evolution with respect to itself, hardly manages to carry a stable ideological content, and mostly sets up a series of semantic displacements aimed at strategically sustaining a metapolitical project.

For instance, the novelist admits that, before his conversion to Catholicism, he embraced in his youth "approximately all the revolutionary nihilisms of the moment,"[11] switching among Trotskyism, royalism, anarchism, and neo-fascism, and then rejecting each of them

8. "Atlanticism" is the term used in France to define political views that are in accordance with the North Atlantic Treaty Organisation (NATO).

9. Lindenberg, *Le rappel à l'ordre*, 90.

10. Jean-Marie Donegani and Marc Sadoun, "Les droites au miroir des gauches," in *Histoire des droites*, vol.3, *Sensibilités*, ed. Jean-François Sirinelli (Paris : Gallimard, 2006) 759–85.

11. Dantec, *Laboratoire de catastrophe générale*, 561.

almost immediately. Even if one can argue convincingly that in 2006 these forms of contemporary nihilism henceforth constitute Dantec's favorite targets, to what extent can we then assume that the strong Catholic and Atlanticist orientation of *American Black Box* represents the final stage of development of a thought that has reached its full maturity? At the very most, Dantec accepts being labeled "conservative" on condition that he can redefine this notion in his own general terms, deprived of any precise ideological content:

> A "conservative"—in a sense in which I could include myself—is someone who considers that State, that is to say POLITICS, is a *necessary evil.* This position prevents the conservative, at the same time, from falling into an infantile state of regression called anarchy and enhancing an overpowering form of State-Matrix. As well as a psychopathological blending of both ideologies. (*American Black Box*, 428)

We must first underline that such a pragmatic approach to conservatism enables the author to displace the common understanding of that notion. While the conservative is commonly depicted as a moral and political individual who defends traditional values inherited from the past, and who obtusely expresses his/her hostility toward any sort of social evolution, Dantec purposely dismisses this meaning, and emphasizes that the conservative's perspective is more in line with reality because it precisely takes into account what Bataille would call "the accursed share [*la part maudite*]" of humanity. The writer can then skillfully contrast his own pragmatic conservatism with all forms of progressivism, which remain, according to him, structurally reliant on a totalizing and utopian apprehension of the world that generates, beyond its naivety, a resentment against present times and a certain kind of nostalgia for an idealized past.

In the same way that Dantec uses Bataille to promote his own conception of conservatism, he appeals to Nietzsche in order to displace the usual meaning of the word "reaction." As a matter of fact, it appears that the multiple references to these two unorthodox thinkers, in Dantec's diary, not only serve to clarify the writer's philosophical orientation, but also to confuse a French reader who was used to linking traditionally their work with left-wing political thought.[12] While

12. See for example Lyotard, Foucault, and Deleuze's famous interpretations of Nietzsche in the 1960s and the 1970s, and also, on Bataille, the standard reference work by Michel Surya, *Georges Bataille. La mort à l'œuvre* (Paris: Séguier, 1987).

"reaction," in political terms, generally names a will to restore previous state institutions in order to respond to the crises and the conflicts that affect the present times, it also designates, in Nietzsche's terminology, the quality of inferior and dominated forces—such as nutrition, reproduction, and memory—that prevent an active force from reaching the end of its power.[13] According to Nietzsche, reactive forces participate passively in the constitution of nihilism, in the sense that they accelerate the depreciation of superior values in favor of a form of life that remains meaningless and aimless. By taking over this Nietzschean understanding of the word "reaction," Dantec allows himself to tactically counter the charge of being reactionary: on several occasions, he stresses the fact that the polemical and metaphysical violence of his writing is precisely based on a feverish quest for meaning that relegates the simple narration of his daily (and perhaps passive?) tasks to a position of secondary importance. He can then argue that his subjectivity, in spite of the continuous transformations carried out by the chaotic process of writing, still manages to remain under the influence of an active force that imparts an ethical value and a meaning not only to his literary project, but also to his life. Commenting on the philosophical aim of his work, he points out for example, in one of his numerous considerations about his duty as a writer, that "meaning is a human production aimed at enlightening the abysses created by the events that humanity spreads along its path. The onus is on literature to revive meaning after Auschwitz and also to give back a meaning to life" (*Le théâtre des opérations*, 264).

Under the pretext of the rhetorical subterfuges used by Dantec to depreciate the common meaning of the notion of "reaction," and also because of a general feeling of suspicion toward analyses biased by their political agenda, shall we definitely abandon the possibility of considering Dantec's work through the prism of the literary history of political ideas? Inaugurated in France by Jean Touchard, this discipline proposes in fact a precise set of theoretical and conceptual tools that allow the reader to widen considerably his or her critical perspective. In his essay focused on right-wing literature that takes into account a large palette of French authors, from Joseph de Maistre to the "Hussards" group in the 1950s, Alain-Gérard Slama acknowledges that these writers share a "political temperament" that he defines as "a

13. Gilles Deleuze, *Nietzsche et la philosophie* (Paris : Presses Universitaires de France, 1998), 66. I am paraphrasing Deleuze's stimulating interpretation of Nietzsche's philosophy.

certain orientation of the mind, which refers to specific affects and also to a specific memory, and which rests on a particular exercise of reason."[14] One of the main advantages of this notion of "temperament" is that it actually allows us to rethink the main opposition between the Right and the Left, no longer in terms of stable ideological contents but in terms of affective intentions. From this global shift of perspective, Slama sketches a new fundamental line of demarcation between the two sensibilities: whereas, on the one hand, the leftist temperament would assume in history the responsibility of dialectical conflict, the rightist temperament, on the other hand, would rather attempt to circumvent or avoid it. Nevertheless this rejection of conflicts, according to Slama, should not be mistaken for a rejection of violence. As a consequence it would be necessary to differentiate two kinds of political violence: first, a left-wing violence that would make up the mainspring of revolutions, and then a right-wing violence, caused notably by fear, that would explode for example during civil wars.

In the conclusion of his essay, however, Slama questions the possibility of maintaining his classification beyond the limits of the specific historical period on which he has focused. Dantec's work, as far as it can actually be labeled as the product of a right-wing temperament, seems indeed partially to invalidate the transhistorical dimension of this distinction. If, of course, the novelist, who fights relentlessly against all possible socialist and anti-globalization utopias, carefully avoids appealing to the coming of a salutary revolution, he still violently denounces the extreme futility of pacifist positions that often lead the alternative and impotent "man of the Left" to be easily satisfied with the status quo. In a French context where the difference of views expressed by the Right and the governmental Left, both resigned to the domination of capitalism, become more and more indistinguishable[15] in the beginning of the

14. Alain-Gérard Slama, "Portrait de l'homme de droite : Littérature et politique," in *Histoire des droites*, vol.3, *Sensibilités*, 797.

15. We must here remind U.S. readers of two historical facts that help to understand the singularity of Dantec's positions toward French politics. 1) The massive contribution of the French Left to the paradoxically triumphant re-election in 2002 of the center-right President Jacques Chirac, who was opposed in the second round by the National Front leader Jean-Marie Le Pen, famous notably for his revisionist talks and his aggressive positions toward North African immigrants. 2) The united stand taken by the Left and the Right—and I should also add the great majority of the French population—around Jacques Chirac and his Foreign Affairs minister, Dominique de Villepin, against the military intervention of the United States in Iraq.

twenty-first century, Dantec makes the decisive choice to support George W. Bush's United States: in other words, the choice of supporting the only world power that is capable in his eyes of actively perpetuating a military crusade against a form of nihilism of which Islam would be the most accomplished representative. Facing accusations in the French media of being a man of the Right, if not a right-wing extremist, Dantec however always makes it a point of honor to refute these classifications:

> Am I a man of the Right? Does this question still have a meaning at a time when a third type of industrial revolution spreads . . . a new moral and political space where such conceptions, inherited from the Euclidian and parliamentary pattern, are no longer relevant (just like the notions of "top" and "bottom" extra-terrestrial space)? (*Le théâtre des opérations*, 136)

Beyond the polemicist's sometimes peremptory sense of rhetoric, which consists in systematically dismissing both right-wing dogmatism[16] and left-wing fanaticism without pronouncing in favor of either, it seems essential to point out here that it is not so much the label "right-winger" that Dantec rejects as the anthropological and political paradigm that it presupposes. We have to remember that this opposition between right-wing and left-wing was born during the Revolutionary era: it is part and parcel of the same set of ideological concepts that comes straight from the Enlightenment and that is based on criteria imposed by reason. Keeping in mind Dantec's global hostility toward both the Enlightenment, which is accused of having evicted metaphysics from thought in order to promote a rationalized conception of Nature,[17] and toward philosophers such as Hegel or Marx who emphasize the idea of reason within history,[18] we can then offer a new hypothesis. Knowing that the writer disregards the notions of "reactionary" or "right-wing" when applied to his work, this rejection could be understood first and foremost as a refusal to take part in a debate whose progressivist, and thus teleological, foundations, according to him, are already questionable in themselves. We may wonder indeed if the real *différend* that opposes the diarist and his critics

16. See Dantec's repeated attacks not only against Le Pen and the National Front (for instance, *American Black Box*, 333), but also against Christian fundamentalists in the United States and in Poland (*Le théâtre des opérations*, 216; 222).

17. Dantec, *American Black Box*, 75; 321–22.

18. Dantec, *Laboratoire de catastrophe générale*, 831 ; 63–65.

has actually anything to do with politics, at least if by "politics" we mean the rational post-revolutionary framework in which not only two opposite views of the world, but also two conflicting sets of mythologies, clash with each other. Let us remember that, once released from its rational and communicative use, language is compared by Dantec to a weapon meant to bring metaphysics back into thought. Under these conditions, it could also become a virus aimed at contaminating the stable consensual ground shared ideologically by both the Right and the Left since the eighteenth century. To a certain extent, the three volumes of the *Metaphysical and Polemical Diary* can then be read as an experimental project that addresses the political unconscious of the Western reader, and brings back to the surface a series of ancient metaphysical fears and threats that were supposedly overcome.

Given that Dantec's ambitions seem to be more metapolitical than strictly political, is it still relevant to confine the discussion within a strictly ideological perspective? We could argue, on the contrary, that the global opposition between the Right and the Left, unsuited for understanding this writer's work, should be relocated within a more operative paradigm that would contrast Gnosticism with agnostic reason. References to gnosis are in fact numerous in his diary, and instead of carrying out the fastidious work of compilation, I am using the concept of gnosis as a guide to unveiling the nature of Dantec's metaphysical project. In this perspective, we need to propose a minimal definition of gnosis, beyond the ongoing debates that still address the problem of its origin. As Simone Pétrement explains, gnosis must be understood as a generic term that groups together certain mystical discourses that have been rejected by the official churches of monotheist religions and that therefore have been considered as heretical.[19] Beyond their differences, these irrational discourses share a common feature: they all presuppose a radical split between God and the world that leads them to an extreme devaluation of the empirical world, and consequently, to the refusal to submit to the temporal authority of the churches. On many occasions in his diary, Dantec praises the virtues of gnosis, which he considers to be "the greatest achievement of religious thought within the three branches of monotheism,"[20] and with

19. Simone Pétrement, *Le Dieu séparé: les origines du gnosticisme* (Paris : Les Editions du Cerf, 1984).
20. Dantec, *Le théâtre des opérations*, 511.

which he contrasts an agnostic France that suffers from a lack of moral points of reference. We can thus postulate the existence of a possible link between Dantec's metapolitical project and the persistence, throughout his books, of a gnostic thought that refuses to compromise in the major political categories established within the Western world.

To this end, one must first underline, following the central argument developed by Gilles Grelet in his ambitious essay on gnosis,[21] the recurrence of a metaphysical war between Western reason, which aspires to the domination and the exclusivity of thought, and a gnostic Orient that claims a violent form of rebellion against this supremacy. If one can certainly question the belonging of gnosis to the East, even at a symbolic level, the conceptual distinctions made by Grelet are nonetheless essential for apprehending Dantec's discursive positions more precisely.[22] In his book, he argues that neither agnostic rationalities nor theologico-political systems can prevail if they simply reject the absolute otherness of the divine outside of themselves. On the contrary, they must first cover themselves with the attributes of the divine, in order to become fully emancipated afterwards. But whereas agnostic reason dialectically initiates a synthesis with the divine and profits from this unifying assimilation, gnosis conversely tends to maintain divinity beyond any possible synthesis with theologico-political structures. It therefore imposes an ultimate form of irrational resistance toward the totalizing conceptions of the Master, who can be embodied indifferently by the religious or the political leader.[23] In essence, gnostic discourse thus opens a breach in the mind of the modern reader, in the sense that it reveals the repressed fear that the state apparatus might have failed to contain the irrational within the limits imposed by modern democracies. Dantec, who refuses to separate faith and madness, presents himself as the writer who

21. Gilles Grelet, *Déclarer la gnose : D'une guerre qui revient à la culture* (Paris : L'Harmattan, 2002).

22. Many scholars, including Pétrement, have attempted to demonstrate the Christian roots of gnosticism. There is no doubt in my opinion that Dantec's gnosticism falls within the scope of this tradition, even if he has great regard for Sufi masters and cabalistic writings (*Le théâtre des opérations*, 511), and if he also shares some of the views expressed by Raymond Abellio in *Manifeste de la nouvelle gnose* (Paris: Gallimard, 1989). We must notice, however, that Grelet criticizes in his essay the improper use of the term "gnosis" by Abellio, since Abellio's "new gnosis," according to him, rather indicates a scientist and totalizing form of wisdom.

23. Grelet, *Déclarer la gnose*, 49–55.

infiltrates this breach and who envisions his diary as a "cybergnosis that comes close to the prophets' ancient work" (*Laboratoire*, 419; 785). It would be misleading to take for granted the reduction of such an irrational discourse to a sort of right-wing extremism, since the gnostic word revived by the writer precisely denies the legitimacy of the rational authority that is behind this political classification. In Dantec's case, the artist, who defines himself as a "gnostic guerilla" (*Laboratoire*, 237), can rather be portrayed as a prophetic diarist who reintroduces the gnostic virus into writing, and assumes consequently the necessity of being misread by his critics. Without claiming to be exhaustive, and at the risk of being too rational myself, I should like to display three different modalities of this heretical use of metaphysics, through which the language of the guerilla manages to destabilize our Western representations. These modalities, to be specific, will successively attempt to unveil the driving principle that controls the writing of the diary, then the topological site favored by Dantec as a perfect place for its activation, and eventually, the eschatology to which its constant process of actualization inevitably leads.

Let us first deal with the founding principle that sets up the grounds of Dantec's spiritual rebellion, one that is undoubtedly a principle of division. "To create is to separate," asserts the writer in *Le théâtre des opérations*. And also, several hundred pages later: "In order to create anything at all, any creator must separate himself from his creation; any creator must divide himself and let a part of him . . . exist according to its own rules. This principle was applicable to God; in His absence, it became applicable to Man" (*Le théâtre des opérations*, 102; 494). At a simply descriptive level, these sentences obviously summarize the basic rule of any artistic creation. Dantec's argument however exceeds this primary dimension, since this principle of division is originally endowed, for the writer, with metaphysical properties. We must indeed imagine the God of the gnostics as a god that is radically separated from the world, in other words as an "absent" and unreachable god whose absolute transcendence cannot be experienced or even felt by mankind through the object of its creation. Within this dualistic conception, the attributes of the divine, which can only be apprehended negatively, should not be used under any circumstances in order to consolidate the power of an empirical religion or a preexisting theologico-political structure. That is why, from my point of view, it is far from insignificant that Dantec particularly enjoys depicting himself under the features of a soldier armed with a saber or a sword, who regularly "toughens and sharpens his blade on the granite of received ideas" (*Laboratoire*, 600). Unlike firearms, the saber actually represents the perfect weapon for the gnostic guerilla, in that its main function consists not only in cutting, separating, and dividing, but also in settling disagreements and bringing them to an abrupt conclusion. We must nonetheless mention that the author's saber is just as well aimed at converting agnostics as to subverting the attempts at modernization of official religions, suspected of misusing divine transcendence in order to consolidate their temporal power. In this way, the Second Vatican Council, for instance, as it symbolizes the increasing process of secularization of the Catholic Church and its opening to the modern world, is openly accused by Dantec of treachery toward Christianity. Facing the compromises made between religion and the secular world, the gnostic therefore embodies the voice of the heretic who comes to break up the stability of theologico-political unions, and who separates himself from the world in order to "dresser, redresser, faire se tenir droit" ("to put up, straighten up, make one stand up straight") (*Laboratoire*, 176), in other words to restore the radical transcendence of his God in the latter's absolute verticality.

Because the world is cut off from transcendence, it is also cut off from the soul. Since the relationship between man and god is not mediated by the world, the gnostic experience of the world, according to Michel Henry, is lived in a great suffering.[24] The gnostic, who is otherworldly, attempts at the same time to devalue the world and to escape from it, with the prospect of reaching another world, which would be the world of true life. Among the numerous paradoxes raised by Dantec's work, one of the most disconcerting is no doubt the topographical localization of this other world in a continent called America. The parallel drawn between Dantec's actual move to Canada and his inauguration of a new mode of writing in fact goes far beyond biographical anecdote, since it also has a strong symbolic value: "The future of humanity is being built in America" (*American Black Box*, 158). Indeed, this emigration to North America means much more for the diarist than a simple rejection of the agnostic Europe and its socialist utopias. Thus, we must refrain from regarding both this depar-

---

24. Michel Henry, "La vérité de la gnose," in *La gnose, une question philosophique: Pour une phénoménologie de l'invisible*, ed. Nathalie Depraz and Jean-François Marquet (Paris: Les Éditions du Cerf, 2000) 19–29.

ture and Dantec's "Atlanticism" as ideological adherences to the alleged virtues of capitalism. While composing his novel *Villa Vortex* in America, the writer acknowledges that more than ever he has to "fight the black magic of the world market by means of the 'gnostic science' . . . that the novel is intended to enact" (*American Black Box*, 60). In what way, then, can North America, and more particularly the United States, personify the world of true life in the eyes of the gnostic? Dantec first argues that economic liberalism, unlike left-wing utopias, has managed to triumph on a world-wide scale because it has always accepted to be confronted with the evolutionist reality of humanity. The totalizing power of capitalism, however, is about to come to an end, since the cyber-economy represents, according to him, the final stage of development of the market, and generates some "extreme forms of solitude and alienation which backfire on social values . . . , in a general process of dissolution that represents an immeasurable danger for the whole world-society" (*Laboratoire*, 122). It appears therefore that America only embodies the gnostic's aspiration to a "true life" to the extent that this politico-economical authority holds the key to its own breakdown: the very possibility of such a breakdown then makes all the more indispensable the recourse to eschatology.

Pétrement thus points out that gnosis, unlike Christian tradition, emphasizes the role of a human-shaped savior, different from God, who must not only awaken and enlighten mankind, but also lead it toward its salvation.[25] The gnostic conception of salvation, which questions the sufficiency of human free-will, implies in fact the necessity of a call that comes from outside the world. Accordingly, it is hardly surprising that gnostic eschatology presents itself as a messianism focused on the very figure of Christ. Referring to a vision he had in Philadelphia, Dantec recalls the "mystical flash of lightning" that struck his consciousness when he realized that "the only possible way out for Christianity might be its capitulation in front of Christ . . . , in front of this superhuman figure that Nietzsche searched for throughout his life" (*Le théâtre des opérations*, 82). From the author's perspective, it appears therefore that Christianity must ultimately be surpassed by Christ himself, to such an extent that at the time of his resurrection, "churches will catch fire and temples will turn into dust" (191). No doubt Dantec's heretical views might seem here com-

---

25. Pétrement, *Le Dieu séparé*, 28–29.

pletely outrageous for the reader who does not bear in mind that the function attributed to Christ by the gnostics differs considerably from one that prevails within mainstream Christian churches. As Grelet argues, Christianity, through the myth of incarnation, promotes the figure of Christ as a double principle of deification of the human and withdrawal of the divine from thought.[26] In reminding the faithful of the promise of the resurrection of the flesh on Doomsday, mainstream Christian theology eventually endows not only terrestrial life with a global meaning, but also gives a rationalized legitimacy to theologico-political structures. In sharp contrast with this empirical situation, Dantec, the Gnostic, presents Christ as a "metahuman" and cataclysmic principle that does not compromise with any worldly authorities, but conversely calls for their actual abolition (*Le théâtre des opérations*, 101; 582; 623).

In light of this distinction, which is fundamental for the proper understanding of the diarist's eschatology, one can now clear up a final ambiguity. Dantec's readers might certainly experience a certain confusion concerning the way the gnostic guerilla, who defines himself as an anti-modernist, systematically dismisses the notion of post-modernity, and likens it to a generalized form of nihilistic multiculturalism. Although post-modernity, according to Lyotard,[27] enacts the end of the great narratives (among which we should of course include the gnostic narrative), it still cannot be compared to a passive nihilism that would lead humanity to a state of depressed resignation: what is at stake in post-modernity, at least from Lyotard's point of view, rather consists in proceeding to a transvaluation of all humanistic values through new artistic or philosophical experimentations. We should however refrain from suspecting Dantec of being thoughtless or inconsistent on this specific point. The depreciation of terms such as "post-modernity," "post-human," or even "post-history" in fact goes hand in hand in his diary with the praise of an eschatological "meta-human" principle, which could eventually be nothing but an actualized and updated version of the Gnostic's Savior: "[Unlike the post-human], the meta-human is being built elsewhere, in secret, within a much more invisible and operative conspiracy. It is being built in a narrative process that annexes not the most probable future, but the

26. Grelet, *Déclarer la gnose*, 42–46.

27. Jean-François Lyotard, *La condition postmoderne* (Paris: Editions de Minuit, 1979).

most singular, the most devouring, in other words the only future that cannot mix with the others" (*Laboratoire*, 849).

In this article, I have mostly attempted to displace the political question, in showing how the supposedly "reactionary" dimension of Dantec's work has primarily to be understood as the expression of a gnostic resistance within a global system widely dominated by agnostic or religious discourses. One may nonetheless wonder to what extent Dantec's gnosticism can actually be heard and also remain sustainable, as its singularity is constantly threatened by loss and dissolution, at least at a superficial level, in the currents of esoteric "spiritualities" (new age thought or scientology, for example) that have proliferated since the turn of the twenty-first century. Far from ignoring this peril, the writer, in the last volume of his diary, seems to develop an acute perception of its gravity. This might however not be sufficient. Though Dantec asserts that, during the first five hundred years of the Christian era, "there used to be a genuine Christian gnosticism . . . that succeeded in fighting some charlatans who called themselves gnostics," he also admits that nowadays, "we all became second-hand gnostics, with new religions in kit-form for third-generation humanoids. Each to his own beliefs, each to his own program that keeps repeating that all religions are equally good, that God is the same for everybody, etc." (*American Black Box*, 101, 98). Taking into consideration the temporal progression of the diary and above all the narration of Dantec's christening at the end of *American Black Box*, we could then be tempted to conclude that Saint-Maurice's heretical positions, in our postmodern times, were finally doomed to be absorbed into a more orthodox Christianity.[28] After all, as the writer remarks on the example of the Cathars, didn't Christianity always strive to welcome the gnostics to its bosom?

---

28. We must point out that Dantec's most violent condemnations of Islam appear in *American Black Box*, in other words in the volume of the diary where the author makes an essential shift from Gnosticism toward a more aggressive form of Christianity. Dantec's christening seems actually to indicate a final and radical rejection of gnosis, to the point where the generic term "Gnostic," in the final pages of the diary, is combined not only with Islam, but also with Satanism and National-Socialism (*American Black Box*, 662).

ARMINE K. MORTIMER

The Third Closet: Sollers's War

In his essay "À travers le vingtième siècle," Philippe Sollers wrote: "There are in fact three poorly resolved 'closets' in French politics: the period of 1940–44; the Algerian war; the explosion of 1968."[1] He elaborated in "Il suffit d'être douze":

> First closet: 1940–1942. The weight of repression is absolutely phenomenal. . . . Second closet: the Algerian war. At the time it was forbidden to speak of war. . . . First closet: a lie. Second closet: a lie. Let's try to see if for the third closet we aren't also right in the middle of a lie. That is the thesis I am continuing to argue.[2]

And in 2003, he called "May '68" the "specter" that continues to haunt French heads of state.[3] May '68 is a specter because it has been put into the closet—hidden by lies—and only its ghost wafts about in the current atmosphere.

It is a commonplace that France has long had difficulty dealing with the Occupation and the Algerian war, and there is nothing new about saying that the "solution" to this difficulty is the closet. The French *placard* contains these two immense skeletons. It is the place to store bad memories, safely out of sight and mind, before that knowledge has been fully dealt with, or "liquidated," as Sollers wrote. His 1983 novel *Femmes* (*Women*), although rather terse about the third closet, recounts the first two in these terms: he says there are two key periods in the history of modern France: 1940–1942, which he calls "the great secret," and 1958–1962, which he calls "the discreet can-

---

1. Philippe Sollers, *Éloge de l'infini* (Paris: Gallimard, 2001), 902. All translations in this essay, except for published referenced translations, are mine.
2. Sollers, "Il suffit d'être douze," *L'infini* 93 (Winter 2005): 20.
3. Sollers, "Liberté surveillée," *L'infini* 82 (Spring 2003): 15.

YFS 116/117, *Turns to the Right?* ed. Johnson and Schehr, © 2009 by Yale University.

cer." "But there are links between the two . . . anti-Semitism, nationalism . . . Censorship, silence . . . Equivocation . . . ."[4] The horrors of the Second World War marked Europeans—and they have been made to repress it: "Even a Frenchman has great difficulty in feeling it genuinely, viscerally . . . We were 'protected' . . . But at what price!" (*Women* 236). The postwar policy of forgiveness protected the French from the continuing impression of horror, from the memory of shame, but at the price of a monstrous lie: "Truth is, since 1940 the French have been living in shame and self-hatred. . . . Can we call it a case of 'family secrets' on a miserable and massive scale? You can be sure of it. Survivors and descendents are doing everything they can to erase this ill-recognized guilt that is often scarcely suspected—stifled, rotting, unspoken."[5]

If there is a social error that haunts Philippe Sollers, it is this need for the French to pretend these things did not happen. He will constantly remind the world of the contrary.

About Mai '68, Sollers says in the journal *Tissage* in 2005, that "anti-68 thinking starts as early as the seventies and has concluded in a generalized normalization in which money takes on its globalizing dimension" ("Il suffit d'être douze" 16–17). He calls this normalization a repression or "refoulement,"[6] in an analysis that oddly coincides with a view from the Right by Paul-Marie Coûteaux writing in *Le Figaro*. In *L'année du tigre*, Sollers refers us to Coûteaux's "hateful" article that appeared at the thirtieth anniversary of the events, in May 1998, in which we can read the following assertion: "Thus a movement purportedly from the Left has insured the perpetuation of the Right in France, and not just any Right: the political Right of money and media that has reigned since that time under different guises."[7] What Coûteaux said with smug irony, Sollers castigates—in particular, the reign of money and media—in all his writing since the early 1980s.[8]

Since that time, Sollers has striven to combat the third closet: France's lies about May '68 and its regression from it. As he writes,

4. Sollers, *Women*, trans. Barbara Bray (New York: Columbia University Press, 1990), 320. Translation modified.

5. Sollers, "Stratégie de Céline," *La guerre du goût* (Paris: Gallimard, 1996), 176.

6. Sollers, *Poker: Entretiens avec la revue Ligne de risque* (Paris: Gallimard, 2005), 63.

7. Paul-Marie Coûteaux, "Une révolution de salon," *Figaro Magazine* 914, May 2, 1998: 47.

8. To satirize the world financial markets, Sollers creates a parodistic, tentacular, terrorist family named Leymarché-Financier in *Passion fixe* (Paris: Gallimard, 2000).

"Who, for instance, would want to return to *before* '68? To be brought back to a buttoned-up country, strangled communication, conformism and fossilization of social behavior, complete discordance with technical progress and new desires."[9] To counteract this regression, as he wrote in 2005, he "transposed" action into his 1982 novel, at a time when "the counter-offensive of mummification had already begun" ("Il suffit d'être douze" 17). It is this 1982 transposition that marks a turning point.

In the sixties and seventies, Sollers was a beacon of the intellectual Left and known chiefly for his activities in support of the avant-garde. A brief list of the indications of his leftist leanings in that period must include the Maoist chapter of the *Tel quel* group; Sollers's trip to China in the company of other *telqueliens*; his study and translation of Chinese poetry; his publication of leftist writers and the avant-garde in art and literature in the book series and journal called *Tel quel* at the Éditions du Seuil; the publication of provocative texts about politically incorrect writers such as Pound and Céline, and writers of "la rupture," in Houdebine's expression, such as Bataille and Artaud.[10] Sollers's key texts of this time, from the mid-sixties to 1981, are the critical essays *Sur le matérialisme* and *Logiques* and the five remarkable, difficult "novels" *Drame, Nombres, Lois, H,* and *Paradis.* Philippe Forest, one of the most perceptive of Sollers's readers, writes: "from *Drame* to *Lois,* the novel is formed in a geometric space of increasing complexity, constructed and consumed at the same time in such a way as to bring forth a pure space of writing beyond any representational purpose."[11] This refusal of representational purpose characterizes the Sollersian avant-garde.

Then, in 1982, there occurs, mysteriously, what looks like an ideological turn. Forest characterizes the moment as a turn away from the "new," an "old" new that remains like a nostalgic era to which Sollers clings and which *H* emblematizes:

> The history of all this is still being written . . . and . . . it is telling us
> how the balance of power between modernity and tradition was reversed
> at the beginning of the eighties, how there occurred at that point a return

9. Sollers, "A travers le vingtième siècle," *Éloge de l'infini* (Paris: Gallimard, 2001), 903.

10. Jean-Louis Houdebine, "Histoires de ruptures," in *De Tel Quel à L'Infini: L'avant-garde et après?* (Nantes: Pleins Feux, 1999), 55–65.

11. Philippe Forest, "Le nouveau est invincible. Sur *H* de Philippe Sollers et *Louve basse* de Denis Roche," in *De Tel Quel à L'Infini: L'avant-garde et après?*, 100.

(a retreat?) toward a whole series of notions on which the "literature of research" had cast doubt, when it hadn't purely and simply swept them away. This history also tells us how there was inaugurated an era of regression, signaling the stifling of any authentic creation, its shipwreck into the Spectacular, etc., etc. ("Le nouveau est invincible" 97–98)

It is noteworthy that Forest could produce this analysis in the context of a conference on *Tel Quel* and the avant-garde. The term "littérature de recherche" refers to the writers mentioned above, and others such as Joyce and Sollers himself, and their revolutionary effect in writing is comparable to the May '68 effect on social life. In the early eighties, then, there was a retreat to a situation in which any authentic creation was swept into the Spectacle.[12] Forest is thus rather cynically describing a turn to the Right in the *Tel quel* context. A sharp observer of the scene, Forest relates the turn to May '68: "The trauma caused by *Tel quel* was so deep and so violent that in the eighties the response was the most complete censure. Philosophers . . . and polemicists [denounced] the dictatorship of the 'moderns,' bringing to light the theoretical impasse into which 'the thinking of 68' had plunged French culture."[13]

The question to ask about this key moment in French intellectual culture is: what is Sollers's position on such a turn to the Right and how do we place him in it? It is certain that something major happened in Sollers's trajectory at this moment, traceable in notable biographical details. He leaves the Éditions du Seuil and moves to Gallimard, which, in *Femmes*, he wittily and tellingly calls "la banque centrale";[14] the last issue of *Tel quel* appears, having exhausted its mission; he starts *L'infini*, which is published at Gallimard after a brief stint at Denoël; he writes *Femmes*, his first novel in a new "readable" style; he publishes book-length interviews such as *Le rire de Rome*, *La divine comédie*, and *Poker* in which he tirelessly exposes his social thought; he continues to write essays collected in important volumes such as *Improvisations*, *La guerre du goût*, and *Éloge de l'infini* as well

12. Sollers is, of course, referring to Guy Debord's concept of spectacle. See Guy Debord, *La société du spectacle* (Paris: Buchet-Chastel, 1967). See also Debord, *Commentaires sur la société du spectacle* (Paris: Gérard Lebovici, 1988).

13. Forest, "Politique du secret," in *De Tel Quel à L'Infini: L'avant-garde et après?*, 212.

14. Speaking in an interview, Sollers comments that the change from Seuil to Gallimard was a surprise to Seuil; he was writing *Femmes*, and he had reached such a point that he recognized that "[his] social reality was going to change." See Jacques-Alain Miller and Sollers, "Une conversation avec Sollers le 19 avril 2005," www.lacan.com/jamsol.htm (accessed June 8, 2008).

as book-length essays like *Casanova l'admirable* and *Mystérieux Mozart*, about a vast array of topics in literature, all the arts, society, and politics, in which certain approaches and themes recur (regardless of the text used as pretext) and which all contribute to the overarching Sollersian theme of the eighties, nineties, and naughts: *society has got it wrong, and only a free man can get it right.*

The free man is, of course, Philippe Sollers, and that autobiographical claim is also the ultimate subject of the entire body of writing since *Femmes*, a remarkably consistent *content* in a wealth of apparently or superficially different *forms*.

WHAT IS MAY '68 FOR SOLLERS?

Sollers's pessimism about society developed gradually in the post-May '68 decades. Late in 1976, Sollers speaks somewhat mildly of a repression of and a regression from May '68: "The fact is, 1968 was for me the explosion in society of phenomena that had until then been considered marginal, hence coming from another culture. This will return, but I think today we are again in a period of regression, a phase of repression. That's what I feel. Until the next explosion."[15] The optimism of "this will return" will disappear as time passes—particularly with the anniversary commemorations every ten years. He is still optimistic in *La part de vérité*, a 1977 television broadcast about Maurice Clavel, where Sollers describes May '68 as a time when "speech resides in living mouths"—as opposed to the cadaverized language of other times.[16] But by *Portrait du joueur* (1984), he has his narrator comment cynically that May '68, "the fun thing to do at the time," no longer exists at all.[17]

At the twentieth anniversary, his article "May '68" published in *L'infini* and republished in *La guerre du goût*, brings the event into the most personal focus: "The woman I married, for instance, *is 68*. We understand each other implicitly about a thousand shattered things, we have definitively shared an experience of the here and now."[18] A

---

15. Sollers and Edgar Faure, *Au delà du dialogue.* Débat présenté et animé par Thierry Pfister (Paris: Balland, Face à face, 1977), 85.

16. *La part de vérité: Maurice Clavel*, television program on TF1, July 4, 1977.

17. Sollers, *Portrait du joueur* (Paris: Gallimard [Folio], 1984), 306.

18. Sollers, "Journal du Joueur II," *L'infini* 23 (Fall 1988): 48. In republishing the "May 68" segment of this article in *La guerre du goût*, Sollers changes "the woman I married" to "one of the women I love." See *La guerre du goût* (Paris: Gallimard [Folio], 1996), 435.

note of nostalgia is sounded, as of something that remains only in privileged individuals.

At the thirtieth anniversary, reprising a paragraph from a publication that same year, he tells the editors of *Ligne de risque:*

> May '68 was a project and a conspiracy to attain the real. Having fun
> was in this case the most superficial aspect of the event. Nothing sud-
> den: a long preparation engendered by society's own negation. Com-
> munication showed how it could be interrupted. Distinctions between
> class, age, sex, and education became radically visible. So it was out of
> the question to rub shoulders with the next guy or treat him as if he
> were what we call a "loved one." Out of the question, as well, to imag-
> ine the unfamiliar as being in the least familiar. Contrary to the eter-
> nal, tenacious dream of the petite bourgeoisie, non-community became
> admissible *at last.* (*Poker* 69, same text in "Réponses aux 'Cahiers du
> cinema'")

If this language seems particularly categorical, it is because Sollers
was responding to terms that were Blanchot's in *La communauté in-
avouable* in a point by point reversal, leading to his final sentence with
its refusal of community, of shared purpose and action. In the same
vein, he wrote in "Il suffit d'être douze," in 2005: "May '68 was not
made for togetherness but for being *outside* a completely smothering
togetherness; that is how singularities appeared multiple" (28). Action
was not political but rather social and especially *individual.* Social effects were undone; only the individual ones remain.

In May 2008, when I asked Sollers what he considered the advances
or gains of May '68, he told me: "what France gained or lost does not
interest me especially. What interests me is the individual adventure,
because I believe that '68 . . . Apart from the individual adventures
that it may have produced, one falls back on a political or politicizing
discourse that, for me, is not very important."[19] But he also accentuates the very favorable period just before 1968, after the end of the Algerian war, where society "radiates" and freedom is gained, in particular sexual freedom—before the punishment of the "années de plomb"
of the seventies (Interview 2008).[20]

Thus Sollers comes to stress the personal and individual experience of May '68. What May '68 won is the freedom *not* to be part of a

19. Sollers, interview by Armine Kotin Mortimer, Paris, May 17, 2008.
20. "Années de plomb," the leaden years, is an expression that refers more commonly to the seventies and eighties in Germany and Italy, victims of terrorist attacks.

community and to proclaim that freedom loudly and without shame. That, to my understanding, is a foundational ingredient in the turn to a new style in 1982–1983.

WHAT TURNED IN 1982?

"I have always said, and am ready to say it again as often as necessary, I belong to the Left, absolutely, without hesitation or reservation! There! . . . So why is it that no one really quite believes me? Why do I yet again have the feeling people think I belong to the Right?" (*Women* 416–17).

The character who speaks these words is the narrator-protagonist of *Femmes,* purportedly an American journalist by the name of Will living in France—but otherwise an image of the author. The question they raise, in a devious manner, may well be asked about Sollers in 1982.

That there was a *before* and an *after* in regard to May '68 is a commonplace: French society changed in several levels, and many commentators, Sollers among them, have expressed a range of opinions. For Sollers, the *after* is characterized by an "affaissement general (general collapse)," as he said in *Poker* (48). The country took a "turn to the Right," visible in what Sollers quite recently claimed to be the most generalizable effect of May '68. Speaking in a May 2007 television program on France 2 called *Esprits libres,* Sollers rhetorically asks who lost in 1968.[21] Not the Right, the Republic, or the foundation of the French state, but the Communist Party, attacked on all sides, bombarded in its quarters, the vociferation of its voice liquidated once and for all. A more metaphorical version of the same opinion is found in *Femmes* in this form: "A high-speed train with the Stalin carriage uncoupled . . . He's in quarantine . . ." (*Women* 356). May '68 sticks like a fishbone in the throat of the historical imposture of Stalinism, he says on France 2. Against his adversary in this dialogue, Luc Ferry, Sollers emphasizes that May '68 was not a communist movement— and to call communism a historical imposture is certainly to take his distance from it. With rich irony, and a measure of insight, Sollers in 2007 predicts that Sarkozy is dreaming of provoking another May '68: "Sarkozy is going to put all his talent, all his energy, into producing a new May '68, through a generalized conformism: work, family, profit. May '68 is tomorrow" (*Esprits libres*). Provocative as always, Sollers

21. *Esprits libres,* television program on France 2, May 11, 2007.

makes himself hard to pinpoint—and I note in passing that such posturing illustrates his self-proclaimed freedom.

In Sollers's opus, this diagnosis of a turn to the Right after May '68 takes a highly personal form. If the *before* was the avant-garde, war is the term I would propose for the *after. La guerre,* as Sollers insists, is simply a continuation of the avant-garde by other means: since 1982, Sollers has spread his war farther and wider. To reach a wider audience was a strong motivation for his change of style in 1982.

The most important of the cluster of events around 1982, as he told me, was his change of publisher, which also means a change of employer, because Sollers is an editor as well as a writer (Interview 2008). In *Portrait du joueur* he describes this change as taking his war into the opposite camp: "I did have to go over to the other side . . . Make war . . ." (18). A key moment comes after the publication in 1981 of the first volume of *Paradis* (much longer than the second published in 1986). The closeness in time between the first appearance of *Paradis* as a book and the publication of *Femmes* accentuates the turn: *Paradis* reaches an acme, a culmination of the revolution in language that grew progressively through the five novels of rupture; the revolution is realized as fully as possible in *Paradis.* From then on, starting with the first novel published by Gallimard, *Femmes,* Sollers's novels abandon abstruse structuralist, text-based programs, geometrical permutations, and punctuation-free writing, choosing instead their famously readable style. On the face of it, this means a change in style that now accommodates narrative (vs. textual) design, plot, characters, chronology, as well as narrator and narrative discourse.

The greatest of these changes appears in the narrator and his discourse. A story is told with a beginning, a middle, and an end, in the familiar Jamesian paradigm. One finds a plot and subplots. Characters act in them and are described by their psychology, intentions, motivations, hair color, sexual behavior. Events can be arranged in a coherent chronology. Or, as the first page of *Femmes* puts it: "There'll be details, local color, one scene after another, mix-ups, mesmerism, psychology, orgies" (*Women* 3). But what most characterizes the novels since 1982 is the central focus on the autobiographical narrator, a multiple portrait of Sollers whose discourse enfolds the novels in their entirety. An omnipresent and masterful self, Sollers speaks in his own voice, not in the voice of an ensemble, as he did during the most characteristic moments of *Tel quel.* All the novels are about Sollers, just as the voice that speaks in his essays is his; his theory is his own; his reference points are no longer other textual theorists, such as Derrida or Kristeva, but poets and writers: Dante, Rimbaud, Hölderlin, Nietzsche, and others. The novels combine events, especially sexual ones, with highly individualistic philosophical essays and reflective dialogues, thus recreating the form of Sade's novels.

Sexual freedom is predominant in the novels from *Femmes* forward. Although sexuality was not absent from the avant-gardist works, and a sexual relation between an adolescent and a woman of thirty was the root of *Une curieuse solitude*, his first novel, the shock of the novel published in 1983 came in large measure, if one believes the reaction in the press, from its free-flowing sexuality and the lavish laying on of sexual relations between the narrator-protagonist and about a dozen women. *Portrait du joueur* (1984) forced the point home, with its stunning passages describing in detail the programmed sexual relations between the narrator-protagonist and Sophie. *Le cœur absolu* (1987) spreads the free-flowing sexuality to a group of five, and the notebooks of the hero, written in code, record his sexual exploits; the narrator deciphers them in detail. *Les folies françaises* (1988) flaunts a sexual relationship between the narrator-protagonist and his eighteen-year-old daughter, France. *Le lys d'or* (1989) describes a pact between the narrator-protagonist and a high-class woman that runs on sexual tension and culminates in a weekend climax. And so on. Sexual relations abound in all the readable novels.

Simply put, sexual freedom is the barometer of freedom in general. Sollers does not hesitate to ground his personal freedom in May '68: "The fact is, I was able to deploy a supplementary freedom that was very personal through all that. The rest, for me anyway, is finally without interest" (Interview 2008). His terse reply to the *Cahiers du cinéma* in 1988 said the same: May '68 brought him "a redoubled freedom."[22]

But do these changes, and these themes, constitute a "turn," for Sollers? Critics may have insisted on the break between the five avant-garde novels and the ones from 1983 on, but for Sollers there is continuity, a continuity that lies in the fight against the Spectacle. If *Drame, Nombres, Lois, H,* and *Paradis* are the voice, *a contrario*, of the Spectacle, "one might believe," Sollers wrote in his 1989 *Carnet*

---

22. Sollers, "Mai 68. Réponses aux 'Cahiers du cinéma'," *L'infini* 62 (Summer 1998): 8. In 2008, Sollers considers this one-page text significant enough to reproduce it in the complete index of the first hundred issues of *L'infini*, published as *L'infini* 101–102 (spring 2008).

de nuit, "that *Femmes, Portrait du joueur, Le cœur absolu, Les folies françaises* are the only novels with a systematic critique of the integrated spectacle."[23] Thus what may appear as a turn, with the change in style, masks a continuity that for Sollers at least is important.

That the turn from avant-garde to war means continuity for Sollers receives further explanation in commentary on *Tel quel* by the critic most qualified to comment, Philippe Forest, author of *Histoire de Tel quel.* His description of the change is laced with irony: "Those who praise the adventuresome rigor of *Tel quel* generally condemn the futile regression toward commercial literature or critical impressionism in *L'infini.* Those who salute in *L'infini* the most vital of journals today sometimes do a bad job of hiding their relief that the *Tel Quel* page has been turned."[24] Of course Forest's purpose is to insist on the continuity, especially in terms of a movement forward, between *Tel quel* and *L'infini.*

Sollers portrays himself in the character S. in *Femmes* quoting Joseph de Maistre and proclaiming loudly his adherence to a classical style, while his double, Will, questions: "So where does that leave the avant-garde, modernity, the whole area to which he is usually consigned?" (*Women* 74). I take this as a subtle affirmation of the change in style for this book—and at the same time, a provocative claim to continuity. "[S. has] always wanted to indulge his classical talents . . . It's a rest from his hazy modern opera" (a periphrastic description of *Paradis*) (*Women* 341). As for Sollers himself, the continuity he claims lies not in the claim to be classical even in his radical experimentation with the French language, as in *Lois* and *Paradis,* but rather in the continuation of the war by other means, starting with *Femmes.* That there is continuity in *content* if not in means or methods he has reaffirmed recently: "There is a perfect coherence between *Paradis* and *Femmes.* It's just—I felt the need to make the content explicit" (Interview 2008). To make the content explicit—to bring the war into the open —thus identifies the change.

On the topic of May '68, the discretion of *Femmes* might be considered rather surprising. One finds a few references, for the most part allusive or off-handed: "The good old days, 1968, if you can call it

---

23. Sollers, *Carnet de nuit* (Paris: Plon, 1989), 29.
24. Forest, "Tel Quel à l'infini," in *De Tel Quel à L'Infini: L'avant-garde et après?,* 167.

that . . ." (*Women* 83); "The old topics of the '60s and '70s . . . '68 . . ." (195). May '68 has no obvious relation to the explosion that kills Cyd near the end of the book; the police investigation suggests such a cause, but it is dismissed: "Were you involved in political movements of the extreme Left ten years ago?" Reply: "It's been a thing of the past for ages now" (492; similar passage on 293). My sense is that in 1982, Sollers's preoccupation with the manifestations of the third closet had not yet reached the pitch it would attain when continuing commemorations every ten years encrusted May '68 with more and more lies.

Moreover, the *before-after* typology in Sollers's opus does not have the abruptness that characterizes the common view of May '68. One cannot describe the change in Sollers's writing as a moment. The turn to Sollers's Right occurs in segments. During the first half of the eighties, Sollers continues to produce *Paradis* (which began to appear in *Tel quel* in 1974) and to publish it, now in *L'infini*; the second volume, much shorter than the first, comes out in 1986, at Gallimard as opposed to Seuil; videos produced during this period with the videographer Jean-Paul Fargier continue the textual experimentation into the visual domain, an important evolution that will influence Sollers's later writing. *Femmes* carries the banner forward: the fresco of the human being's misfit in the world and society's flattening effect continues from *Lois* and restates, in different language, the themes of *Paradis*. In the background, *Paradis* continues; but after the 1986 publication, nothing new in that vein appears, in spite of the fact that Sollers proclaims that *Paradis* continues without end. He told me this in 2003. More publicly, but perhaps more ambiguously, in 2005 he wrote of the 1972 *Lois* that it prepares *Paradis*, "where things go on to infinity, with no other end than my own" (*Poker* 141; this interview dates from 2002). Largely because of this claim, I have described *Paradis* as the *basso ostinato* of his obsession—but there is no longer any printed manifestation of it. The absence of this avant-garde manifestation, last seen in 1986 when two "figurative" novels had already been published, must certainly be counted as another indication of a turn, in spite of Sollers's creditable claim that what he did to language with *Paradis* will finish only with his death.

"Figurative" is the adjective that others have used to describe the difference in the writing of the novels starting with *Femmes*. André S. Labarthe in the 1998 television film *Philippe Sollers, L'isolé absolu*, for the series "Un siècle d'écrivains," speaks of the productive vein of what he calls Sollers's "romans figuratifs (figurative novels)," begun with the spectacular "changement à vue (visible change)" of 1983.[25] And in *Femmes*, the autobiographical narrator, one of the "Multiple Related Identities" (or MRIs) of the author, uses the adjective "figurative" with the off-hand comment, "Not all Picasso's paintings were cubist" (*Women* 59). The war continues in his figurative writing, in which the theme of freedom and its stylistic expression focalize what is for Sollers the war against the closet of May '68.

THE ADVENTURE OF LANGUAGE

> "I always see events through language and not as if events
> determined the language" (Interview 2008).

Sollers quite spontaneously spoke these words, in response not to a question about his writing or his relation to language, but in reply to a general question: what has May '68 brought to you, and to France, that has since been lost? The turn in Sollers is a specific reaffirmation of the relation to language. Sollers readily affirms that his only guide and compass are his writing—what he is writing at any given moment; he has reiterated that he always coincides with his writing. Since at least Jean Ricardou's formulation opposing the adventure of language to the language of an adventure, novels of the avant-garde, including the range of phenomena known as the *nouveau roman*, were considered to have abandoned the language of an adventure—plot, story, etc. —in favor of the adventure of language: language had become the topic of the novel. This opposition can be updated to mark the change from the avant-garde to the "pleine guerre" [all-out war] in Sollers's work. As of 1982, experimentation with language *seems to* cease; or as Forest suggests, textual writing became saturated with *Lois* and perhaps could go no deeper ("Le nouveau est invincible" 100).

But Sollers would rather claim that textual writing goes underground; experimentation with language becomes more subtle with *Femmes*. The adventure of language has taken a different form. As recently as 2005, Sollers, invoking Heidegger, grants to language the ability to escape absolute anthropomorphism, thus allowing spontaneous revolution; the writer has the ability to create the language of this revelation, as he calls it: "I'm keeping the word 'revelation' to indicate that what society buries, a writer can bring to light" (*Poker* 111). Similarly, in 1977, in speaking about Maurice Clavel, with whom Sollers

25. *Philippe Sollers, L'isolé absolu*, film by André S. Labarthe, 1998.

published a dialogue, *Délivrance,* Sollers had asserted: "As best I can, I pursue an experiment in the depths of language which is an experience of truth in writing" (*La part de vérité*). Clearly Sollers considers that his writing both *before* and *after* has this anti-closet power of revelation, a claim he makes explicitly in *Poker:* after Heidegger, he has tried to "think and consider simultaneously and in a lively manner everything that has been said and thought in the language that I speak," and he cites as examples not only *Paradis* but also the 1997 novel *Studio* and his collection of essays, *La guerre du goût* (*Poker* 78).

Ultimately, change is observable on a superficial level; the *content* to which Sollers points remains his writing, his relationship to language, including the signal importance of the vocal expression.

FREEDOM AND THE PILE OF BOOKS

In 1998, Sollers chose not to grant an interview to *Les cahiers du cinéma,* and his written response to their questions, which he published, merely says that May '68 brought him "une liberté redoublée." To those to whom he does choose to answer, he will of course give the same message: "My books constantly bear witness to this way of living, which must be described as . . . very free. As free as possible" ("Il suffit d'être douze" 16). Similarly, with Philippe Labro, in the televised program *Ombre et lumière* in 2002, asked to define himself, Sollers simply replies "a free man."[26]

Yet people are not necessarily "getting it." Sollers complains most frequently that people are not reading his books. This complaint has taken many forms and appears in novels as well as essays. In a May and June 1983 interview published in *Le rire de Rome,* Sollers describes what he perceives as a censuring of *Femmes,* saying: "The main effect has always consisted in an obliteration of all the female portraits, in a general putting forth of the 'anti-feminist' theme and in the accent placed on the male portraits."[27] Speaking with me in May 2008, he still emphasizes exactly the same censure: his women have been put into the closet. The *content* is there—and ignored. Nor is this effect limited to a simple turning away of the majority from the stack of his books, which Sollers indicates with an expressive gesture

26. *Ombre et lumière:* Sollers and Philippe Labro, television program on France 3, September 18, 2002.

27. Sollers, *Le rire de Rome: Entretiens avec Frans De Haes* (Paris: Gallimard, 1992), 47.

of both hands in the film *L'isolé absolu* and creates anew for my benefit during our conversation in 2008. It is as if the twenty-five years of *L'infini* did not exist, as if his stack of books did not exist, he says with palpable irony.

What is it about the content of a "readable" book like *Femmes* that is not grasped by the reading public? In his own quirky way, Michel Houellebecq pinpointed the problem parodistically in *Les particules élémentaires.* Bruno first confuses the name of Sollers with a brand of mattresses, then tries to read: "he tried immersing himself in *Une curieuse solitude,* gave up pretty quickly, succeeded nevertheless in reading a few pages of *Femmes* —especially the sex scenes"—and even those passages do not sit well with him: "reading *Femmes* gave living proof: the only women [Sollers] succeeded in screwing were the old whores from the cultural set; the chicks obviously preferred singers."[28] It is a minor and ironic point that old whores and young chicks are notably absent from the cadre of women in *Femmes.* Houellebecq's Bruno can only be an ironic guide for the alert reader, but in the very exaggeration of this parody he drives home the point that the content is misread. And that is Sollers's chief complaint today. Freedom—his personal freedom—has been put into the closet, along with May '68 and the other cadavers. The censure, active repression, and even hatred of which he is the object amount to a closet of falsification that Sollers, inverting the usual expression, scathingly calls "the closet in the cadavers" (Interview 2008). To call his falsifiers "cadavers" is to take the defensive war into the offensive realm. Against such misreaders, Sollers again asserts his freedom.

In the Labarthe film, Sollers speaks of his books, his purpose in writing, the strength of the self that comes out in the writing. He refers to all his writing as "One single book, actually, one single voice." If instead of diagnosing a superficial turn to his Right we reread everything to discover how all the works speak, deeply, fundamentally, with the same voice, we will see how the war continues. Sollers writes even now with his fountain pen and blue ink, fighting to keep his war out of the closet, and shunning the computer screen, because, as he says, "Everything's written with sound, with the internal voice" (Interview 2008).

28. Michel Houellebecq, *Les particules élémentaires* (Paris: Flammarion, 1998), 229–30.

Contributors

BRUNO CHAOUAT is Associate Professor of French at the University of Minnesota. In 1999, he published a book on Chateaubriand and an autobiography (*Je meurs par morceaux. Chateaubriand*); has edited a volume on shame: *Lire, écrire la honte* (2007); and has published many articles in the field of twentieth-century French studies.

VERENA ANDERMATT CONLEY teaches in Comparative Literature and in Romance Languages and Literature at Harvard University. Her publications include *Ecopolitics: The Environment in Post-structuralist Thought* (1997) and *Littérature, politique et communisme : Lire 'Les lettres françaises,' 1942–1972* (2002). She is currently finishing a manuscript on space in recent French culture.

BÉNÉDICTE COSTE received her PhD from the University of Montpellier and has written on English and French Literature. She is currently a researcher at the Université de Montpellier-III and is working on a project on nineteenth- and twentieth-century forms of belief in English and French prose.

RICHARD J. GOLSAN is Distinguished Professor of French and Head of the Department of European and Classical Languages at Texas A&M University. He is the author of *French Writers and the Politics of Complicity* (2006), *Vichy's Afterlife* (2000), and *René Girard and Myth: An Introduction* (1999). His edited volumes include *The Papon Affair* (2000), *Fascism's Return* (1998), and *Memory, the Holocaust, and French Justice* (1995). He is Editor of the *South Central Review*.

MICHEL GUELDRY is Professor of European Union Studies at the Monterey Institute of International Studies. He has published numerous works on France and Europe, French politics, and contemporary French society, including *France and European Integration: Towards a Transnational Polity?* (2001) and *Les États-Unis et l'Europe face à la guerre d'Irak* (2005), and is the editor of *Languages Mean Business: Integrating Languages and Cultures in/for the Professions.*

NACIRA GUÉNIF-SOUILAMAS has a Ph.D. in sociology from l'École des Hautes Études en Sciences Sociales in Paris. She is Associate Professor at the University of Paris Nord and research fellow at Experice (Paris 13-Paris 8). Her publications include *Des beurettes aux descendantes d'immigrants nord-africains* (2000), and she has co-authored, with Éric Macé, *Les féministes et le garçon arabe.*

MICHAEL A. JOHNSON is Assistant Professor of French at the University of Texas at Austin. He has published articles on both medieval and 20th-century writing that examine questions of textual culture and embodiment, and is particularly concerned with matters of sexuality and interpretive orthodoxy. His current book project, *Rhetoric of Sodomy: Reading the Body in Medieval Literary Debate,* examines a set of literary debates concerned with the practice of reading in the European High Middle Ages wherein sodomy is frequently invoked both to describe misreading and to enforce orthodox reading practices.

ADRIAN JOHNSTON is Assistant Professor of Philosophy at the University of New Mexico at Albuquerque. He is the author of *Time Driven: Metapsychology and the Splitting of the Drive, Žižek's Ontology: A Transcendental Materialist Theory of Subjectivity,* and *Badiou, Žižek, and Political Transformations: The Cadence of Change.* With Catherine Malabou, he is presently co-authoring a book on affects reconsidered at the intersection of psychoanalysis, neuroscience, and philosophy, and is working on a project addressing forms of materialism.

DOUGLAS MORREY is Associate Professor of French at the University of Warwick. He has published widely on French cinema and is currently preparing a comparative study of Michel Houellebecq and Maurice G. Dantec.

ARMINE K. MORTIMER is Professor of French Literature and of Criticism and Interpretive Theory at the University of Illinois. She works particularly on Balzac and Sollers, and she is the author of six books and numerous articles. Her book-length study on Sollers's *Paradis* appeared in *L'infini* 89 (Fall 2004).

FRANÇOIS NOUDELMANN is Professor at the Université de Paris 8 and Visiting Professor at Johns Hopkins University. His most recent books are *Hors de moi* (2006) and *Le toucher des philosophes. Sartre, Nietzsche et Barthes au piano* (2008).

KARL POLLIN is Assistant Professor of French and Comparative Literature at the University of Tulsa, Oklahoma. His research focuses on modernity, contemporary French literature and theory (Deleuze, Laruelle, Lyotard). He has published articles in *Symposium, Europe,* and *La revue des sciences humaines,* and he is currently preparing a book about singularity in Alfred Jarry's work.

LAWRENCE R. SCHEHR is Professor of French at the University of Illinois. He has published on nineteenth- and twentieth-century French narrative, as well as in the field of gender studies. Recent volumes include *French Gay Modernism* and a translation of Willy's *The Third Sex.*

The following issues are available through **Yale University Press,** Customer Service Department, P.O. Box 209040, New Haven, CT 06520-9040. Tel. 1-800-405-1619. yalebooks.com

73 Everyday Life (1987) $22.00

75 The Politics of Tradition: Placing Women in French Literature (1988) $22.00

Special Issue: After the Age of Suspicion: The French Novel Today (1989) $22.00

76 Autour de Racine: Studies in Intertextuality (1989) $22.00

79 Literature and the Ethical Question (1991) $22.00

81 On Leiris (1992) $22.00

82 Post/Colonial Conditions Vol. 1 (1993) $22.00

83 Post/Colonial Conditions Vol. 2 (1993) $22.00

84 Boundaries: Writing and Drawing (1993) $22.00

85 Discourses of Jewish Identity in 20th-Century France (1994) $22.00

86 Corps Mystique, Corps Sacré (1994) $22.00

87 Another Look, Another Woman (1995) $22.00

88 Depositions: Althusser, Balibar, Macherey (1995) $22.00

89 Drafts (1996) $22.00

90 Same Sex / Different Text? Gay and Lesbian Writing in French (1996) $22.00

91 Genet: In the Language of the Enemy (1997) $22.00

92 Exploring the Conversible World (1997) $22.00

94 Libertinage and Modernity (1999) $22.00

95 Rereading Allegory: Essays in Memory of Daniel Poirion (1999) $22.00

96 50 Years of *Yale French Studies,* Part 1: 1948-1979 (1999) $22.00

97 50 Years of *Yale French Studies,* Part 2: 1980-1998 (2000) $22.00

98 The French Fifties (2000) $22.00

99 Jean-François Lyotard: Time and Judgment (2001) $22.00

100 FRANCE/USA: The Cultural Wars (2001) $22.00

101 Fragments of Revolution (2002) $22.00

102 Belgian Memories (2002) $22.00

103 French and Francophone: the Challenge of Expanding Horizons (2003) $22.00

104 Encounters with Levinas (2003) $22.00

106 Jean Paulhan's Fiction, Criticism, and Editorial Activity (2004) $22.00

107 The Haiti Issue (2005) $22.00

108 Crime Fictions (2005) $22.00

109 Surrealism and Its Others (2006) $22.00

110 Meaning and Its Objects (2006) $22.00

111 Myth and Modernity (2007) $22.00

112 The Transparency of the Text (2007) $22.00

113 French Education: Fifty Years Later (2008) $22.00

114 Writing and the Image Today (2008) $22.00

115 New Spaces for French and Francophone Cinema (2009) $22.00

ORDER FORM   **Yale University Press,** P.O. Box 209040, New Haven, CT 06520-9040

I would like to purchase the following individual issues:

____

For individual issues, please add postage and handling:

Single issue, United States $2.75   Each additional issue $.50

Single issue, foreign countries $5.00   Each additional issue $1.00

Connecticut residents please add sales tax of 6%.

Payment of $__________ is enclosed (including sales tax if applicable).

MasterCard no._______________________________ Expiration date _______________

VISA no._______________________________ Expiration date _______________

Signature ____

SHIP TO ____

____

See the next page for ordering other back issues. Yale French Studies is also available through Xerox University Microfilms, 300 North Zeeb Road, Ann Arbor, MI 48106.

The following issues are still available through the **Yale French Studies Office,** P.O. Box 208251, New Haven, CT 06520-8251.

19/20 Contemporary Art $3.50	42 Zola $5.00	54 Mallarmé $5.00
33 Shakespeare $3.50	43 The Child's Part $5.00	61 Toward a Theory of Description $6.00
35 Sade $3.50	45 Language as Action $5.00	
39 Literature and Revolution $3.50	46 From Stage to Street $3.50	
	52 Graphesis $5.00	

Add for postage & handling

Single issue, United States $3.85 (Priority Mail)   Each additional issue $1.25
Single issue, United States $1.90 (Third Class)   Each additional issue $ .50
Single issue, foreign countries $3.75 (Book Rate)   Each additional issue $3.00

YALE FRENCH STUDIES, P.O. Box 208251, New Haven, Connecticut 06520-8251
A check made payable to YFS is enclosed. Please send me the following issue(s):

Issue no.   Title   Price

____

____

                                                          Postage & handling _______________

                                                                      Total _______________

Name ____

Number/Street ____

City _______________________________ State ___________ Zip __________________

- -

The following issues are now available through Periodicals Service Company, 11 Main Street, Germantown, N.Y. 12526, Phone: (518) 537-4700. Fax: (518) 537-5899.

1 Critical Bibliography of Existentialism	19/20 Contemporary Art
2 Modern Poets	21 Poetry Since the Liberation
3 Criticism & Creation	22 French Education
4 Literature & Ideas	23 Humor
5 The Modern Theatre	24 Midnight Novelists
6 France and World Literature	25 Albert Camus
7 André Gide	26 The Myth of Napoleon
8 What's Novel in the Novel	27 Women Writers
9 Symbolism	28 Rousseau
10 French-American Literature Relationships	29 The New Dramatists
11 Eros, Variations...	30 Sartre
12 God & the Writer	31 Surrealism
13 Romanticism Revisited	32 Paris in Literature
14 Motley: Today's French Theater	33 Shakespeare in France
15 Social & Political France	34 Proust
16 Foray through Existentialism	48 French Freud
17 The Art of the Cinema	51 Approaches to Medieval Romance
18 Passion & the Intellect, or Malraux	

36/37 Structuralism has been reprinted by Doubleday as an Anchor Book.
55/56 Literature and Psychoanalysis has been reprinted by Johns Hopkins University Press, and can be ordered through Customer Service, Johns Hopkins University Press, Baltimore, MD 21218.